Improving Processes for Health Care Delivery

Chester Chambers • Maqbool Dada
Kayode Williams

Improving Processes for Health Care Delivery

Lessons from Johns Hopkins Medicine

 Springer

Chester Chambers
Carey Business School
Johns Hopkins University
Baltimore, MD, USA

Maqbool Dada
Carey Business School
Johns Hopkins Hospital
Baltimore, MD, USA

Kayode Williams
Anesthesiology & Critical Care Medicine
Johns Hopkins University, School of Medicine
Baltimore, MD, USA

ISBN 978-3-031-19042-1   ISBN 978-3-031-19043-8   (eBook)
https://doi.org/10.1007/978-3-031-19043-8

Mathematics Subject Classification (2020): 90B90, 90B22

This Springer imprint is published by the registered company Springer Nature Switzerland AG
The registered company address is: Gewerbestrasse 11, 6330 Cham, Switzerland

I have had many talents given to me and I feel they are in trust. I shall not bury them but give them to the lads who long for a wider education.

Baltimore, MD   *Johns Hopkins*

Foreword

Quality comes not from the inspection, but from improvement of the production process.

William E. Deming

Dr.'s Chambers, Dada and Williams crafted a timely and excellent body of work providing real-time examples from a large, highly matrixed Academic Medical Center of Johns Hopkins Medicine. Those of us buffeted by the winds of the current public health crisis know all too well the collective challenge of caring for our patients in health systems with high steady state bed utilization, emergency room wait times, clinic visits delayed for months, and operating and recovery room holds. Our current state was challenged by the crisis as we reconfigured care locations and provider networks, and cancelled elective procedures to free up capacity, equipment, and supplies to meet the increased and unpredictably fluctuating load of critically ill patients. With this in mind, innovation in hospital operational processes to improve efficiencies of the system, while maintaining quality and outcome, would enhance equitable access to care and better prepare for future public health crises.

Johns Hopkins University has a rich history as the first in the US to have a department of Operations Research. The authors note the field of operations management leverages work from industrial engineering, economics, and operations to provide insight to how we think about a system and model the functions of hospital medical operations— ultimately, improving efficiency and outcomes, reducing healthcare waste and improving access.

Their work provides exemplars of health care practices in the inpatient and outpatient settings. Our healthcare systems are complex, hence the application of simple methods to analyze and inform would not serve. They bring to light the nuances of healthcare, taking into consideration the myriad, unique variables: multiple care providers, varying geographics and disease prevalence, highly specialized providers, patients with the complexity of chronic co-morbidities, multiple hand-offs, and more. All are interrelated and affect throughput, requiring operational efficiencies to optimize utilization of system capacities. How do we predict the performance of these complicated systems, patients, care providers, shared resources, changes in payer and practices, and unanticipated strains on the system? Applications of the authors' described foundational principles can provide insight to inform strategy and tactics leading to improved efficiencies and predictability of performance.

As the field moves forward, increased application of artificial intelligence tools will engender a shared future where one could imagine every hospital's operational strategy based on a digital twin to inform ongoing decisions (Erol et al (2020)). The creation of hospital digital twins could facilitate testing a system under varying permutations of design and operations to better predict performance. Building on the authors' foundational principles, along with the further application of artificial intelligence tools, will allow modeling of data in these complex systems, to better position health systems to allow for planning and access to care at baseline and for future public healthcare crises.

Gainesville, Florida, USA   *Coleen Koch, MD, MS, MBA*
August 2022   *Folke H. Peterson Dean's Distinguished Professor*
                                              Dean, University of Florida College of Medicine

Preface

Its not a question if - just a question of when!

Regardless of current background, position, or demographic characteristics, a time will come when you will be deeply concerned about the function of systems that provide health care services. The person most directly involved may be you, but it may be a parent, a child, a friend, or some other loved one. No life will escape the need for a functioning system to deliver health related care. Thus, millions of hours have been spent developing, managing, and working to improve the functioning of such systems.

Early efforts to develop health care systems surely began before recorded history. The desire to avoid or manage pain is instinctive to all sentient beings. The earliest writing that is commonly labeled as a medical text stems from six papyri from ancient Egypt and date to between 2000 and 1500 BCE (Stiefel et al (1996), Castiglioni (2019)). These earliest recorded efforts include the use of herbs and practices thought to be helpful based on series of recorded observations. The effectiveness of such efforts was a mixed bag, but over time humans made more discoveries about how different practices, and ingestion of various elements eased pain, or prolonged life.

Much later, the enlightenment and the development of the scientific method yielded more formal ways to experiment, test methods, and measure results in efforts to identify better approaches. (Bernard (1957)) The need to co-locate varied resources and newly discovered elements of care eventually led to the consolidation of such efforts and the collection of resources in larger spaces that became formal hospitals and clinics.

Beginning in the 19th century a various areas of engineering and applied math were directed to the problem of building and managing the hospital and its housed processes. The need to improve these systems was a primary driver of the first American universities that focused on research in addition to teaching. One of the earliest leaders in this regards was a small school in Baltimore, Maryland founded by Johns Hopkins (French (1946)). This early medical school and associated collection of smaller schools was a leader in the creation of many practices still used today including grand rounds, a system of interns and residents, and the formation of specialties that focus on a subset of diseases or patients such as neurosurgery and pediatrics (Long (1991)).

Efforts to make the hospital run better and serve a growing population quickly included expertise from faculty with skills in engineering and mathematics. Consequently, Johns Hopkins developed the first department in an American university focused on what eventually become known as Operations Research in 1952 (Flagle (2002)). The tools developed in Operations Research departments included such esoteric topics as Queueing theory, Discrete Event Simulation, and other forms of mathematical modeling in which an abstract representation of an actual system could be constructed and analyzed as part of the search for better ways to get things done (Gass and Assad (2005)). Thus, the link between hospital operations and Operations Research was institutionalized in the US. (Similar efforts took place simultaneously in the UK.)

The economic reality of the country evolved at the same time. In the early 1800's bartering for services was common because the typical worker had very limited ability to pay for health care delivery. At the same time, the skills and education needed to deliver medical care grew rapidly as scientific approaches to care produced thousands of new ideas, drugs, devices, and procedures. It quickly became very difficult and time consuming for one to learn all that needed to be understood for the general practice of medicine. The need for more devices, equipment, space, and training inevitably led to increases in both the quality of care and the cost to deliver it.

Social responses to increasing expenses included the rise of many benevolent societies, religious charities, insurance companies, and even government programs to help individuals manage the cost of these essential services. Over time this industry grew to become the largest single sector in the world's largest economy and that growth shows no sign of stopping in the foreseeable future. (CMS (2020), Lorenzoni et al (2014)) Such growth has consequences not imagined in the 19th century.

Government efforts to deal with health care costs include ever expanding bodies of regulations and a myriad of ways to restrict payments that are presented as efforts to "manage" costs. The need for means to improve efficiency and manage costs are readily apparent from consideration of a few simple facts. For full service hospitals in the United States, the median profit per patient discharge is negative (-$82) (Bai and Anderson (2016)). In other words, most hospitals lose money on the typical admitted patient. Administrators struggle not just to maximize patient satisfaction, but to simply keep the doors open. Most rural areas have a shortage of care providers, and almost every hospital administrator or clinic manager will report that the shortages of nurses (Lasater et al (2020)) and general practitioners (Majeed (2017)) show no sign of relenting.

The high cost of inpatient care leads to increased demand for outpatient services. The shortage and growing costs of providers for outpatient services drives the search for increased throughput from fixed levels of resources. Consequently, the role of engineers and mathematicians that was first seen in the early construction of medical facilities emerges once again in a very different context. The engineers needed to design the buildings and spaces must now be supplemented with those needed to improve the processes that take place within those spaces.

This monograph is meant to be a small contribution to the body of knowledge directed toward this endeavor. Over the past decade the authors have worked on dozens of quality improvement projects, supervised many efforts to gather data on system performance and quality, taught thousands of students from business and medical disciplines, and constructed many models, cases, research publications, and readings on this critical topic. All of this work has been carried out within the environment of the world's most famous hospital.

We make no claims to have all of the answers or even to fully understand all of the many nuances of the problems. However, it does seem fair to say that the reader may be aided by exposure to what we have witnessed, tested, and applied in this setting.

Organization of Content

If we think about improving the operations function of a small to medium sized service unit we can easily find recipes for the task as a series of simple steps. First, define the processes in place to deliver the service and analyze them in terms of resource usage, capacity, quality, and output. Assuming that pricing is exogenous to the unit manager, (as is almost always the case in health care delivery) one then focuses on the connections between the value delivered, and the cost incurred to deliver that value. Once this understanding is in hand we can compare the performance of one unit to that of another as part of the mission to seek ways to improve one or both parts of this performance metric.

Unfortunately, when we apply many common tools of this approach to the processes of health care delivery, they often break down. This is not to say that the inherent logic of process analysis, cost reduction, and performance measurement do not apply in health care. Rather, we repeatedly find that special care and adjustments are needed in their application. For example, introductory approaches to process analysis tend to focus on the identification of a bottleneck resource, and a parallel search for sources of variability that can be eliminated. This approach facilitates a matching of capacity to demand, and increases the efficiency and predictability of process performance. However, several distinctive characteristics of health care services complicate this approach. These characteristics include patient participation, simultaneity, perishability, intangibility, and heterogeneity (Fitzsimmons and Fitzsimmons (2006)).

To this list, we add two additional elements that we have found to be quite common. First, many resources are shared among an ever changing collection of jobs. Resources float from room to room, or patient to patient with frequent interruptions, repeating some tasks and splitting others into smaller parts that must be performed by multiple specialized resources. The high division of labor in hospitals and the hierarchical structures that result interfere with efforts to define, measure, and compare performance. Therefore, improving these processes requires additional tools and modified approaches are needed.

Second, the psychology and culture of health care providers is such that thinking of cost reduction as a first priority is anathema to their nature. Few providers hold a clear idea of what a process costs because their minds will not allow this consideration to be their primary concern. Some providers simply refuse to speak in terms of costs, because to do so feels like it is implicitly pricing human suffering. On the other hand, administrators cannot escape the reality that most hospitals lose money and that if no action is taken, they will cease to function. Costing is not widely understood in health care but the system will collapse if it is not addressed.

This complexity also affects the notions of quality of service and value of outcomes. Health outcomes for the many must be balanced against attention to the relative few who are on site right now in ways that effect health outcomes, costs, waiting times, and many other elements of patient and provider experience. The fact that outcomes lay along so many dimensions simultaneously makes simple metrics such as profit and loss woefully inadequate. Again, this is not to imply that such measurements are immaterial, but that their treatment must be managed in a style that respects the context and culture of the industry.

After we do develop an understanding of process performance, quality, and costs we can easily identify a set of issues to be addressed. With these issues in mind, we will address new questions in the second phase of this text. How are we going to make this system better? Can we identify an approach that can be replicated and applied across systems with such complex issues and varying settings? It is clear that managers need tools that are robust enough to be used in many settings, and yet powerful enough to help get this job done.

This short book is a compendium of readings, examples, exercises, and case studies intended to help identify both areas in need of improvement, and some means to bring that improvement about. In Chapter 1 we begin with a primer on basic elements of Process Analysis with a special effort to place the terms, and approaches within the context of Health Care Management. The reader will quickly realize that many complicating factors common in health care settings warrant additional tools and adjustments to these generic approaches. Chapters 2 and 3 deal with tools to help in this regard, and present examples to show why they are needed. More specifically, Chapter 2 discusses simple tools including Gantt Charts and the Critical Path Method as aids to presenting and understanding complex systems. Chapter 3 considers issues related to shared resources and schedules that can be repeated as cycles throughout a session, or shift. Chapter 4 introduces Queueing theory as a way to formalize the consideration of variability related to inter-arrival and activity times. Chapter 5 wrestles with the question "how much will an episode of care cost?" These 5 chapters constitute the first major section of the text.

With an understanding of this foundational material in hand, we turn to the question of how to move from analysis to improvement. In Chapter 6 we lay out a framework that has often helped us in this regard. A six step process is depicted to move from process mapping to eventual process improvement. Technically speaking the center piece of this methodology is the use of Discrete Event Simulation as a management tool. Consequently, Chapter 7 explores why this tool is needed, and what types of insights it is likely to produce. Examples of implementations and issues uncovered are interspersed in these chapters to highlight applications of the approach. We conclude with a collection of case studies as Chapters 8 through 11 that relate to major portions of the preceding chapters and help contextualize their application.

Readers are encouraged to work from start to finish. However, each chapter is written with the idea that most people will pick and choose what is most relevant to them at any point in time. Consequently, we have made an effort to allow each chapter to serve as a stand alone reading on the relevant topic. This design results in a bit of redundancy, but hopefully reinforces key messages without becoming tedious.

Background and Intended Audience

Over the past decade we have taught courses on Services Management, Health Care Services, Fundamentals of Health Care Processes, Introductions to Process Analysis, Business Analytics, and a host of Immersion courses focused on various processes in the settings of clinics, hospitals, and insurers. In addition, we have published a collection of works in various medical and business journals, and have been involved in a host of quality improvement projects, business planning efforts, and operational studies. Over the course of this work a guiding framework emerged that can be taught and repeatedly applied in process improvement efforts (Dada and Chambers (2019)). This framework and its associated readings, cases, assignments, lectures, videos, and projects that we developed or led became the source content for this text.

The primary audience for this text is students in courses similar to ours that may be taught in schools of Business, Nursing, Medicine, and Public Health with a focus on health care delivery processes. The first eight chapters easily map onto an 8 week course on the topic. We typically use one or more of the included case studies as an end of course project or as part of a final exam. These cases fit most directly into MBA, or MS programs on the topic. However, we strive to present the content in a way that makes it accessible to undergraduate students in advanced electives as well. A second audience includes administrators such as clinic managers, and department heads working in this space.

The sequencing of the chapters is designed to fit within a course structure, but each chapter stands on its own as a reference for anyone in need of one of the tools discussed. While the work presents a variety of tools we note that the book is not a substitute for more detailed training material on the most technical topics. The primary example is the use of Discrete Event Simulation. Many other texts fill this void. Our objective is to present the logic of the ideas and to explain their use.

We submit that any reader who has ever pondered questions like, "why is this place so slow," or "why is this charge so high" will benefit from exposure to this material. We strongly suspect that this group includes anyone who has ever inter-acted with this system at a stressful time, which is virtually everyone. Again, its not a question of if you will ever be in that group - only one of when.

Finally, we wish to thank the hundreds of health care professionals involved in our prior studies, projects, and publications that have led to this point. This includes the technicians, nurses, doctors, administrators, and patients who allowed us to view their activities and care. Thanks also goes to the dozens of readers, reviewers, and presentation audience members who have added content, clarity, and focus.

Most importantly we thank our families who have suffered long hours as read-ers, supporters, and sounding boards along the way. Chester Chambers particularly thanks S, L, and C: the Queen of All, The Light of the World, and the Joyous Con-tinuation respectively.

Maqbool Dada particularly thanks his wife Shamim and our children Natasha and Myra for their love and support over many decades while tolerating innumer-able long-winded discourses on all things academic.

Kayode Williams dedicates this work to his wife Oyinkansola without whose love and support his career achievements would not be possible, their sons and daughter-in-law, Olatunji and his wife Victoria, Oluwatomi, and their granddaugh-ter, Rosie, all of whose enquiring minds have spurred his quest to acquire knowl-edge.

Baltimore, MD, USA   *Chester Chambers*
July 2022   *Maqbool Dada*
                                                                                                   Kayode Williams

Prologue

As we seek to build intuition regarding the management of health care processes, we must wrestle with the vastness of the system under study. For example, if one looks into the breadth of the systems connected with Johns Hopkins medicine one finds a vast array of outpatient clinics and surgical centers in the US that handle almost a million patient visits per year, and hospitals that handle over 4 million visits per year including more than 350,000 emergency department visits (Chambers and Williams (2017b)). The system also includes hospital management and facilities in China, Singapore, India, Japan, United Arab Emirates, Saudi Arabia, Turkey, Lebanon, Pakistan, Chile, Peru, Mexico, Brazil, Panama, Columbia, and Canada. In addition, the system adds insurance companies, and schools of medicine, nursing, and public health.

In the consideration of such a large and complex network, it is imperative that we focus on lessons and tools that are applicable across a plethora of settings. With this in mind we will focus on smaller problems in proto-typical settings to help develop insights that can be generalized and adjusted to fit whatever system you wish to improve. It is instructive to focus on bite sized chunks of a care delivery system such as a single clinic, emergency department (ED), operating room (OR) suite, hospital ward, or hospital. Narrowing the focus facilitates calculations and allows for the exploration of small examples that can be created to convey key points.

Unfortunately, this approach flies in the face of the fact that health care is the largest single industry in the world's largest economy (for Economic Co-operation and Development (2020)). As a result, it involves a vast network of facilities, staff, physicians, and resources spread across almost every community. This vast landscape creates a multitude of hand-offs between units, and coordination among far-flung agents. Any analysis of these parts suffers if connections to the rest of the system are ignored. The simultaneous need to break large problems into manageable portions and to understand the nature of connections among system parts makes the study of health care processes uniquely difficult and complex. With this in mind, it is helpful to envision a virtual system that can serve as a microcosm of the larger reality. We will frequently refer to this mental model throughout the chapters that follow.

Envision a large hospital located in a moderate sized city on the east coast of the United States. Let us refer to this unit as Eastern University Hospital. We use this construct as a literary device. While the bulk of our research and experience has taken place within the Johns Hopkins system, Eastern is not intended to be a replication of any particular clinic, ward, unit, or hospital. As a result, the problems presented here are fully informed by our study of actual settings, but not meant to be duplications of any singular unit. The data presented are a composite of sources that we have gathered over the past 10 years.

Eastern happens to be a teaching hospital, meaning that many processes will involve residents in addition to the nurses, clinical assistants, attending physicians, and a host of technicians and other staff. We will consider patients entering Eastern through at least 3 routes. Some patients will arrive at the ED. We will assume that these patients arrive one at a time with random times between arrivals. We will also assume that the ED has some fixed number of examination rooms, but we will treat the waiting area as though it has infinite capacity. Most patients who enter via the ED will later be discharged and sent home. However, some portion of these patients will need to move to an OR suite. The OR suite will have a fixed number of rooms. Most surgeries in this suite will be scheduled in advance (elective surgeries) whereas those that stem from ED visits will not (emergency surgeries). After patients leave the ED, they may travel to a ward such as medical, orthopedic, or neurology ward. Other patients will be in critical condition and will be sent to an intensive care unit (ICU). The ICU will have finite capacity as well.

Most patients who interact with Eastern will do so through the Eastern Hospital Outpatient Clinic (E-HOC). This clinic deals with patients by appointment, and has scheduled opening and closing times each working day. The vast majority of patients that enter E-HOC will go home after their visit. However, it is possible that they will need to move to an OR, ward, or very rarely the ICU. Managers at E-HOC and other clinics routinely deal with the problem of developing, and fine-tuning an appointment schedule. This schedule is designed to strike a balance between waiting times and overtime operations for the clinic. Any patients still in the clinic at the proposed closing time will be seen, meaning that the clinic does not really close until all of the patients on the schedule have been treated.

0.1 A Patient's Journey Through the Eastern University Hospital System

Frank Caldwell resides in the same city as Eastern Hospital and is in generally good health. Frank doesn't think much about the health care system, even though he recognizes it as the largest sector of the economy, and the largest employer in his town. Frank has health insurance through his employer but hasn't paid much attention to its cost because he is young, he doesn't use the system much, and his co-pays are pretty low. One afternoon Frank suffers an injury to his right hand during a pickup basketball game after work and decides to drive himself to the ED. This is his entry point to the Eastern Hospital System.

0.1.1 Entry Through the ED

Frank has suffered an injury to his right hand during the pickup basketball game, but has also had some pain in this hand before. He is pretty sure that this particular injury is just a sprain, but the ED was close by and he wanted to be sure. Either way, this is certainly not a life-threatening condition.[1] As he enters the ED he sees a line of 7 patients waiting in front of what looks like a Nurses' station. Frank is pretty sure that there are more than one of these stations but the others are around the corner so he does not see exactly how many are in place. While he is waiting he notices that patients are walking into the ED at a rate that he estimates to be about 1 per minute. (actually 55 patients per hour.) During a short triage step that takes roughly 4 minutes he is told that, typically 10% of the patients who enter the ED are admitted to the hospital. The rest are released and go home; usually with a prescription and some instructions about how to deal with the malady. Frank is told that since his condition is not critical he will have a short wait before seeing the doctor. He is also told that for patients who are admitted the time with the doctor averages about 30 minutes, but for simpler cases like his it is likely to be around 10 minutes. Frank walks over to a waiting area and takes a seat. When he looks around he counts 34 patients in the room with him. Frank is concerned that the wait will be rather long, but is told that more than one doctor is in the ED that day; and that the staff can process patients quickly enough to maintain a fairly stable number of patients in the waiting room.

Frank also happens to be a fairly new student in an evening MBA program in town, and recalls some readings about process management. He wonders if he can figure out a few things about how this system is working. Like most patients he is primarily worried about his health, but since he has a few minutes to think, he wonders if he can determine how long the average patient spends in the ED, how many doctors are working in the ED that day, and how many patients are in the ED in total.

---

[1] This vignette parallels a problem presented in Anupindi et al (1999) and will also be revisited in the review material after Chapter 1.

0.1.2 Specialty Outpatient Clinic

It turns out that Frank has not broken any bones. However, the doctor recommends that Frank visit Dr. Twofer, who is a specialist in sports medicine. This particular specialist is renown for his use of arthroscopic procedures to remove floating bodies in wrist and hand joints and the ED physician suspects that this issue is contributing to Frank's problems. However, before the procedure can be scheduled Frank will have a visit to a clinic that this surgeon shares with several other physicians in the Orthopedics department to determine whether the surgery is really necessary. Upon arrival at the clinic, Frank checks in and is informed that, since this clinic is affiliated with a teaching hospital he will be seen by a resident first, before seeing Dr. Twofer. Frank sees Dr. Twofer chatting on the phone in the hallway and wonders why he has to wait. He is told that the doctor is on the phone getting information on another case, and that Frank should not have to wait long because the resident and the attending physician will work in parallel, at first, and then come back together to complete Frank's visit.

When Frank made this appointment several slots were available. Frank selected the first appointment for the day hoping that this would minimize his waiting time. He was surprised to find that another patient had the same appointment time that he did, but the clinical assistant (CA) at the desk informed Frank that this was a normal practice for this clinic. While standing at the desk Frank notices a template next to the screen that the CA was viewing labeled "Appointment Schedule for Dr. Twofer". It looked something like this,

TABLE 1: APPOINTMENT SCHEDULE FOR ORTHO CLINIC 1

Metric	Average Value
New 1	8:00
Return 1	8:00
Return 2	8:30
New 2	8:50
Return 3	8:50
Return 4	9:30
New 3	10:10
Return 5	10:10
Return 6	11:30

As Frank looks over the scheduling template he thinks to himself, these people make everything so complicated they can't simply add two numbers together. Why can't they just have patients come in every half hour? They have 9 patients on the schedule so they can easily finish at noon. It's obvious to Frank that this would be a much simpler schedule and it would have to work better than the odd looking mess posted here. [2]

0.1.3 Procedure Capacity and Parallel Processing

At the end of the visit, Dr. Twofer schedules a simple arthroscopic procedure to clean out some floating debris within Frank's wrist. Dr Twofer is well known for these procedures and has worked over the past 20 years to streamline his operating process. In his consultation with the surgeon, Frank learns that the surgeon uses 2 rooms in a procedure suite at the same time. A patient is prepped, and positioned in Room 1. This process, which takes 35 minutes involves one OR and the staff assigned to that case. Dr. Twofer then enters Room 1 and completes his portion of the process over the next 25 minutes. After each case, it takes 15 minutes to clean the room, but only 5 minutes for the surgeon to scrub and change gowns before moving to Room 2 to work on the next patient, who is already prepped and ready by this time. This cycle then repeats so that the surgeon can complete 3 surgeries in one session. [3]

Frank is curious about this odd process. It seems like a waste to assign 2 OR's to one surgeon who can only be in one place at a time. He once read that the OR is among the most expensive resources in the hospital and thinks to himself, "no wonder health care costs are so high".

0.1.4 Patient Flows and Transfers Between Units

Frank's time in the OR goes according to plan, but the effects of the anesthesia linger much longer than is typical, and the surgeon believes that Frank should be held overnight for observation. Dr. Twofer explains to Frank that this happens in 1 to 2% of his patients and is nothing to be alarmed about. Frank will wait in the post-anesthesia care unit (PACU) until he is moved to a bed on one of the hospital floors. Frank is still groggy but alert enough to ask how long it will be before he is moved to a room. Dr. Twofer explains that it can take anywhere from a few minutes to a few hours, and that the nursing staff will take care of him from here. The doctor then moves on to the next case.

As Frank lies in wait in the PACU he gets a bit irritated thinking about the wait. "This hospital has over 800 beds and I have to wait to find just one?" Frank vaguely

---

[2] This schedule parallels that used in the clinic discussed in detail in Chapter 10, and is also discussed in the review material after Chapter 3.

[3] This vignette is inspired by that depicted in Bohmer et al (2007) and will be revisited in the review material after Chapter 2.

remembers that Eastern usually has an occupancy rate of around 70% (AHA (2017)) and wonders, "if 30% of 800 beds are empty, it doesn't make any sense for me to be waiting this long. There doesn't seem to be any way to make sense of this mess."

0.1.5 Billing and the Cost of Care

Frank is moved to a bed in the medical ward after a half hour or so and spends the night. He is a little uncomfortable at first, but his medical symptoms dissipate over the next 8 hours. By morning he is ready to go home and a nurse informs him that he will be leaving soon. His surgeon comes by about 8 AM and tells Frank that he is cleared to go. There are just a few administrative issues to work through and a few forms to sign, but it shouldn't take too long. For some reason that Frank doesn't understand his discharge is not completed until the middle of the afternoon.

About a week later Frank gets a statement from the hospital that shows costs of $18,000. Stamped across the top of the statement is a note that reads, "THIS IS NOT A BILL" but it sure looks like a bill to Frank. In the coming days Frank gets a similar statement from the surgeon's office and another from some anesthesiology partnership. Frank is a little upset by these statements. When all of these charges are totaled they are close to $30,000. Frank wonders if some of these "costs" occurred because the hospital was so slow in moving him from the PACU to the bed, and then not allowing him to go home as soon as he was ready. Eventually, Frank gets a bill from his insurance provider. The bill shows the total charges of close to $30,000, but it seems to indicate that the insurer pays roughly $12,000 and that Frank owes about $600 of that amount. Frank doesn't really understand what is going on here, but he is so relieved that this $30,000 in charges translates to a $600 check from him that he decides not to ask any questions. However, he does wonder how the hospital can survive if the gap between its costs and revenues is that high.

0.2 Health Care Process Analytics

As we follow a patient's journey through an episode of care we are struck by the number of intersection points between the patient and the medical system. A single event easily leads to interactions with an ED, a specialty clinic, a PACU, an OR suite, a medical ward, and a billing system. This list omits the interactions with pharmacies, counseling services, social workers, and government agencies that are common when considering older patients who make up the bulk of the patient population.

In the coming pages we introduce a collection of tools, and observations used to shed light on the myriad of questions that naturally arise through the patient's experience with this large, complex system. We will frequently refer to Frank's story to provide context to the discussion of a number of the analytical techniques that we use. However, the larger issue is that these settings and problems are really mini-laboratories in which we develop tools that can be applied generally to settings of the reader's interest.

Contents

0.1 A Patient's Journey Through the Eastern University Hospital System xvi
    0.1.1 Entry Through the ED xvii
    0.1.2 Specialty Outpatient Clinic xviii
    0.1.3 Procedure Capacity and Parallel Processing xix
    0.1.4 Patient Flows and Transfers Between Units xix
    0.1.5 Billing and the Cost of Care xx
0.2 Health Care Process Analytics xx

1   **A Primer on Process Analysis for Health Care Delivery** 1
  1.1 Introduction 1
  1.2 Basic Definitions 2
    1.2.1 Process Management 8
    1.2.2 Goals of Process Management 11
  1.3 Key Process Measures: Throughput, Work in Process, and Cycle
    Time 12
    1.3.1 Little's Law 13
    1.3.2 Example 1 14
    1.3.3 Example 2 16
    1.3.4 Example 3 16
    1.3.5 Example 4 17
  1.4 Putting the Pieces Together: Instrumentation Preparation 18
  1.5 Key Take-Aways 24
  1.6 Review Material and Prior Works 25
    1.6.1 Process Analysis for ED 25
    1.6.2 Process Analysis for Hernia Clinic 25

2   **Special Issues in Process Analysis for Health Care: Visualization, &**
  Project Management 27
  2.1 Introduction 27
  2.2 Data Collection 28

2.3   Gantt Charts: A Valuable Tool to Understand Health Care
            Delivery Processes 31
            2.3.1   Creating Gantt Charts 33
    2.4   Examples of Clinic Visits 34
    2.5   Collected Comments on Gantt Charts 41
    2.6   Makespan and the Critical Path Method 43
            2.6.1   Earliest Start, Earliest Finish and the Forward Pass 44
            2.6.2   Latest Finish, Latest Start, and the Backward Pass 46
    2.7   Putting the Pieces Together: Appointment Scheduling at Eastern
            Hospital Outpatient Clinic 46
    2.8   Key Take-Aways 50
    2.9   Review Material and Prior Works 50
            2.9.1   Surgeon Using Two Rooms: Normal Cases 51
            2.9.2   Surgeon Using Two Rooms Double Cases 51

3   **Special Issues in Process Analysis for Health Care: Shared
    Resources and Cycles** 53
    3.1   Introduction 53
    3.2   Process Mapping 55
    3.3   Parallel Processing 55
    3.4   Combining Resources 58
    3.5   Sharing Resources 60
    3.6   Scheduling Jobs with Variable Activity Times 61
    3.7   A Cyclic Approach to Appointment Scheduling 62
            3.7.1   Problem Setting and Identification 64
            3.7.2   Finding an Optimal Schedule 67
            3.7.3   Composite Jobs 69
            3.7.4   Application in the AMC 69
            3.7.5   Heuristics for Appointment Scheduling 71
            3.7.6   Gantt Chart of Simple Heuristic 73
    3.8   Key Take-Aways 75
    3.9   Review Material 76
            3.9.1   Cyclic Scheduling Template with NEW and RETURN
                    Patients 76
            3.9.2   Cyclic Scheduling Template with only RETURN Patients .. 77

4   **Management of Queues** 79
    4.1   Introduction 79
    4.2   Problem Setting 81
    4.3   Analysis of Waiting Times 84
            4.3.1   Resource Utilization 85
    4.4   Theoretical Foundations for the Study of Queues 87
            4.4.1   Anatomy of a Queueing System 87
            4.4.2   Exponential Time Distributions 88
            4.4.3   Contributions of Markov 91

	4.4.4	Little's Law & Queues	93
	4.4.5	M|M|1 Queues	94
	4.4.6	M|M|s Queues	96
4.5	Examination of Vaccine Delivery Process		98
	4.5.1	System Capacity	98
	4.5.2	Average Cycle Time and Census	98
	4.5.3	Average Waiting Time	99
	4.5.4	Process B: Two Servers with a 50/50 Split	99
	4.5.5	Process C: Two Less Experienced Servers with Reduced Speed	100
4.6	Key Take-Aways		101
4.7	Review Material		103
	4.7.1	Large Scale Vaccination Site: Process A	103
	4.7.2	Large Scale Vaccination Site: Process B	104

5 Cost Estimation and Process Improvement 107
5.1	Introduction		107
	5.1.1	Cost are Just a Percentage of Charges - Right?	109
5.2	Cost Measurement at a Prototypical Outpatient Clinic: Process 1		111
5.3	Time-Driven, Activity-Based Costing		115
	5.3.1	Cost Measurement at Eastern Hospital Outpatient Center: Process 2	117
	5.3.2	Process Metrics Using Process 1	120
	5.3.3	Process Metrics Using Process 2	121
5.4	Key Take Aways		123
5.5	Review Material & Prior Works		124
	5.5.1	Cost for Blood Test with Attending Follow-Up	124
	5.5.2	Cost for Blood Test with Nurse Follow-Up	124

6 A Process Improvement Process 127
6.1	Introduction		127
6.2	A Representative Clinic: Part I		129
6.3	How to Fix Health Care Processes		131
6.4	The Process Improvement Process		133
	6.4.1	Step 1: Process Description	133
	6.4.2	Step 2: Data Collection	134
	6.4.3	Step 3: Create a DES of the System	136
	6.4.4	Step 4: Metrics of Interest	138
	6.4.5	Step 5: Propose Process Changes	140
	6.4.6	Step 6: Predict Impact of Process Changes	140
6.5	Experiments, Simulations, and Results		141
	6.5.1	Arrival Process	142
	6.5.2	Physician Processing Times	143
	6.5.3	Private Practice versus the AMC	145
	6.5.4	Pre-processing	146

6.5.5   Cyclic Scheduling 147
6.6   Key Take-Aways 148
6.7   Review Material 150
   6.7.1   Searching for a Better Appointment Schedule 150
   6.7.2   Searching for a Better Appointment Schedule 150

7   **Discrete Event Simulations: Concepts, Metrics, and Canonical Models** 153
7.1   Introduction 153
7.2   Outpatient Clinics 156
   7.2.1   Variability and System Performance 161
   7.2.2   Pooling Resources 162
   7.2.3   Mixing Patient Types 165
   7.2.4   State Dependent Face Time 166
7.3   Emergency Departments 169
   7.3.1   Downstream Resources and Blocking 171
   7.3.2   Length of Stay from ED to Discharge 172
7.4   Key Take-Aways 174
7.5   Review Material & Prior Works 175
   7.5.1   Patient Unpunctuality 176
   7.5.2   An Academic Model with Distributions of Teaching Time .. 177
   7.5.3   State Dependent Activity Times 178

8   **Case Study: Miller Pain Treatment Center** 179
8.1   Introduction 179
8.2   Eastern Hospital and E-HOC 180
8.3   Private Practice 181
8.4   Efficiency of Clinic Operations 182
8.5   Patient Tardiness and Waiting Times 184
8.6   Merging Clinics 186
8.7   Miller Pain Treatment Clinic 187
8.8   Issues in the AMC 190
8.9   Review Material 193

9   **Case Study: Collecting Activity Times Using a Real Time Location
   System** 195
9.1   Collecting Activity Time Data in Eastern Hospital 195
   9.1.1   Kick-Off Meeting 196
   9.1.2   Additional Issues 198
9.2   The GI Team 199
   9.2.1   Processing AMS and RTLS Data 200
9.3   Review Material and Prior Works 205

10   **Case Study: The RadOnc Clinic Expansion** 207
10.1   Analyzing Flow Data 207
10.2   Visualizing Key Data 208
10.3   Review Material 212

11 Case Study: Safe Birth Clinic 219
11.1 Introduction 219
11.2 Process A: The Earlier Process (Followed by Patients Until December 2018 220
11.3 Process B: The Current Process (Being Followed by Patients Since January 2019) 223
11.4 A New Potential Addition: Genetic Counselling and Physical Therapy Session 224
11.5 Process Redesign: Separate Upfront Examinations by the Doctor . . . 226
11.6 Discussion Questions 226

12 Epilogue 229
12.1 Introduction 229
12.2 Complications in Projects to Improve Health Care Processes 231
12.3 Searching for Improvement Ideas Using Prior Works 233
12.3.1 Finding Ideas 233
12.3.2 Screening Ideas..................................... 236
12.4 Closing Comments 237

References 239

Index 245

Acronyms

Unless otherwise noted, these acronyms are used consistently throughout the text.

ACA   Affordable Care Act: The Patient Protection and Affordable Care Act expanded Medicaid, and altered individual insurance markets.

AMC   Academic Medical Center: Medical facility that includes an educational mission as part of the routine process flow.

CA   Clinical Assistant: The role of a CA is to directly assist physicians, nurses and other health care professionals in providing patient care, with the focus being on performing clinical duties rather than clerical tasks.

CDF   Cumulative Distribution Function: The probability that the realization of a random variable will be less than a given level. The CDF is expressed as a general function that can be used for any possible realization level.

CMS   Centers for Medicare and Medicaid Services: A federal agency within the United States Department of Health and Human Services that administers the Medicare program and works in partnership with state governments to administer Medicaid, the Children's Health Insurance Program, and health insurance portability standards.

CPM   Critical Path Method: An approach to finding the longest path through a network representing a project to determine Makespan and to explain how changing start times or durations for activities affects project length.

CT   Cycle Time: The time a flow unit spends within process boundaries.

DES   Discrete Event Simulation: A mathematical model that tracks changes in element status at discrete moments in time such as a patient arrival, or the start of end of an activity.

DRG   Defines groups based upon primary diagnosis. Useful in allowing comparison of costs, outcomes, mortality rates etc. across units or countries. The list has been revised 10 times and thus, produces ICD-10 codes.

ED   Emergency Department: An entity that accepts patients who arrive randomly for any medical condition. Many (but not all) of these patients will arrive with life-threatening conditions.

EFT   Early Finish Time: The earliest that an activity can be concluded given that the activity start time is contingent on the completion times of earlier activities.

EMR   Electronic Medical Record: The dominant format for storage of medical patient information in the US. Includes information for billing, test results, doctor's notes, etc.

EST   Early Start Time: the earliest it is feasible to begin an activity given that its start time is contingent on the completion times of all earlier activities.

ICD   International Classification of Diseases: Classification system that typically specifies a lump sum payment to cover all charges from admission to discharge based on which group is designated by the main diagnosis.

ICU   Intensive Care Unit: Area reserved for high acuity patients in need of care beyond the normal capability of a typical hospital ward.

IE   Industrial Engineering: Engineering profession that is concerned with the optimization of complex processes, systems, or organizations by developing, improving and implementing integrated systems of people, money, knowledge, information and equipment.

LFT   Late Finish Time: The latest that an activity can be concluded without increasing Makespan given that subsequent activity start times may be contingent on the completion times of this activity.

LST   Late Start Time: The latest it is feasible to begin an activity without increasing Makespan, given that each activity's start time is contingent on the completion times of all earlier activities.

OECD   Organization for Economic Co-operation and Development: An intergovernmental economic organization with 38 member countries, founded in 1961 to stimulate economic progress and world trade.

OM   Operations Management: Field of social science focused on the design, management, and improvement of systems that deliver goods and services.

OR   Operations Research: An area of applied mathematics that used analytical models focused on problems related to the management of processes or other industrial or business functions.

ORS   Operating Room Suite: A collection of 1 or more Operating Rooms that may be designated for a specific type of surgery or may be equipped for general use.

PACU   Pre (or Post) Anesthesia Care Unit: An area where patients are prepped for surgery including any final pre-surgery steps that may include administration of pain medicines and anesthesia. The same unit is also often used for the same patients post-surgery if they do not need to proceed directly to an ICU.

PP   Private Practice: Medical facility that does not include an educational mission.

RTLS   Real Time Location System: An electronic system including receivers and transmitters that indicate the location of selected or "tagged" items in real time. Often used in hospitals, universities, and warehouses to track goods and personnel.

TDABC   Time-Driven Activity-Based Costing: An approach to estimating the cost of an activity based on products of busy times and cost rates for individual resources.

WIP   Work-in-progress: Flow units within process boundaries at a moment in time.

Chapter 1
A Primer on Process Analysis for Health Care Delivery

Abstract Before we can begin to improve health care delivery processes we need a language and methodology to describe them. In addition, we need clear metrics to express their performance. With these elements in hand, we will be prepared to discuss how to improve them with confidence that all parties involved agree on what is being described and what it means to achieve improvement. To accomplish this task we borrow a collection of tools from Industrial Engineering that has proven to be useful. We make no claim that this presentation is exhaustive, or even the most effective. We simply set out to present a coherent framework for the necessary discussions that follow.

1.1 Introduction

To improve the performance of a system we need ways describing that system and its performance that are readily recognizable and understandable to the agents involved. After the industrial revolution many of the earliest efforts to systematically study systems that deliver products and services were undertaken by Industrial Engineers (Emerson and Naehring (1988)). These early efforts started in the 19th century, and were key in the development of both mass production processes for manufacturing and data-driven approaches to managing the delivery of services. Over time the field of Operations Management (OM) developed when work from Industrial Engineering (IE) was merged with additional insights from the fields of Economics and Operations Research (Sprague (2007)). Since the early 20th century, experts and scholars in OM have collaborated with practitioners and scholars in health care to extend the use of IE and OM tools to improve the performance of systems that deliver health care services.[1]

---

[1] While we will note a number of specific text along the say, a comprehensive review of this work can be found in Jha et al (2016).

C. Chambers et al., *Improving Processes for Health Care Delivery*,
https://doi.org/10.1007/978-3-031-19043-8_1

It is useful to have a working understanding of a number of tools from these scholarly areas and to present them in the context of Health Care Delivery processes. More specifically we aim to introduce elements of <u>Process Management</u> and <u>Process Analysis</u> to create a vocabulary and framework with which we can view health care delivery systems in a way that facilitates their improvement. We begin with a brief collection of terminology that we shamelessly borrow from earlier works (In particular, see Anupindi et al (1999), Hopp and Lovejoy (2012), Ozcan (2009), and Karuppan et al (2021).)

Though the most common terms are often not a perfect fit for health care settings, for the most part we will stick with this terminology so that users will find it easy to locate supporting documentation in other articles and textbooks. However, at each point we will work to position these rather generic terms in the health care context. With this vocabulary in place we consider the most common measurements used in Process Analysis. We close with a few examples to illustrate how these ideas can be applied in a variety of health care settings.

1.2 Basic Definitions

<u>**Flow Unit:**</u> The discrete entity that is being altered by a process. Many textbooks and articles use the term <u>job</u>. The Flow Unit is most likely to be a physical item in a production setting, or the customer in a service setting. However, it can be a virtual item such as a file or data packet. It may also be some other manifestation of the process such as a test result, x-ray, or collection of records or data points.

Note: One key distinction between production settings and service settings is that in almost all service settings the Flow Unit holds a special relationship to the customer before any transaction takes place. In some cases the Flow Unit is the customer's information. In other settings it is the customer's property. The hardest systems to manage are those in which the flow unit is the customer him/herself, which is true in most of the problem settings under consideration here.

Activity: A discrete, identifiable, task or step involved in transforming the Flow Unit. To be a useful point of analysis, each activity should be defined so that important aspects of its functioning are measurable.

Note: To have a coherent discussion of improvement, it is extremely useful to have some measurements to focus upon. These can include physical counts, spans of time, measurements of quality, proxies for satisfaction, or some other attribute or score.

Resource: An item, or actor essential to the completion of an activity. Resources can include personnel, tools, equipment, or spaces.

Note: The personnel resources that we will consider most frequently are medical professionals including doctors, nurses, and technical staff. The spaces involved are often examination rooms, hospital beds, or operating room (OR) suites.

Route: The physical or virtual connections between a series of Activities that are needed to deliver the desired change to the Flow Unit.

Note: In most cases that we describe, Route is a virtual device, and not a physical pathway. If Activities A, B, and C are needed in that order, then we have a Route from A to B to C. The Route may or may not involve any physical movement of the Flow Unit. For example, different resources may all enter and exit a common space such as an examination room or OR suite to perform the needed Activities.

Process: A plan to move a Flow Unit from its original state to a desired state. More concretely, a process can be defined by a Route along which Resources perform Activities designed to alter the state of a Flow Unit.

Note: In health care this "Route" can be quite complex. Patients in a maternity ward and patients in an Oncology unit will follow completely different Routes within the system. The key point is that for a clearly defined population or "job type" we should be able to specify a series of steps that we anticipate happening when a member of the relevant population arrives.

Process Map: A diagram depicting the Routes, Resources, and Activities defining a process, along with selected metrics needed to convey the most pertinent information for understanding or analysis.

Note: In our work, we have found that it is best to begin the analysis using a very simple process map. Many health care professionals become distraught when feeling that such diagrams are incomplete, and they are certainly correct. The fact is that all process maps are incomplete. The key is to identify the Activities most critical to the process metrics of primary interest. Ultimately, this list may prove to be much shorter than one might think. In addition, the Process Map that guides discussions of a process will evolve over time as greater attention is focused on key details under consideration. We recommend building maps at the level of detail that fits the analysis, as additional information is likely to hinder understanding.

Flow Time: This is the amount of time that a Flow Unit spends between selected points in some segment of a process. A segment may include one or more process steps. The Flow Time within that segment includes processing time as well as any time spent between steps (waiting time.)

Note: Many texts define Flow Time more narrowly to be time spent from the start to the end of a process. We emphasize that a Flow Time may be calculated between any two points on a process map. This may span the entire process, or it may only focus on some smaller part or segment. When a process involves multiple decision making units, it is often useful to focus on different segments in turn. For example a care delivery process may include activities in a clinic, a pharmacy, and a lab. What takes place in these spaces may be thought of as segments, sub-processes, or discrete parts of the larger process.

Cycle Time: When Flow Time is measured using the beginning and the end of a process to define the relevant process segment we will call this special case the Cycle Time (CT). Improving CT is a very common objective in process management. Just as with any Flow Time, Cycle Time includes processing time, waiting time, rework time, inspection times, and transportation times as long as these events take place within the boundaries of the process of interest.

Note: For our purposes, the CT will often be the duration between patient arrival and exit from some clearly defined space or facility. In many instances, this time is synonymous with Length of Stay (LOS). However, in other settings the definition can be quite different. For example, many payers are concerned with the span of time from the start of the first visit for a condition to the end of the last follow-up visit. Thus the CT may involve multiple episodes of care. The key point is to define CT relative the process of interest and the goal of the analysis.

Takt Time: The average time between consecutive exits from a process.

Note: The term originates from the German work "takt" meaning a beat or pulse. Thus, we can think of Takt Time as defining the pulse or realized pace of the process. If patients exit a clinic after completion of their visit, Takt Time is the average duration between those exits. Thus, Takt Time reflects the realized inter-exit times of Flow Units. Many process improvement processes boil down to efforts to reduce Takt Time.

Throughput: Throughput is the rate at which Flow Units actually move through the process, and thus, Throughput is the inverse of Takt Time. Throughput may be expressed as units per hour, patients per clinic session, operations per day, cases per shift, etc.

Note: We emphasize that Throughput is a rate, and not simply a quantity. Consequently, counting the units of analysis and measuring the durations of time involved are both necessary to define this value. In addition, we are typically concerned with the realized rate; not simply what we wish the rate to be or what it "should" be. This rate will be the inverse of Takt Time. For example, if we average 5 minutes between exits, then Throughput equals one Flow Unit every 5 minutes. [Takt Time

= 1/Throughput]

If demand is not too high, the exit rate will equal the arrival rate. In these settings increasing the speed or efficiency of the system will not reduce Takt Time, as it is being dictated by the arrival rate of the Flow Units. However, in the vast majority of health care settings significant spans of time exist in which the average time between arrivals is less than the time between exists. In these instances, reducing Takt Time will reduce congestion in the system and the resulting waiting times.

Critical Time: The minimum time that can be sustained as the duration between the completion of successive units. It is a lower bound on Takt Time given the current structure of the process.

Note: We emphasize the term sustained in this definition. In almost any process involving highly skilled labor it may be possible to "rush" a job or two to reduce the time between the completion of successive jobs for a while. The key question is often whether this increased speed can be sustained for an entire shift or clinic session. Thus, the manager must be careful not to mistake a special case for a useful measure of Critical Time. Consequently, measurement across multiple cases, sessions, or even weeks is needed to find this value in practice.

For most (but certainly not all) settings of interest here the Critical Time will be the longest busy time per Flow Unit for a Resource involved in at least one (but often more) Activities in a defined process. It is often useful to keep the following fact in mind: if Resource A is busy for y minutes for every flow unit, then it does not matter how many other resources we bring to bear – Throughput can never exceed 1 unit every y minutes.

Capacity: The maximum sustainable rate of Throughput stated as Flow Units per unit time. The unit of time may be of any length: a second, minute, hour, shift, day, week, quarter, etc. We typically find that Capacity = 1/Critical Time.

Note: Given the definitions in place here it should be clear that to change Capacity, we must do something that reduces the Critical Time. We note that some texts do not differentiate between Takt Time and Critical Time. We differentiate between the two because Takt Time will be easy to find by direct observation, whereas Critical Time may be hidden. This is true because it may not be immediately clear how far Takt Time can be reduced before some constraint in the system stops it from dropping further. Since, managers want more Capacity, identification of the minimum Takt Time is often a useful starting point for analysis.

Bottleneck: A production Resource that limits how fast Flow Units can exit a process.

Note: The Bottleneck is typically (but not always) the resource whose busy time per Flow Unit defines the Critical Time. Stated a bit differently, it is the Resource with the lowest overall capacity. If each Resource is assigned to one and only one step, then identifying the step with the longest Activity Time also identifies the Bottleneck resource. If a resource is involved in multiple steps, then the Bottleneck may not be connected to the longest Activity at all. The Bottleneck may be labor, equipment, space (such as an examination room) or material.

In our experience this is the term on the list that is most often misused. No matter how many times we stress that the longest step is not necessarily tied to the Bottleneck resource, many people instinctively focus on the longest step and insist on referring to it as the bottleneck. This line of thinking is quite likely to lead to incorrect conclusions in health care settings for at least three reasons. First, many activities involve multiple resources that travel from patient to patient and must be carefully tracked and coordinated. Second, it is very common for a key resource such as a Nurse or Attending to be involved in multiple steps involving a single patient. Third, many activities such as reading x-rays or conducting tests occur outside the view of the observer. Consequently, we generally look at a process from start to finish and sum busy times for each Resource in search of the one with the greatest cumulative busy time per Flow Unit. Thus, in most settings that we consider discovery of the Critical Time and identification of the Bottleneck resource take place simultaneously.

Batch Size: The number of Flow Units that are processed or held as a group.

Note: In many cases Batch Size is the number of Flow Units processed before a Flow Unit of a different type can be worked upon. A common rationale for using batch sizes greater than one is that if changing from one job type to another requires an extra task to be performed, then this is a new batch. Consequently, every Process has a Batch Size, but for most cases of interest here that Batch Size is simply one.

Some are surprised to see processes in health care with batch sizes greater than one. However, many items related to patient care such as x-rays, lab tests, or drug packaging will be handled in larger batches. Mixing tasks that are carried out in batch sizes of one such as examinations with other tasks that are completed in larger batches such as delivery of a collection of x-rays can greatly complicate process analysis.

Setup Time: The fixed time involved in processing a Flow Unit or batch of Flow Units. If Flow Units are handled in a batch or group, this time is independent of the batch size.

Note: Many Activities involve time spent preparing to perform a particular task or operation. However, some processes will also have set actions that must take place during or even after a process step, such as data recording, or error checking. Even though these actions do not literally "set up" the Activity, they may still be fixed amounts of time associated with an Activity and therefore are still characterized as Setup Time.

Many health care settings have Setup Times that are quite literal such as positioning a patient for surgery or adjusting machine settings for radiation oncology, or x-ray. Other Setup Times are more subtle and may include actions such as pre-visit charting or post-visit dictation. Many efforts to analyze patient flows miss these times because they are out of sight or outside the clinic walls. Any setup time that must be incurred for a process to be completed should be accounted for when calculating Flow Times and Critical Times.

Lead Time: Span of time from the initial request for service to the start of service.

Note: The concept of Lead Time is critically related to access to care. In some systems the time between the request for an appointment and the actual visit can be days, weeks, or even months. Thus, when focusing on some problems related to public health, managing Lead Time may be more important than managing Cycle Time.

Work-in-Process (WIP): The number of Flow Units within the process boundaries at any given moment in time. This includes units being worked on and those waiting within the process boundaries.

Note: Some texts refer to this as Work-In-Progress. In our work this value is often referred to as the Census. Technically the Census is the number of inpatient-occupied beds in a service, unit, ward, or in the entire hospital or health care facility, but practitioners often use the term to refer to patients in a clinic as well. In the context of bed management it is important to note who is and who is not counted, and when the Census is actually taken. In some instances the official Census is taken at midnight, and newborns are not counted. Thus, the analysts must be careful to ensure that everyone involved with the analysis is using the term in the same way.

Turnover: The rate at which WIP in the system is replaced. Thus, Turnover is the inverse of Cycle Time. For example if the Cycle Time in a system is 2 hours, then we expect the WIP turnover to be one turn every 2 hours. Stated differently, all of the WIP in the system right now is "replaced" with new jobs over the next 2 hours, and the Turnover can be stated as once every 2 hours or 0.5 turns per hour.

Note: This term is of special interest to those who manage beds or other critical resources such as lab spaces, ORs, or examination rooms. One common misconception is thinking that increasing Turnover is the same as increasing Capacity. This is generally true if resource levels are held fixed but may not be true in general. For example, compare a process (Process A) with three Activities that each take 1 minute and another process (Process B) with a single Activity that takes 2 minutes.

The Cycle Times are 3 minutes for Process A and 2 minutes for Process B. Thus, we might say that turnover is 1/3 per minute for Process A and 1/2 per minute for Process B. However, the Critical Time is 1 minute for Process A and 2 minutes for Process B. Therefore, a process change can reduce Cycle Time, and thus increase turnover, while also increasing Critical Time, thus reducing capacity.

Makespan: The span of time from the start of the first job to the completion of the last job.

Note: This odd sounding term, is much more important than it may appear. Many outside observers assume that time after the stated durations of sessions, or shifts represent times when Resources become idle, but this is often untrue. For example, if patients remain in a clinic or OR at the scheduled end time, the staff will stay until the last patient on the schedule has been seen.

Utilization: Ratio of the amount of a Resource actually used over the amount of that Resource made available.

Note: In many settings labor utilization is expressed as actual time spent processing Flow Units divided by the duration of a shift. However, it is common in health care for providers to continue to function until all jobs are finished. Therefore, it is more useful in our settings of interest to define labor utilization as cumulative time spent on activities related to flow units divided by Makespan. Given this definition, Utilization will never exceed 100%. The key point is that all parties who are involved in the analysis or use its results should hold the same definitions in mind.

Additionally, we stress that we must not confuse utilization with productivity. Keeping a Resource busy doing work that could be done by a less expensive Resource (even if that Resource is slower) will almost surely increase Utilization of the more expensive Resource, but may be counter-productive. The large gaps between the cost rates for medical personnel makes this distinction particularly salient (Kaplan and Porter (2011)). One painful lesson for many new managers is that a health care delivery system with 100% Utilization of the most expensive Resource is almost certainly not the most productive system.

1.2.1 Process Management

Although the main focus of this note is on Process Analysis, it is useful to point out that this analysis is actually part of a larger, ongoing practice of Process Management. The term Process Management encompasses Process Analysis, as well as the design, assessment, control, and continuous efforts to improve process performance.

In this note we place particular emphasis on the role of Process Analysis in efforts to improve working processes. The ongoing nature of care delivery and process management mean that many steps discussed here will occur multiple times as the situation dictates. Given our role in the projects that we work on, we will speak about much of this work from the perspective of an outside consultant working with a unit seeking improvement. This work will typically begin with some assessment of the existing process.

1. **Process Assessment:** This phase consists of defining a process, and evaluating its current performance. A clear definition of a process includes identification of the Flow Units involved, Resources employed, and Activities needed. It must also include the development of an understanding of what the process hopes to accomplish.

   Note: When considering a larger system, it is important to identify the processes that are performing least well, and that need the most, or the most immediate improvement. In some cases the process of focus is obvious. However, in other settings we need to analyze multiple processes to figure out where the greatest need for improvement actually is. It is not uncommon to initially believe that the main problem lays in one area, only to find that the performance of one process is actually being constrained by the poor performance of a different process.
   In addition, we must point out that it is very useful to identify some metric or set of metrics that describes what aspect of performance we will focus on. To avoid getting bogged down in superfluous information, we will focus most of our examples on a small number of dimensions of performance such as Makespan, Cycle Times, Critical Times, or Utilization.

2. **Process Analysis:** After process assessment identifies the process steps, inputs, outputs, and metrics of interest, this information is used to depict the process, develop and calculate useful metrics, and identify drivers of system behavior. Typical focal points for analysis include:

   a. Determination of process Capacity

   b. Identification of options to increase Capacity

   c. Identification of current Cycle Times and/or calculation of Theoretical Cycle Times

   d. Identification of options to decrease Cycle Time

   e. Calculation of Makespan and Utilization

   f. Identification of means to reduce Makespan and/or alter Utilization

g. Calculation of the costs involved in delivering the service

h. Identification of means to reduce those costs

Whenever we ask a process manager why a process is not performing as well as one would like, the response is almost invariably "we don't have enough y" where y is some resource. Thus, it is usually good to begin by establishing what resources are used, and the availability of these resources. This task naturally leads to the calculation of process capacity.

As intuition suggests, process Capacity is most often directly tied to the available level of some Resource and identifying this Bottleneck Resource is of immediate concern. In most instances, the Bottleneck dictates Capacity, and any effort to change Capacity must do so by having some effect on the way the Bottleneck functions. In addition, since it is natural to believe that using more resources leads to more output, it is quite common (but not guaranteed) for the Bottleneck to be the most expensive Resource that is being used. Consequently, efforts to manage costs will often center on the productivity of the Bottleneck as well.

When considering the cost of the process we will typically focus on the spans of time that each Resource is kept busy and some measure of the cost per unit time for those resources. (We will consider this issue in more detail in Chapter 5.) In addition, Lead Times and delays are often very important because we want to reduce the time between identification of a problem or ailment and some approach to address it. To account for all of these elements we must become familiar with the resources involved and the rationale for each step so that any steps that do not add value can be eliminated or at least streamlined.

Once a process is fully defined, measured, and understood, possible actions for performance improvement can be developed, and process managers can review the feasibility of these actions to develop a plan for process improvement.

Note: In these first few Chapters, we will discuss processes as though activity durations are deterministic. Once a set of critical ideas are mastered, additional tools will be brought to bear to more formally account for variability. However, we routinely find that analysis based on average values is a good starting point. If a system shows problems before variability is included, it surely will have the same problems (and more) once variability is added.

3. **Process improvement:** In this phase, the proposed improvement is implemented (on a pilot basis if appropriate), feedback on results is obtained, and an implementation plan may be developed or revised as needed prior to system wide adoption. The process performance should then be continuously monitored and controlled to facilitate an ongoing cycle of improvement.

1.2.2 Goals of Process Management

Though we have mentioned several possible objectives, we want to underscore the idea that agreement on the goals of the improvement effort is key. As observers, we can fall into the trap of seeing what we believe to be the problem and assuming that everyone involved is committed to addressing the same issue, without realizing that they see the situation quite differently. It is important to have a clear (and shared) understanding about the objectives when conducting the analysis.

As a general rule "making things run better" is a concept that everyone welcomes, but it is far too vague to be of much use as a process improvement goal. This phrase also fails to adequately capture the idea that we will be balancing competing concerns. Some agents will have multiple concerns, and different agents interacting with the process at different points will develop very different ideas about what "running better" actually means. In addition, working to improve any particular performance metric will involve tradeoffs that become evident when changing the levels of some other metrics. If the agents cannot agree on what is most important it will be almost impossible to make much progress.

For example, if all other things are equal, shorter waiting times are preferred, particularly true from a patient's perspective. Of course it is also true that if all other things are equal, most patients feel that more face time with the physician is also preferred. The obvious catch is that increased face time for one patient essentially guarantees that Throughput will be reduced and waiting times will rise for other patients. Thus, even if we only consider users of the system, we have competing objectives that must be balanced.

Given the economic realities facing health care providers today, reducing delivery cost while holding all other things equal is preferred. Again, if something is done to reduce cost, some other aspect of performance will also be affected. If resources are viewed as having a cost per minute, then reducing time spent on each flow unit should reduce cost. However, there will also be some relationship between time spent and the quality of the experiences created for both patients and providers. Thus, we have competing objectives even if we only consider managers of the system and tradeoffs must be recognized to guide our efforts.

If we are looking for a good place to start in thinking about this collection of issues, it is quite often advisable to consider time as the metric and language of the analysis. Obviously, waiting times are easy to calculate and all will agree that less is preferable to more. If reducing or controlling cost is important and labor involves a significant cost per unit time, then minimizing Cycle Time is likely to be an attractive goal. If the objective is to increase the use of a system and users are sensitive to Lead Times, then a focus on such times may be a good place to start. When other issues such as quality are the dominant concern, then reducing the time between error commission and error discovery, and the time between discovery and correction will almost always leave us in a better position. In all of these instances, a focus on measurements of time is the natural starting point.

1.3 Key Process Measures: Throughput, Work in Process, and Cycle Time

The definitions provided so far were listed one at a time. However, it should be clear that many pairs of metrics are related to each other in rather formal ways. Takt Time is the inverse of Throughput, and Critical Time can be thought of as the inverse of Capacity. Cycle Time is the inverse of turnover, etc. It turns out that three critical metrics are related in a way that is particularly useful.

In the simplest of processes, we have Flow Units entering the process at a single point and leaving at a single point. For example, if we consider a walk-in clinic we have patients entering to start the process and departing once the visit is completed. However, it is also possible to have multiple points of entry and/or exit for flow units. For example, it is routine to have patients enter an Intensive Care Unit (ICU) after leaving an OR. However, it is not uncommon to have patients enter from the Emergency Department (ED). Alternatively, some patients experience a deterioration of their condition while on inpatient status in another ward and need to be moved to the ICU. Therefore, the ICU has multiple entry points. Similarly, most patients leave the ICU and are moved to another ward. However, some will not survive. Thus, multiple points of exit exist as well.

At any instant a process can have multiple inflows at multiple rates. Speaking a bit more formally, we can let $r_i(t)$ refer to the inflow rate of type i at time t. If this occurs, we refer to the total inflow rate $IN(t)$ as the sum of these rates. If there is only one type of inflow then $IN(t) = r_1(t)$. Similarly we can have a total outflow rate $OUT(t)$ that combines multiple outflow levels. We note that these levels $IN(t)$ and $OUT(t)$ are not likely to be identical at any time point. For example, there is no reason to believe that a patient will walk out of the clinic at the exact instant that another patient walks in. Figure 1.1 depicts inflow and outflow rates for a simple process. Note that the levels are rarely if ever identical, but balance each other when averaged over time.

If the average values of the total inflow rate and total outflow rate are equal over a reasonable span of time, we will say that we have a stable process. For example, over a 4-hour clinic session we will expect that the numbers of entering and exiting patients will be the same. When we have a stable process, we can refer to either the average inflow or outflow rate as the average flow rate or the Throughput of the process. For ease of exposition, we generally refer to Throughput simply as R since

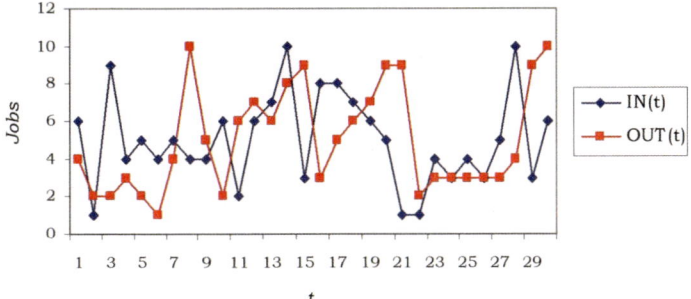

Fig. 1.1 Flow Units Entering and Exiting a Process Over Time

it reflects a balancing of rates over time.

We have already noted that WIP is the number of Flow Units within the process boundary at any given time. Even if the inflows and outflows vary moment to moment, if we have a stable system it is useful to think about the average WIP in the system as a useful metric which tells us about how busy the system is.

As mentioned earlier, we will often find that we are particularly interested in the average Cycle Time for a process. We note that if the system is stable, then the average Cycle time, CT will be stable as well.

For many cases of interest to us Throughput will be synonymous with the rate of Patient Arrival , WIP will be synonymous with the Census , and Cycle Time will be synonymous with Length of Stay. Patient Arrival, Census, and Length of Stay are simply context-specific expressions of the same ideas.

1.3.1 Little's Law

With definitions in place for Throughput, WIP, and CT we are able to state a major result describing the connections among them known as Little's Law (Little (2011)). Even though the pattern of flows through the system and the corresponding inventory levels can vary greatly over time and can be extremely complex when we focus on average values we can write that,

$$WIP = R * CT \qquad (1.1)$$

Again, WIP will typically be the Census in our examples; R refers to the throughput rate which will often be something similar to a patient arrival rate, claims per hour, phone calls per shift, etc., and CT is cycle time which for us is often LOS.

This relationship must hold for a stable system. If arrival rates were always greater than exit rates, the system would accumulate an infinite amount of WIP which is not physically possible. If the outflow rate were always be greater than the inflow rate then the system would be left with a negative number of Flow Units which is also impossible. Consequently, over some reasonable time frame the inflow rate and output rate must equal Throughput $= R$. The average time in the system is CT, and the average census must be the product of these two values, thus $WIP = R * CT$.

One useful analogy for Little's Law is to think of it as a manifestation of the "conservation of mass." Something is flowing into a vessel (our system) and something is flowing out. The differences between what came in and what went out must be what remains within the vessel. If patients arrive at a rate of 10 per hour and stay in the system for 2 hours, then it is easy to see why the average Census must be 10 per hour * 2 hours = 20 patients.

Another analogy is to recall the old lesson from physics that "Rate times Time equals Distance." In Little's Law we have a Throughput rate, a Cycle Time, and a Census or inventory level that is analogous to distance. Thus Rate * Time = Distance becomes $R * CT = WIP$.

The power of Little's Law often lays in the fact that its application allows us to "bend" the definitions. For example, we may have a pharmacy that sees 20 customers per hour on a typical day between 8 and 11 AM, but then receives 50 customers per hour around lunch time from 11 AM to 1 PM.

This system may be fairly stable during the first block of time, but its WIP inventory (meaning the customers in the system) is likely to grow rapidly during the second block. It is also common for the arrival rate to be sharply lower for later hours, say from 1 – 4 PM and then to pick up again when customers get off of work after 4 or 5 PM. Clearly this system is not perfectly stable from minute to minute or hour to hour. However, it is still useful to think about average rates during low and high demand periods, as well as average rates over periods in which the system starts and ends in a similar state. To generate additional insights into the usefulness of Little's Law let us consider a few examples in more detail.

1.3.2 Example 1

An X-ray lab processes 150 patients per 15 hour day. Patients arrive for an x-ray, and then leave after the process is over. The files are later sent to a Physician or Nurse who reviews them with the patient if needed. On average, 7.5 patients are in the X-ray lab at a time waiting to be X-rayed, in the X-ray room, etc. How long does an average patient spend in this part of the system?

Note that 150 patients per 15 hour day must be 150/15 = 10 patients (pat) per hour. This system is empty at the start of the day and is emptied at the end. Thus it is useful to define the Throughput R as 10 pat/hr. This does not guarantee that exactly 10 patients arrive every hour, or any hour for that matter. We also see that we are thinking of the Flow Units as patients in this example. In other instances it would be more useful to think about the X-rays being prepared as the Flow Units because some patients will have many more X-rays than others. Thus, the definition of a Flow Unit may differ for the same system depending on the focus of the analysis.

Given this context, the average WIP level is the average number of patients in the clinic. This is given as 7.5. Again, this does not mean that the clinic always has 7.5 patients as we hope not to have any half bodies waling around the hospital. This is only an average, but it is useful to consider $WIP = 7.5$.

We would like to know about how long the average patient spends at the facility in such cases. Because the process is defined by the patient's time in the X-ray lab, we can say that the patient's entry and exit are the process boundaries. The time between these two points is the Cycle Time. Little's Law tells us that $WIP = R*CT$. Hence, $CT = WIP/R$ or,

$$CT = \frac{7.5 \text{ pat}}{10 \text{ pat/hr}} = 3/4 \text{ hrs} = 45 \text{ min} \tag{1.2}$$

This analysis begs the question, "why can't I simply count or measure each of these things directly," or "why do I need an equation when I can simply count units?" Part of the answer to this question is that data based on counting in real time often is not nearly as reliable as we would like to believe. For example, when we collect data on clinic performance it is common to have check-in times for patients that are fairly reliable because patients sign in using an automated system such as a kiosk or a staff member at the front desk. However, check-out times are not as reliable. Patients who do not schedule a follow-up visit sometimes, simply leave the office after a visit without interacting with the staff. In such cases, direct measurement of CT breaks down. If we are willing to assume that the system is stable, and therefore that the arrival rate equals the exit rate which also equals Throughput, then we may be able to periodically count patients in the system to estimate average WIP and then find CT indirectly using Little's Law.

Data regarding the Census can be more complex as well. For example, when we consider a walk-in clinic we may be interested in the number of patients in the system. Counting bodies in a waiting room sounds like a good way to find WIP for that area but may not be such a good estimate if our analysis considers patients as the Flow Units because many bodies in waiting areas are not patients. They may be spouses, parents, friends, etc. In these cases we may need a different way to estimate the relevant WIP value. If we create a setup in which check-in and check-out times are reliable, then we can deduce Throughput and CT values, and use Little's Law to fill in the gap.

In other cases, patient no-shows and lateness distorts our measurement of arrival rates. In these instances it may be useful to have a different way to account for it. Let us consider another simple example that does not involve a clinic setting.

1.3.3 Example 2

Eastern Insurance Company processes 10,000 claims per year. The average processing time is 3 weeks. Assuming 50 work weeks per year, what is the average number of claims in process?

Here we have output over a yearly period (10,000 claims per year.) It is useful to think of this as 200 claims per week, given 50 working weeks per year. We are also given a processing time of 3 weeks and we may feel confident using this as a measure of average CT. Thus, if we think of the number of claims within the process boundaries as WIP we can use Little's Law to argue that the average number of claims in the process must be,

$$WIP = \frac{10,000 \text{ claims / yr}}{50 \text{ wk/yr}} * 3 \text{ wk} = 600 \text{ claims} \tag{1.3}$$

1.3.4 Example 3

Frank has a sample sent to Made-Up Labs for processing. Made-Up Labs processes an average of 5,000 samples per week. The typical inventory of items to be processed is 2500. What is the expected Cycle Time (CT) for Frank's test and what is the Turnover in the system?

In this example, we want to speak about the CT for an individual lab test, but only have aggregate data, (which is not unusual). Consequently, Little's Law may not be entirely sufficient to address the problem. However, it does provide a good starting point. Because we know that average $WIP = 2500$ samples, and $R = 5,000$ tests/week, we see that $CT = WIP/R = 2500/5000 = 0.5$ weeks, and we can say that a typical sample stays in this system for roughly 3.5 days.

1.3.5 Example 4

We mentioned earlier that part of the power of Little's Law lays in the way that we can bend definitions. One meaning of this idea is that we can apply the law to sub-sections of a process, or to sub-populations of the Flow Units involved. With this in mind, let us consider a slightly more complex setting.

Eastern Hospital is part of Eastern University. The University has a student health clinic with open scheduling. In other words, students are free to arrive without an appointment. One third of these arrivals are NEW patients who require up 30 minutes of a physician's time. The other two thirds are RETURN patients who spend 15 minutes with a physician. The basic process flow is very simple. Students check in (Activity A). They then wait to see a physician (Activity B). Being seen by a physician is Activity C. Among these patients, 50% require some Lab work. For these patients an additional step takes place (Activity D) that takes 10 minutes. A Process Map is shown in Figure 1.2.

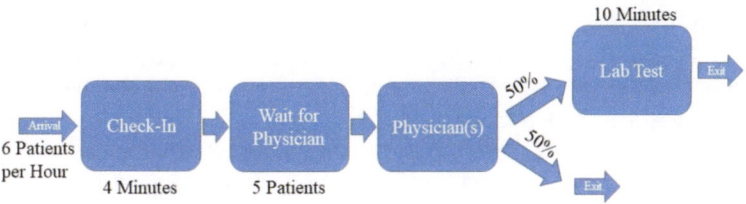

Fig. 1.2 Process map for Eastern University student clinic

The map provided adds a few relevant details. For example, we see that the arrival rate is 6 patients per hour. (We will assume that this is a stable process.) The waiting room includes 5 patients waiting for physicians. Note that we are treating Waiting as an Activity even though no paid resources are involved and it does not involve any effort. Waiting is being treated as an activity because it represents a significant part of the patient's time in the clinic and we want to account for this. As a general rule, any time span that we wish to single out for analysis can be given a name and measured. We also note that we do not yet know how many physicians are working in the clinic at this time. We might like to find several additional pieces of information including:

1. On average, how long do NEW patients spend in the clinic?

2. How many physicians are working in the clinic today?

3. How many patients are in the clinic?

Even for small processes such as this one we find that some questions deal with a single step, whereas others deal with multiple steps or the entire process. Similarly, some questions deal with the entire population of Flow Units while others deal with a subset. Let us address the questions listed here in turn.

NEW patients have two slightly different possible paths. Those who not need lab work proceed through Activities A, B, and C before exiting. Those who need lab work proceed through A, B, C, and D. We are not given the average time in Activity B - Wait for Physician. For that step we have an arrival rate, $R = 6$ pat/hr. The WIP for this step is 5 patients. We can refer to the time spent in this step as the Cycle Time for this step. From Little's Law we know that $WIP = R * CT$ or that $CT = WIP/R$. Thus the average time spent in this step is 5 pat/(6 pat/hr) = 5/6 hr, or 50 minutes.

The CT for NEW patients that do not need lab work becomes, 4 + 50 + 30 = 84 min. The CT for NEW patients who do need lab work is, 4 + 50 + 30 + 10 = 94 min. Therefore, the average CT for NEW patients is simply (84 + 94)/2 = 89 min.

For physicians in the clinic we know that the average time for Activity C is (1/3 * 30 min + 2/3 * 15) = 20 min. If the process consisted of only one activity this would be the CT for that process. Thus, we can label this value as the CT for Activity C. The arrival rate for this activity is $R = 6$ pat/hr. By Little's Law we know that $WIP = R * CT = 6$ pat/hr * 1/3 hr = 2. Therefore, we can conclude that the clinic must have at least 2 physicians on site at this time.

For $RETURN$ patients, half have a CT of 4 + 50 + 15 = 69 min and half have a CT of 4 + 40 + 15 + 10 = 79 min, for an average of 74 minutes. This makes sense, because it is 15 minutes less than the time for NEW patients. Since 2/3 of the total population of Flow Units are $RETURN$ patients, we get an average CT of $(1/3 * 89 + 2/3 * 74) = 79$ min. We can apply Little's Law to the entire process and get $WIP = R * CT$. Since 6 pat/hr is 0.1 pat/min, the Census = 0.1 pat/min * 79 min = 7.9 patients. For practical purposes, we can round this to 8.

The two most common errors made in this type of analysis are;1) mixing units, and 2) ignoring proportions. When some times are given in hours and other are in minutes it is easy to confuse them. Also, when a population does not have a 50/50 split of types, we need to account for the relative sub-population sizes.

1.4 Putting the Pieces Together: Instrumentation Preparation

Eastern Hospital has established a special unit known as the Eastern Hernia Surgery Center. This unit performs a single procedure (with minor variations) on a number of patients each day (5 days per week.) The list of instruments used for this procedure has been standardized to increase efficiency and consistency. The instruments used each day are delivered to a vendor that handles sterilization. Each evening the instruments are delivered to the vendor's location to be processed so that they can be re-used the following day. In simplest terms, the instruments go through a process that can be described in 4 Steps:

1. Decontamination

2. Assembly and Packing

3. Sterilization

4. Distribution

We can think of each of these 4 steps as consisting of 1 or more smaller steps, which we can refer to as Activities. A more complete description of the process includes the list of these smaller steps as shown below:

1. Receiving

2. Scrubbing & Soaking

3. Cart & Load Decontaminator

4. Decontamination

5. Remove & Repack

6. Sterilizer

7. Cart for Pickup

8. Pickup

This small unit employs two dedicated workers who we will call Albert and Barry. Albert has been working in this unit longer than Barry. Consequently, Albert makes $30 per hour whereas Barry makes $20. We can describe the Activities in this admittedly stylized example as a simple sequence.

Activity 1: Items are received in small bins corresponding to a single procedure. Barry receives the bin, records the relevant data, prints and attaches a bar code for tracking, and positions the bin near a decontamination sink. Since the collection of instruments is fairly standard the activity time for this step is highly predictable; 7 minutes per bin.

Activity 2: Albert visually inspects the instruments by the sink, scrubs those that have visual signs of contamination, and then loads the items onto a tray that is designed to facilitate the next step. Barry is a bit squeamish and is therefore not a good fit for this task. Fortunately, Albert has no such problems and enjoys this work. This step takes 15 minutes per bin.

Activity 3: Barry loads the tray(s) into the Turbo-11 Decontamination Unit. This machine is akin to a very high pressure dish washer. The water pressure is roughly 10 times greater than that of a typical car wash. This particular machine handles 1 tray/bin at a time. Loading the machine takes 5 minutes per bin. Management is considering the purchase of a larger machine that can hold 2 trays at a time.

Activity 4: The Turbo-11 washes the instruments for a programed time of 45 minutes. The tray is automatically pushed out of the machine when this step is completed.

Activity 5 Albert inspects each instrument, places the instruments into a clean bin following a precise placement pattern, and loads the bin into a sterilizer. This takes 10 minutes per tray/bin.

Activity 6: The sterilizer (which is essentially a fancy steamer) runs through a standardized cycle of 40 minutes. The model in place can handle either 1 or 2 bins at a time and ejects the load automatically upon completion.

Activity 7: Barry loads the bins onto a clean cart and records information, both on a paper form and into the IT system which tracks the location of every bin in the facility. This task takes 10 minutes and Barry can process either 1 or 2 bins during this time span. If he had to handle 3 or 4 bins this activity would take 20 minutes.

Activity 8: Barry hands control of a cart of bins to an orderly who picks up up the cart to be delivered to the OR suite. This activity takes only 5 minutes regardless of how many bins are involved.

Let us apply some basic tools of process analysis to address a few simple questions.

1. If the system is empty when a single bin arrives, how long will it take to process a bin?

2. What is the bottleneck resource, and what is the Critical Time (in minutes)?

3. What is the capacity of this process?

4. How many bins can the unit process in a night assuming that the technicians operate for no more than 5 hours?

5. How much of Albert's and Barry's valuable time will it take to process a single bin, and what is the resulting labor cost in dollars per bin if no other labor is accounted for?

6. What is the capacity of this process if one of the workers is out sick leaving only one worker to perform all of the needed tasks, and what is the Critical Time on such days?

7. The hospital is considering leasing a larger decontamination machine: the Turbo 22 which can process 2 bins at a time. If this happens what is the capacity of this modified process?

Let's consider each of these questions in turn. The first question simply asks for a Cycle Time, CT. Since this is a serial system, meaning the steps progress directly from first to last, this is simply the sum of the time spent at each step so,

$$CT = 7 + 15 + 5 + 45 + 10 + 40 + 20 + 5 = 137\text{min} \qquad (1.4)$$

To be a bit more precise, we often refer to this value as the Theoretical Cycle Time. (Some texts call this the Rush Order Flow Time.) This is the CT value when no waiting is involved for things like employee breaks, or other delays caused by congestion. Since we are ignoring variability at this point, we will assume that the realized Cycle Time is the same as this Theoretical Cycle Time value.

We can consider questions 2 and 3 together by considering each of the main resources in turn. Albert and Barry are each labor resources whereas the Decontaminater, and Sterilizer are the main equipment resources. Albert is involved in Activities 2 and 5. Barry is needed for Activities 1, 3, 7, and 8. The Turbo 11 is used in Activities 3 and 4. The Sterilizer is used only in Activity 6. Based on this data we can calculate how much time is required from each resource to process one bin.

- Albert is needed for 15 + 10 = 25 minutes. Therefore, his capacity is (60 min/hr)/25 min/bin = 2.4 bins/hr

- Barry is needed 7 + 5 + 10 + 5 = 27 minutes and his capacity is (60 min/hr)/(27 min/bin) = 2.22 bins/hr

Considering the equipment involved we see that the Turbo 11 is needed for 5 + 45 = 50 minutes/bin, and its capacity is (60 min/hr)/(50 minutes/bin) = 1.2 bins/hr. The Sterilizer is used only in Step 6 for 40 minutes and its capacity is 1.5 bins/hr. In this simple serial process we can say that the Critical time is:

$$\text{Max}(25, 27, 50, 40) = 50 \ \text{min}$$

The values 25, 27, 50, and 40 correspond to the busy times for Albert, Barry, Turbo 11, and the sanitizer respectively given the way the process is currently designed and managed. Thus, the Critical Time is 50 minutes, the Bottleneck resource is Turbo 11, and system capacity is 1 job every 50 minutes. Recall that capacity is the the inverse of Critical Time. We can think of Critical Time as 50 minutes per bin. If we write 50 minutes as 50/60 hours per bin, we see that capacity is 60/50 or

1.2 bins per hour.

For Question 4 we can use the fact that the system capacity is 1.2 bins/hr. If the system runs for 5 hours per night, the system capacity is 5 * 1.2 = 6 bins per night. Note that there is a special assumption being made here that carts can start the process and stop mid-process at the end of the shift or continue when another shift of workers takes over. This assumption may be reasonable for many back-office operations such as instrument cleaning. If this is not a reasonable assumption then this calculation may not be precise. For settings in which a job cannot be split across two sessions we must be explicit about how such instances will be handled in our calculations.

For question 5 we can use some of the work we did earlier. The processing of a single bin occupies Albert for 25 minutes and Barry for 27 minutes. Assuming that the hourly costs provided include any relevant overhead we have $30 per hour or $0.50 per minute for Albert and $20 per hour or $0.33 per minute for Barry. Thus the total labor cost is, 25 * $0.50 + 27 * $0.33 = $21.50. This is the allocated cost of useful work. Alternatively, the labor cost is 50/1.2 or roughly $45 per bin.

Notice that if one of the workers is unavailable for any reason the remaining worker has to perform 25 + 27 = 52 minutes of direct labor. We also see that the Critical Time for this setting becomes Max(52, 50, 40) = 52 minutes, and direct labor becomes the Bottleneck. Thus, for the setting laid out in Question 6 identification of the Bottleneck resource is key.

Question 7 presents a slightly different scenario because the resource in Activity 4 can handle 2 bins at a time. Note that if only 1 bin is in process at a time nothing has changed. However, if 2 bins are to be processed we have a slightly different system.

In the original process design a Flow Unit was a single bin and Critical time was 50 minutes. If this process is used twice to process 2 bins, it is as though we have an "order size" of 2 units.

If the Turbo 11 is used for a job of this size we see that the total time needed includes 2 iterations of Activities 1, 2, 3, 4, and 5. However, we need only one iteration of Activities 6, 7, and 8 because the sterilizer can handle two bins at a time, and Barry's busy time does not change for Activities 7 and 8 as long as the order size does not exceed 2 bins. Thus, we have busy times for each resource of:

- $(15*2+10*2) = 50$ minutes for Albert

- $(7*2+5*2+10+5) = 39$ minutes for Barry

- $(5*2+45*2) = 100$ minutes for Turbo 11

- 40 minutes for Sterilizer

Each of Albert's tasks must be replicated to handle 2 bins. Thus Albert's busy time doubles when the load doubles. Two of Barry's tasks must be replicated but the other two do not, so his busy time increases but does not double. The Turbo 11 must run through 2 cycles to handle 2 loads so its busy time doubles. The sterilizer can handle either 1 or 2 bins/trays at a time so its busy time does not changed.

Given this process design Critical Time becomes Max(50, 39, 100, 40) = 100 minutes. Thus we can say that the capacity is now 1 order every 100 minutes. However, because the order size has changed we need to note that this is still 2 bins every 100 minutes or 1 bin every 50 minutes. Thus, capacity has not changed at all. The key point here is that analyzing the process as a whole is required to see how capacity changes when the process is altered. Intuitively, it seems obvious that increasing the apparent capacity of some resource will increase the capacity of the system, but as we see here, this is not necessarily true.

It is instructive to consider *CT* for this new arrangement as well. Based on Activities 1 through 8, CT = (14 + 30 + 5 + 90 + 20 + 40 + 10 + 5) = 214 minutes. This is clearly much greater than the value of 137 minutes calculated for question 1. However, note that while this value is greater, it is not twice as great. Because some of the Activity times do not double when the order size is doubled. This is one reason we always must be careful to be clear on whether we wish to change *CT* or Capacity as they are not at all the same things.

Now let us consider the introduction of the Turbo 22 that can handle 2 trays at a time. What changes is that Activity 4 does not have to be replicated to handle 2 bins and the busy time for the Turbo 22 to process 2 bins stays at 55 minutes (5 * 2 + 45), compared to 100 minutes for the Turbo 11. Now the Critical Time becomes Max(50, 39, 55, 40) = 55 minutes. Critical Time for orders of 2 bins becomes 55 minutes per order and capacity is now 1 order every 55 minutes.

By moving from the Turbo 11 to the Turbo 22 we have "apparently" doubled the capacity of this resource. We add the word "apparently" here because in actuality the useful capacity of this resource is defined by the structure of the system.

The Turbo 11 was the Bottleneck when the order size was 1 bin. It had a busy time of 50 minutes, which was greater than any other resource. When the order size rises to 2 bins, and we use the Turbo 22 we have a busy time of 55 minutes. However, the capacity of the system does not double. The Critical Time of this new construct is now 55 minutes. Why does the capacity of the system not double, even though we doubled the capacity of the Bottleneck resource? The answer to this question is that this resource has be set up by another resource and we did not double the capacity of that resource. Barry loads the Turbo 11 or Turbo 22. For Activity 3 both Barry and the sterilizer are involved. The fact that resources must be combined to complete an Activity implies that capacity cannot double unless the ability of each resource doubles for that Activity.

Increasing the capacity of a Bottleneck resource increases the capacity of the entire system, but this works only until the capacity of some other resource becomes a constraint. Thus, doubling the capacity of a resource does not necessarily double system capacity even when that resource was the Bottleneck.

We can take this insight a step further. Imagine that the sterilizer became twice as fast, and Activity 6 could be done in 20 minutes instead of 40. At first glance this may seem like a good idea. However, if we focus on the busy times for the resources per job we find that Critical Time becomes Max(50, 39, 55, 20) = 50. Since the sterilizer is not the Bottleneck resource, increasing its 'apparent' capacity has no impact on system capacity at all. This conclusion is immediately obvious in the context of this simple example. However, it is often not obvious in practice. It is quite common for organizations to become enamored with the idea of increasing the capacity of some resource and later finding that the increase did not bring about the desired change in process capacity. In these settings, providing a thorough process analysis can add great value.

1.5 Key Take-Aways

To facilitate the more general application of these terms and ideas, let us collect many of the insights involved into a short list.

1. A process includes a <u>Route</u> that <u>Flow Units</u> follow, along which is a collection of <u>Activities</u>, performed by <u>Resources</u>, that alter inputs to create desired outputs.

2. Efforts to improve processes need a coherent definition of what improvement means. These definitions can center around process metrics such as Lead Time, Cycle Time, WIP, Throughput, Capacity, or Makespan.

3. Process Improvement involves assessment of a process, defining what we mean by improvement, focusing on metrics consistent with that idea, devising ways to improve those metrics, and implementing these changes.

4. Process metrics are inter-related, meaning that changing the level of one metric will always have some impact on at least one other metric.

5. The first steps in process analysis typically include mapping the process flow, and selecting the relevant metrics to consider.

6. The impact of changing any element of a process must be evaluated in light of its role in the process as a whole.

7. Basic tools of process analysis can give us a good starting point in our efforts to bring about system improvement.

1.6 Review Material and Prior Works

Many of the examples discussed above are stylized versions of settings that we have studied in detail. Names are changed as a courtesy to all parties involved. To consider supporting data and analysis in more detail consult Chambers and Williams (2017b), Chambers and Williams (2017a), Conley et al (2016), Dada and Chambers (2019), Elnahal et al (2015c), Williams et al (2012), and Williams et al (2015).

To ensure that the material covered here can be applicable to your settings develop your responses to the scenarios laid out below.

1.6.1 Process Analysis for ED

Consider the ED that Frank Caldwell entered, as described in the prologue. Let us assume that the observations Frank made are typical. In other words the number of people he sees in line is average and the number of servers is stable.

1. Under these assumptions, draw a simple process map of the ED process.

2. On average, how long does a patient spend in the ED?

3. On average, how many patients are being examined by doctors? (There may be more than one doctor in the ED at a time.)

4. On average, how many patients are in the ED?

1.6.2 Process Analysis for Hernia Clinic

The Eastern Hernia Clinic is a single-condition medical facility that performs hernia surgeries. Some surgeries are for single hernias and others are for double hernias. (If you don't know what a hernia is, consider yourself lucky.) On average, one third of the patients checking in each day have double hernias. These patients generally stay for 3.6 nights. This duration is twice as long as the average patient with a single hernia.[2]

---

[2] This vignette is inspired by actual operations at the Shouldice Hernia Clinic as described in Heskett (2003)

1. Assume that on an average day 135 patients check in. How many patients of each type are in the clinic on a given day?

2. How many times per month does the clinic turn over its inventory of patients? (Assume it operates 7 days per week and has 30 days in each month.)

3. Assume that a fee for the actual procedure is paid by the government, but the patient pays for the room. The average double hernia patient pays a rate of $250 per day and a single hernia patient pays an average of $210 per day. What is the average revenue the clinic receives from these fees per day per occupied room?

Chapter 2
Special Issues in Process Analysis for Health Care: Visualization, & Project Management

Abstract Collecting and presenting data are key to both gaining understanding of a process and sharing information in efforts to improve process performance. Health care settings become quite complex for a variety of reasons including the use of shared resources, overlapping jobs, and dynamic routing of jobs within the system. Consequently, improving process performance requires the use of robust tools that can depict a wide variety of settings. These tools need to simultaneously serve as communication devices about why a proposed change will make the system perform better. With these facts in mind we introduce two tools from industrial engineering that we find particularly useful for improvement projects. The first is a graphical tool known as a Gantt Chart, which we use as an alternate depiction of system behavior. This presentation of process flow lends itself to useful analysis. The second is a form of the Critical Path Method (CPM) which is usually used in project management. It is useful for organizing and scrubbing detailed data on activity times. These tools helps to translate raw data into a narrative about process performance and cut through much of the fog created by contradictory and/or incomplete data.

2.1 Introduction

In the health care settings where we have worked, data are collected continuously on process performance. Information is routinely recorded on case loads, staff levels, appointment schedules, arrival times, waiting times, throughput, and length of stay. In theory, these data can be used to facilitate detailed process analysis. We use the phrase "in theory" for several reasons. First, the data are often inaccurate. Staff involved in patient care are dealing with more pressing matters. Consequently, efforts to collect process data are often executed in a haphazard fashion. Second, the data collected are often stored in multiple systems that do not talk to each other. Hospitals include appointment systems, bed management systems, scheduling systems, billing systems and other reporting systems that overlap in functionality, but differ in format, data structures, and reporting methods. As a consequence, the same event is recorded in different ways, by different people, using data that does not match. Third, the collection of this data does not usually imply a meaningful use for the data collected. Information systems do not lack in the types of reports they can produce. In fact, they provide an overload of options for data processing and presentation. Ironically, it is often this overload that prevents their use. (Carvalho et al (2016))

Data that are of spotty quality, are interspersed with contradictory values, are hard to compile, and have unclear usefulness in process improvement do not beget successful improvement projects. In this chapter we discuss several approaches to data collection that we have employed when seeking more useful information. We then turn our attention to tools borrowed from industrial engineering that help interpret and display this information in ways that are more likely to lead to success.

In almost any process improvement effort we need a base of understanding to work from that includes at least three key metrics of process performance: Throughput , Cycle Times , and Utilization . Throughput is the rate at which jobs move through a process. For example, treating an average of 3 patients per hour is synonymous with the statement that patient throughput is 3 per hour. Cycle Time refers to the duration between a flow unit's entry to and exit from a process. In many settings we can match this to Exit Time minus Arrival Time. Utilization can often be thought of as the busy time for a resource divided by Makespan which is the duration from the start of the first job to the completion of the last. For example, if a nurse is engaged in process-related activities for 120 minutes over a 240 minute session, we might say that nurse utilization is $120/240 = 50\%$.

This is obviously not an exhaustive list of metrics, but we can think of these three as the bare minimum needed to speak coherently about system performance. Each of these metrics can be uncovered if we have three pieces of information about each flow unit that enters the system: the Entry Time, the Exit Time, and the Activity Times for the tasks done in between. At first blush it may seem that this is not much to ask from a sophisticated information system. However, in practice, collecting accurate data along these lines is deceptively difficult and most often done incorrectly.

2.2 Data Collection

We have seen and used a variety of methods to collect the data needed for process analysis. In particular, we have used at least five distinct methods listed below:

1. Queries from existing databases (Elnahal et al (2015b))

2. Electronic recording of data by health care staff and/or physicians as part of the workflow (Elnahal et al (2015a))

3. Paper forms that travel with jobs or records for data collection (Williams et al (2012))

4. Automated systems for data collection such as Real Time Location Systems (RTLS) (Chambers et al (2016))

5. Direct observation (Williams et al (2012))

To elaborate on each of these approaches let us consider the example of a clinic that handles patients by appointment. Such clinics will use an appointment system along with a linked system for data collection that records **Check-In** and **Check-Out** times. An electronic medical record (EMR) system will also provide time stamps when a staff member or physician opens or closes a patient record. These data can later be queried to produce reports that tell us something about clinic performance.

As a general statement, time stamps for patient arrivals tend to be quite accurate and useful. In many modern clinics this time stamp is generated by a kiosk or tablet that records when the patient first accesses it. Exit times are most commonly generated when desk staff closes a patient record as the patient checks out. Unfortunately, the activity times in between are much more difficult to ascertain.

Consider the duration of an examination in an exam room. The examination is often the central task in a clinic visit and its duration is a core piece of the information needed. It is common to expect a nurse or physician to open the patient record upon entering an examination room and close it just before leaving. Other systems make use of a badge or card that is swiped upon entry or exit. However, many variables complicate this process. Some staff or physicians will engage in conversation with the patient before opening the record. Thus, the time stamp for opening the record becomes an unreliable estimate of activity start time. The same thing can happen at the end of the visit making this value unreliable as well. In other settings the physician will open the record anticipating patient interaction, and the patient may or may not be present when this occurs.

In addition, face time with a patient is often interrupted by a call or the need to gather some information, assistance, or equipment. As a result, what appears to be a single activity time is actually an amalgamation of the times for multiple, overlapping activities. If this happens, then the duration between the opening of the file and its closing is not a reliable estimate of the duration of any single activity. Consequently, we may have a mountain of data that is too inconsistent to yield satisfactory information about the nuances of process flow.

The inconsistencies motivate some process managers to supplement this approach with information recorded by desk and/or nursing staff. For example, we have seen several instances in which staff at a nurses' station are expected to record when they have completed a step such as rooming a patient (placing the patient in an examination room.) However, this recording step is often delayed when the nurse is called away on another task.The information is eventually recorded from memory. We have even seen cases in which the information is recorded at the end of the shift, compromising its accuracy.

A variant of this approach is to attach an old-fashioned paper form to a patient record. Desk staff, nurses, and physicians can record a time whenever they interact with the record. Surprisingly, this approach tends to work much better than either of those mentioned earlier. In situations involving low case loads, this process produces very good data. Unfortunately, the data are most needed for settings with excessive case loads.

A fourth approach to data collection is the use of electronic recording such as with a Real-Time Location System (RTLS). These systems use sensors around doors and other spaces to record when a provider enters and exits a space such as an examination room or a procedure suite. In our experience, this is the gold standard for long term collection of this information. This raw data must be scrubbed and interpreted in light of a good understanding of clinic layout and the patient schedule to discern when the relevant activities start and stop. We have found project management tools to be quite useful in scrubbing the data. In addition, these data can be paired with other data from the information system to generate an excellent depiction of actual movements and activities. Unfortunately, this is a surprisingly time consuming process and is available in only a minority of settings.

Finally, we must discuss the best way to collect this information - by direct observation. Many nuances of process flow, provider interactions, and patient behavior are discernible only through direct observation. We routinely find that paid observers provide the best data possible for the simple reason that they will see and record information that we did not ask for up front because we did not think of it in advance. The flexibility of human data collectors is unmatched by any technological system. In addition, we routinely find that researchers who skip the step of direct observation carry assumptions into analysis of available data without even realizing it. These assumptions skew the analysis and often leads to errors and misunderstanding.

Once process data are in hand the next step is to convert these files or sheets of data into some form that lends itself better to analysis and communication. Fortunately, this type of problem has been widely studied and a host of tools are readily available to assist in this task.

2.3 Gantt Charts: A Valuable Tool to Understand Health Care Delivery Processes

One tool that is surprisingly useful for summarizing and communicating process performance is known as a Gantt Progress Chart. A Gantt Chart is a simple horizontal bar chart developed as a production control tool in 1917 by Henry L. Gantt. (Gantt (1919)) The chart is a graphical illustration of a sequence of events or activities. It provides immediate visual cues that alert you to violations of key constraints. The central theme of the chart is to present all activities in terms of time. As one historian explained:

> If management is to direct satisfactorily the operation of our industries under conditions of ever-increasing difficulty, its decisions and its actions must be based not only on carefully proved facts but also on a full appreciation of the importance of the momentum of those facts. The Gantt Chart, because of its presentation of facts in their relation to time, is the most notable contribution to the art of management made in this generation. Clark (1922)

Walking through the logic, steps, and usage of the Gantt Chart is instructional and helps to develop a deeper understanding of the system being studied. To facilitate our presentation let us work through patient visits to an outpatient clinic in both a private practice and an academic medical center.

Consider the life of a resident working a rotation in an outpatient clinic. One prototypical process flow for these visits is shown in Figure 2.1. The process map displays a Route that each Flow Unit follows. The route consists of a sequence of Activities that are handled by Resources, along with the related activity durations. The process shown in Figure 2.1 involves 6 activities which we can refer to by number or by name.

The diagram conveys critical information about the process organized by activity including:

1. Activity 1 or **Check-In** is the initial interaction between the patient and a clinical assistant (CA). The resource used is the CA and the duration is 10 minutes.

2. Activity 2 or **Vitals** includes a nurse who leads the patient to an examination room, collects vital sign information, and notifies a physician. The duration for this activity is 4 minutes. This step involves two named resources; the nurse and an examination room (Room).

3. Since this is a teaching hospital the first physician notified is likely to be a resident or a fellow. Thus, in Activity 3, or **Resident**, a resident reviews the patient chart, enters the Room, and interacts with the patient. This step involves both a resident and the room and takes 15 minutes.

4. In Activity 4 or **Teaching**, a resident looks for the attending physician (Attending) to have a discussion about the case. This activity involves the attending, a

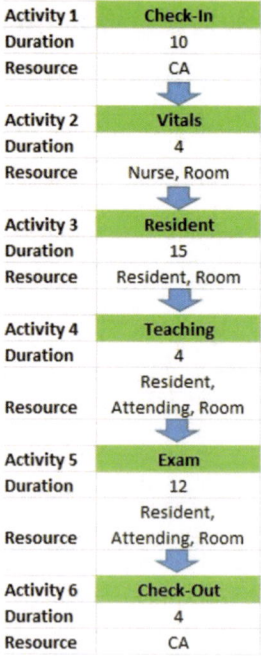

Fig. 2.1 Process Map of Office Visit: Academic Medical Center. Duration is shown in minutes. CA, clinical assistant.

resident, and the room because the patient is waiting in that space while this discussion goes on. The duration here is given as 4 minutes.

5. In Activity 5 or **Exam** the attending physician enters the room with a resident to interact with the patient. This step involves the attending, a resident, and the room simultaneously for 12 minutes.

6. In Activity 6 or **Check-Out** the CA interacts with the patient for 4 minutes.

A wide variety of methods are available to depict a process, and we are neutral about which one is chosen. The important point is that key information is displayed including: the Route or sequence of Activities that is involved, the durations of these activities, and the resources involved at each step. We have chosen this spreadsheet - based arrangement simply as a convenience.

Notice that the attending moves from room to room with teaching-related conversations (Activity 4) occurring in between. This blended approach means that there may be spans of time when the Resident is ready to move to the next step but the Attending is not available. There may also be spans of time when the Attending is available but a resident is busy. Whenever process steps combine resources involved with jobs that can overlap in time, we have to be careful when discussing the utilization levels of each resource. When considering utilization levels we must decide how we will account for any "inserted idle time." By this phrase, we refer to durations in which the structure of a system forces a resource to be idle. Ignoring these times would lead to underestimating utilization levels, and distorting our understating of the congestion present.

To appreciate the added complexity, let us highlight two more factors. First, the attending, and the resident(s) can work in parallel. By this we mean that the attending may work on one case while a resident works on another even though both resources must eventually participate in both cases. This is a common arrangement because the involvement of the Resident is a critical part of the training of the next generation of physicians. In addition, the resident is often managed as a lower cost resource that can handle tasks such as recording patient history, collecting supplies, and making phone calls to gather additional information.

Second, outpatient settings must always deal with some level of patient no-shows; meaning occasions when a patient does not arrive for an appointment. One common response to this phenomenon is the use of double-booking. In other words many clinics will schedule more than one patient to arrive for at least one appointment slot on the schedule just in case one or both patients do not show up. This is particularly common in academic settings because it leverages both the attending and the resident in a way that increases the utilization of both physicians as we shall see later. When both patients scheduled for an appointment slot do arrive, one tactic that we often see is to alter the process flow slightly by using the flow described in Figure 2.1 for one patient while the attending treats another patient without the involvement of the resident in another room. Analysis of this hybrid system is a bit more complex.

2.3.1 Creating Gantt Charts

The process flow diagram shown in Figure 2.1 is a natural starting point for process analysis. However, we need to understand how scenarios will play out over time when two or more activities overlap. In particular, we need to account for how activities overlap in time because resources may be shared and some steps can be carried out simultaneously whereas others cannot (Clark (1922).) To construct the chart we work through four steps.

1. List all activities involved in the process. For each activity state its duration, the resources involved, and what other activities must be completed before the start of this one.

2. Plot each activity-resource pair using horizontal bars such that the left edge of the bar shows the earliest feasible activity start time and the right edge shows the earliest feasible end time. Choose units and scale the drawing so that the chart fits into a convenient space such as one piece of paper.

3. Check the chart and use it to identify any infeasible situations. Adjust the start times and reposition the horizontal bars to eliminate these issues. In other words, "schedule" the set of activities such that no activity starts until the activities that it depends on have been completed, and the number of units of any resource used at any point in time never exceeds the number of units of that resource available.

4. After verifying that no constraints are violated, present the analysis showing when each activity should start and finish along with any additional metrics of interest.

We must comment on what we mean by "schedule" an activity. Originally Gantt Charts were used to create work schedules on projects. However, our use of the term in these examples is a bit different. We will consider sequencing rules, and activity times to show how long it takes for a body of work to get done. Therefore, we are not literally scheduling each task. Instead, we are using the chart to envision how a clinic visit can play out in real time. Thus, we are really depicting a clinic session, rather than trying to dictate how it must be managed.

A plethora of tools for the creation of these charts is available, and we are not interested in recommending any particular product. Our goal is to leverage the logic behind Gantt Charts to help train our minds on how to think about these settings. For the small examples that we present here we will use a spreadsheet template for ease of reproduction (and the reader's eyesight.) However, simple charts drawn by hand are perfectly adequate in most instances. In fact, hand drawing these charts is usually far faster, and easier, and often works better.

2.4 Examples of Clinic Visits

Let us begin with a simplified example of a clinic visit and progress to the more complex setting depicted in Figure 2.1. Consider a setting in which a sole attending works through a schedule of patients and no resident is involved. A simple process map of this setting for a single appointment is shown in Figure 2.2. We work through our steps to create the corresponding Gantt Charts.

Note that Step 1 (listing activities and related information) is already embedded in the creation of the process map shown in Figure 2.2. A process map should convey enough information to allow us to generate a Gantt Chart for a single instance

Activity 1	Check-In
Duration	10
Resource	CA

Activity 2	Vitals
Duration	4
Resource	Nurse, Room

Activity 3	Exam
Duration	12
Resource	Attending, Room

Activity 4	Check-Out
Duration	4
Resource	CA

Fig. 2.2 Process Map of Office Visit: Private Practice. Duration is shown in minutes. CA, clinical assistant

of a process. We have four activities labeled **Check-In**, **Vitals**, **Exam**, and **Check-Out**. We see that a CA is involved in both **Check-In** and **Check-Out**. A nurse is involved in **Vitals** and the attending is involved in **Exam**. We will also assume that an examination room (Room) is involved in both **Vitals**, and **Exam**. Consistent with our earlier examples, let us assume that **Check-In** takes 10 minutes, **Vitals** takes 4 minutes, **Exam** takes 12 minutes, and **Check-Out** takes 4 minutes. For Steps 2 and 3 we make use of templates created in Excel 2016.

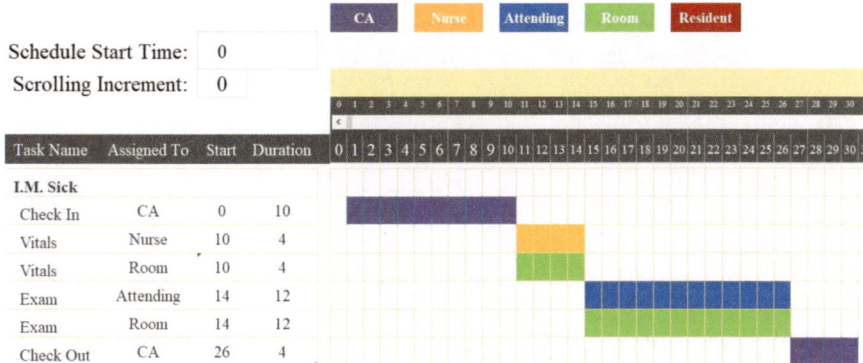

Fig. 2.3 Gantt Chart for Single Office Visit in Private Practice. CA, clinical assistant

Figure 2.3 shows the four activities for one patient (Patient 1). It includes a bar for each activity-resource pair. Consequently, if an activity involves two resources, it will have two related bars that overlap in the span of time that they cover. In this particular example, we have two resources involved in **Vitals**; the room and the nurse. We also have two Resources in **Exam**; the room and the attending. In both instances both Resources are involved for the entire duration of the step, but note that this need not always be the case. It is entirely possible to have one or more resources needed for a portion of a step. This is one reason it is good practice to have a separate bar for every activity-resource pair. We assign a unique color to each resource to cut down on confusion when bars overlap. The start times are calculated to capture the logic that the four activities form a definite sequence. (You can adapt these templates for other settings by adding rows and labels as needed.) As you experiment with the spreadsheet, you will discover that it is easy to change the duration of an activity and immediately see how it is reflected in the chart.

If we assume that the entire clinic schedule consists of only one visit, we can also use the chart in Figure 2.3 to present information needed for additional analysis. (Step 4) For example, we can immediately read the Makespan of this trivial schedule off of the chart as 30 minutes. The left-most column containing a colored bar corresponds to minute 1 and the right-most column used corresponds to minute 30. The chart also depicts the busy times of each resource as $10 + 4 = 14$ minutes for the CA, 4 minutes for the nurse, 12 minutes for the attending and $4 + 12 = 16$ minutes for the room.

Using this information we divide the busy time for each resource by Makespan to determine resource utilization. This calculation yields utilization levels of $14/30 = 47\%$ for the CA, $4/30 = 13\%$ for the nurse, $12/30 = 40\%$ for the attending, and $16/30 = 53\%$ for the room. Even though this chart is quite simple, it allows us to easily visualize a single visit in some detail. It shows start times for each task, resource usage, Makespan, etc. and creates a "quick and dirty" picture of clinic activity.

A more interesting application arises when we consider multiple visits. Figure 2.4 shows the Gantt Chart for a schedule of two office visits. Note that this depiction assumes that the physician cannot be in two places at the same time. (The blue bars representing the attending cannot overlap.) To create this chart we copied the rows related to the first visit down to represent the second visit and adjusted the start time for the first step of the second visit to ensure that we do not have overlapping bars for any of the resources.

If exactly one unit of each resource is involved, we need to adjust the start time of the second patient by the longest contiguous busy time of the resources used for the first patient. Note that this is not necessarily the greatest total busy time for a resource. The CA is used for $10 + 4$ minutes but since this usage is split into two parts and a sufficient gap exists between these pieces, we do not need to have the second patient start at minute 14. In addition, if the office has more than one unit of a resource, we can allow busy times to overlap for that resource type. Since the attending is busy for 12 minutes for each patient, we schedule the second patient to arrive after 12 minutes. Again, the word "schedule" is being used here as a refer-

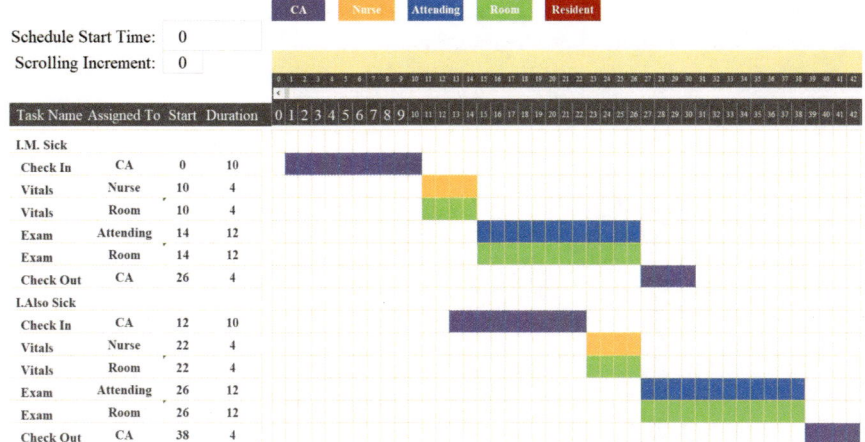

Fig. 2.4 Gantt Chart for Pair of Office Visits in Private Practice. CA , clinical assistant.

ence to our effort to show the most efficient use of resources, meaning that we seek to depict the minimum Makespan that is feasible. In reality, almost no hospital or office would schedule appointments that are exactly 12 minutes apart.

The chart illustrates that we still have an overlap of the bars linked to the room(s). This is acceptable if (and only if) we have access to more than one examination room. This is indeed the case in almost all clinics that we have studied. The general rule to keep in mind is, if we have n units of a resource, then any vertical line (or column) of the chart can have no more than n cells of the corresponding color. Notice that if you look at columns for minutes 23 - 26 we have exactly two instances in each column of the color corresponding to the room. As long as we have two or more rooms available, then this arrangement is feasible. With this schedule in place, we can calculate utilization levels for key resources as,

1. $(14+14)/42 = 67\%$ for the CA,

2. $(4+4)/42 = 19\%$ for the Nurse,

3. $(12+12)/42 = 57\%$ for the Attending, and

4. $(16+16)/(2*42) = 38\%$ for the Room.

When we calculate utilization of the rooms we must account for the fact that two rooms are in place. Thus, we see that adding an additional unit of a resource (room) increases the utilization of all of the other resources at the expense of having reduced utilization of each room.

Figure 2.5 presents the Gantt Chart for a schedule of two patients using the process described in Figure 2.1. (The figure is rotated for ease of viewing. When such figures would extend beyond a page we truncate the depiction by selecting a value for the left-most column shown to reduce the size of the chart.)

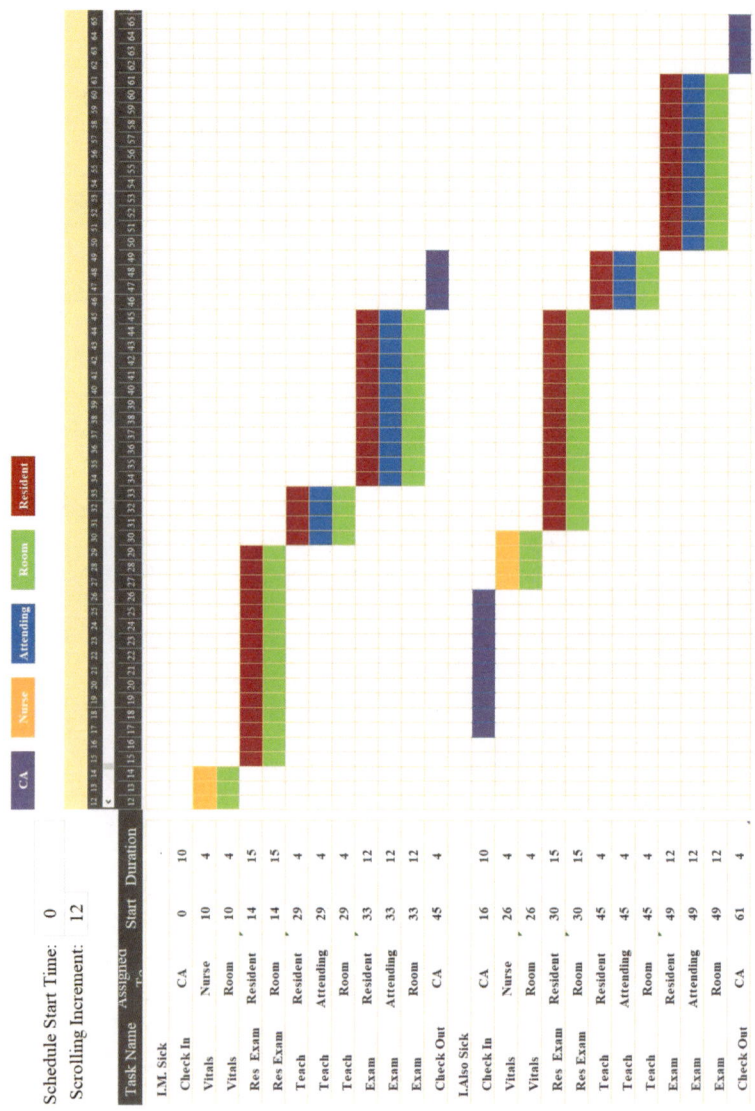

Fig. 2.5 Gantt Chart for Pair of Office Visits in AMC (Infeasible). CA, clinical assistant; Res, resident.

We can think of the process from Figure 2.2 as that of a private practice and the flow shown in Figure 2.1 as that of an academic medical center. Clearly the inclusion of the resident adds process steps and increases Cycle Time. The inclusion of the educational mission also means that we must have the attending and the resident co-located for the steps labeled "Teach" and "Attending". The start of the **Check-In** step for Patient 2 is timed to ensure that the Attending is never assumed to be in two places at one time.

In Figure 2.5 the arrival time of the second patient is adjusted based on the busy time of the attending, as was done in Figure 2.4. Thus, the schedule is feasible for the attending. However, we immediately see that bars corresponding to the resident overlap. If we are informed that only one resident is present in this clinic we have a problem.

Studying these figures makes it clear that the attending cannot stay busy continuously using this process for multiple patients without having the resident be in two places at the same time. The resident "double-booked" from minutes 31 to 45. Again, this is fine if we have at least two residents. However, with only one resident, this is situation infeasible. Consequently, the inclusion of the educational mission of the academic medical center implies that the attending physician is forced to be dormant for 14 minutes (or at least not seeing these patients.) Some texts refer to this period as "Inserted Idle Time" on the attending's schedule and the time alters our utilization calculations.

Since this schedule is clearly infeasible, we developed the chart shown in Figure 2.6 which delays the arrival of the second patient to alleviate this violation. To make this more concrete, consider the utilization levels of the key resources under this schedule. Again, we can easily find Makespan and the busy times for each resource by reading directly off of the chart (Table 2.1).

Table 2.1 Busy Times and Utilization Levels from Figure 2.6

Metric	Busy Times (min)	Value
Makespan	$00-80$	80
Resident Util	15-45, 45-75	$60/80 = 75\%$
Attending Util	30-45, 61-76	$30/80 = 38\%$
Room 1 Util	10-45	$35/80 = 40\%$
Room 2 Util	42-76	$35/80 = 44\%$

Attending utilization has decreased based on the traditional definition of busy time for this resource, whereas Cycle Times have risen. If we include this forced idle time for the attending we see that utilization is actually higher. This implicit utilization should be understood when analyzing these systems. Otherwise one could

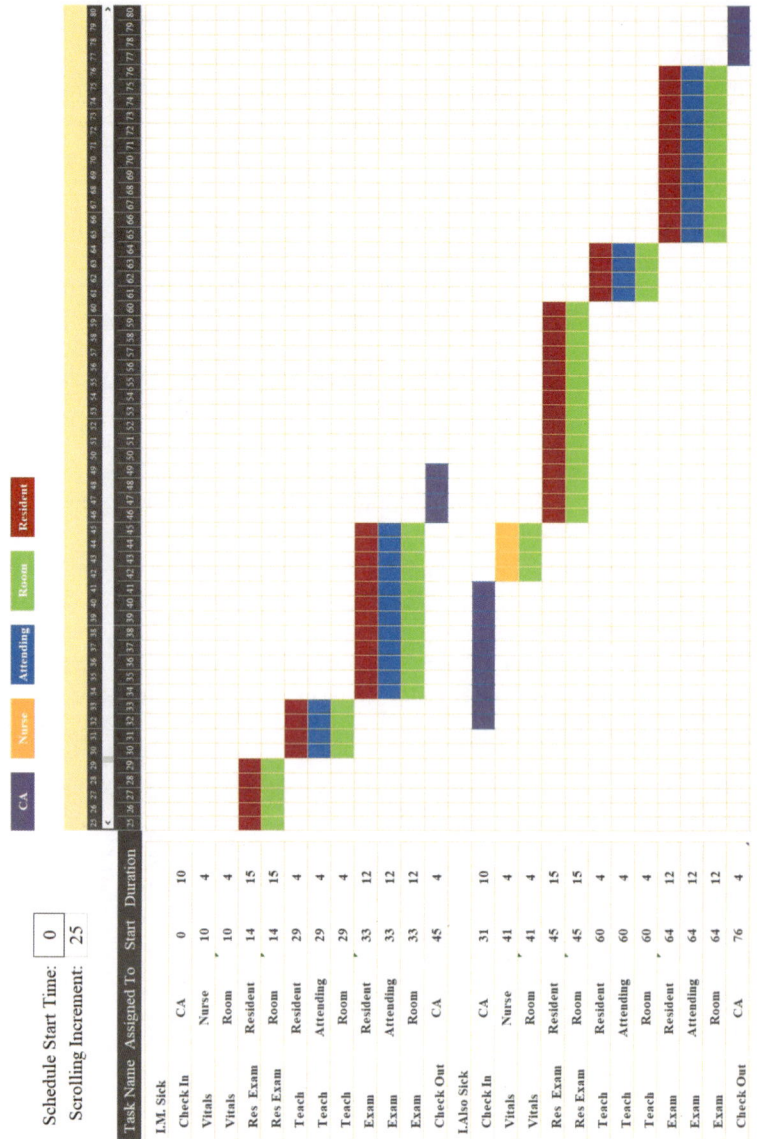

Fig. 2.6 Gantt Chart for Pair of Office Visits in an Academic Medical Center (Feasible). CA, clinical assistant; Res, resident.

erroneously conclude that the system is under-performing because the attending is inefficient.

Figure 2.7 shows a Gantt Chart for the academic medical center when one patient is scheduled to arrive at time 0 using the process described in Figure 2.2, and the second patient is scheduled to arrive 10 minutes later using the process described in Figure 2.1. This schedule has the resident involved in one case and omitted from the other. This is a controversial approach that is acceptable in some settings and unacceptable in others. To understand why this approach may be attractive, consider the utilization levels of the key resources under this schedule (Table 2.2).

Table 2.2 Busy Times and Utilization Levels from Figure 2.7

Metric	Busy Times	Value
Makespan	00 – 59	59
Resident Util	25-39, 40-43, 44-55	31/59 = 52%
Attending Util	15-26, 40-43, 44-55	28/59 = 47%
Room 1 Util	11-26	16/59 = 27%
Room 2 Util	11-45	35/59 = 59%

Note that Makespan has decreased from 80 to 59 minutes, while utilization of the attending has risen from 38% to 47%. We note that this in no way proves that this approach is optimal. It makes a trade-off between utilization of key resources and the educational mission of the clinic. This is not a trivial decision. What the charts do is convey a body of information about the state and evolution of these systems while accounting for some perplexing constraints and complications involved. It informs, but does not dictate a number of related decisions. The key point is that such decisions should not be made without an explicit statement and shared understanding of how such a change affects system performance. Gantt Charts are an excellent way to develop this shared understanding, and may be their greatest value.

2.5 Collected Comments on Gantt Charts

Before moving on to consider additional tools, let us take a moment to gather several key observations related to Gantt Charts here.

1. Process mapping is the first step in process analysis and includes the information necessary to create Gantt Charts.

2. Gantt Charts are horizontal bar charts that depict how a process will play out.

3. Gantt Charts add value when we need to consider multiple instances of a process or some collection of processes that overlap in time.

4. Gantt Charts are designed to provide visual cues that alert us to issues involving resource constraints.

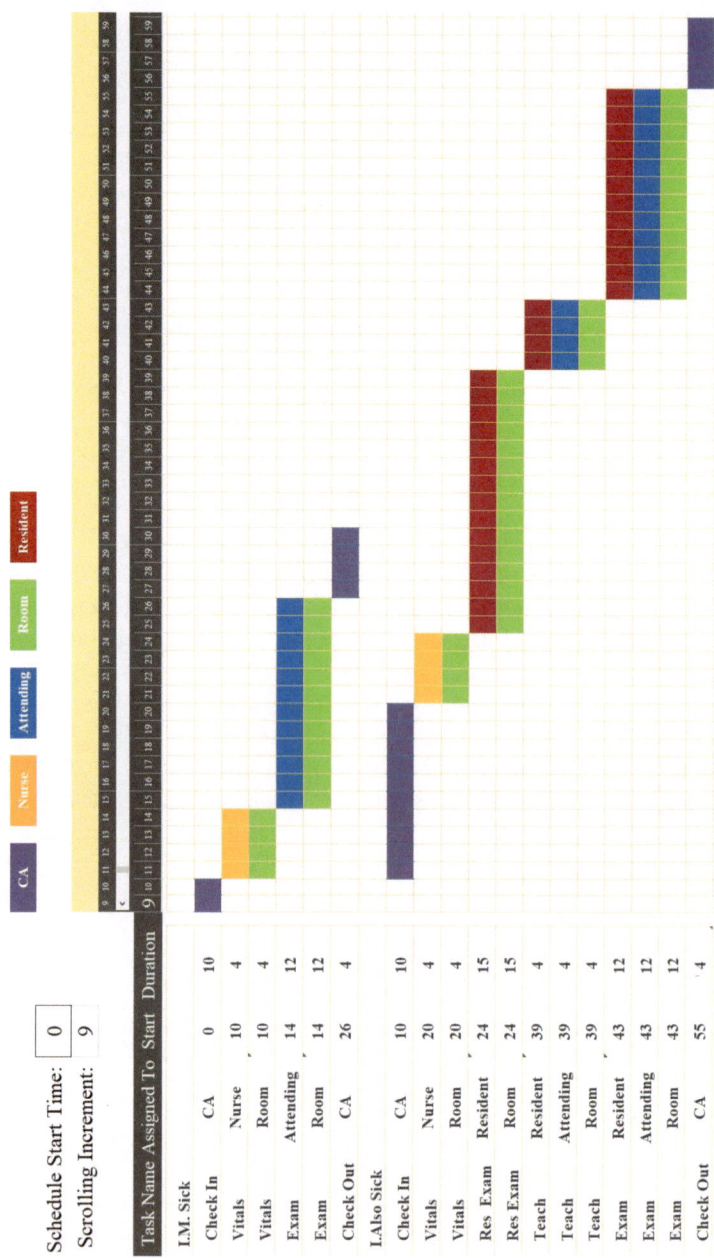

Fig. 2.7 Gantt Chart for Pair of Office Visits in an Academic Medical Center (Hybrid). CA, clinical assistant; Res, resident.

5. Gantt Charts present a way to visualize scenarios and highlight conflicts but they do not dictate any policy or response to the issues raised.

2.6 Makespan and the Critical Path Method

One of the major benefits of creating Gantt Charts for a sequence of events is that they provide visual evidence of any overlapping commitments of resources. When confronted with such a depiction it is natural to look for a way to reorganize or stagger the starting times of activities in hopes of improving process performance. For the simple structures considered so far we were able to do this by inspection - meaning that we simply looked for conflicts and found a way to slide start times to make things fit. For larger problems that can easily emerge in a health care setting this ad-hoc approach can be unreliable. To expand the applicability of the ideas presented so far we need to introduce another tool that helps to keep track of activity start times for more complex systems.

Fortunately, several tools can provide the needed insight. In particular, we have found the concept of a Critical Path to be a good way to help illuminate issues about process structure when a larger set of activities is involved. When we present a sequence of steps as a diagram using nodes to represent activities and arrows between them to indicate the order of events we can see paths from the start to the finish of a schedule. The longest such path is labeled the Critical Path and defines the Makespan for a problem setting. The Critical Path Method (CPM) can be used to uncover this path in a manner that facilitates an exploration of changing process design or an appointment schedule to improve performance.

CPM is a project management technique developed in the 1950's to help predict completion times for large projects and to help organize the scheduling of activities related to those projects. It has found many applications in a variety of fields, but perhaps its most famous applications were found in large engineering projects such as the construction of the World Trade Center in the 1960's.

The logic of CPM is embedded in a sequence of steps. The first step is to construct a model of the project. In this context the term "model" simply refers to a graphical representation of the inter-connected events involved. Note that we are also using the term "project" rather loosely here. In our contexts this will often refer to a schedule of cases, or patients to be seen during a single session. Therefore, a model of the project will double as a depiction of events over a session. This model will need to include a number of components.

1. A list of all activities required to complete a project or schedule

2. A time or duration needed to complete each activity

3. A list of resources needed for each activity

4. The dependencies between the activities

5. Logical start and end points for the project or schedule

Note that almost all of this information is provided either implicitly or explicitly in the Process Map. Once these elements are defined we can lay out the project and display it as a network. Using this representation we look for the longest path through this network. In addition, we will be able to see how changing a start time affects the Critical Path and whether moving the start time of an activity changes the Makespan.

The term "dependencies" here has a rather specific meaning. When we think about a sequence of activities we have instances in which an activity cannot begin until some number of other Activities has been completed. If Activity B cannot begin until Activity A has been completed and Activity C cannot begin until both A and B have been completed, then we have dependencies. A is said to have B as an immediate successor and B is said to have A an immediate predecessor. Note that Activity C has both A and B as predecessors but only B is its immediate predecessor. Fortunately, when the dependencies are recorded, as long as we list the immediate predecessors and successors for each activity we can reproduce the entire network structure.

2.6.1 Earliest Start, Earliest Finish and the Forward Pass

All activities that lay along the Critical Path from the network developed are labeled Critical Activities. Hence any delay in the start of any of these activities guarantees that the completion time for the last activity on the schedule will be delayed, and Makespan will be increased. By contrast we may find that some activities could be delayed by some amount of time without increasing the Makespan. The amount of time that an activity can be increased without increasing Makespan is referred to as the Slack Time of the associated activity. In other words each activity has a slack time (which may be 0) and as long as a delay or increase in activity time is below this value, the Makespan will not be increased. To compute slack times, we must calculate four values for each activity:

1. Early Start Time (EST): The earliest possible time that an activity can begin

2. Early Finish Time (EFT): The earliest possible time that an activity can end. Calculated as EST plus activity time.

3. Late Finish Time (LFT): The latest possible time that an activity can end without increasing Makespan

4. Late Start Time (LST): The latest possible time that an activity can begin without increasing Makespan. Calculated as LFT minus activity time.

With these definitions in place, we can say that for any activity, Slack Time = LST - EST = LFT - EFT. What remains is a systematic approach to handling these calculations. To organize the calculations we work through the network diagram twice. First we make a forward pass from Start to End and calculate the EST and EFT values along the way. Then we make a backward pass from End to Start and calculate LFT and LST values along the way. On the forward pass we begin at the start and schedule each activity in sequence as early as possible. Once this is complete, we move to the backward pass in which we consider each activity in reverse order and compute the latest time we can complete and start each activity without increasing the Makespan.

To find the EST and EFT we begin with a "dummy" node that we label as "START". This node has an EST and duration set to 0. Any activity that has no other predecessor is declared to have START as its only immediate predecessor. We also add a dummy node labeled END. This node as a duration of 0. Any activity that has no successors is declared to have END as its only immediate successor. We then proceed from START to END repeating the following steps:

1. Find an activity such that the EFT(s) of each of its immediate predecessors have been calculated.

2. Set the EST of this activity as the maximum of the EFT values for its immediate predecessors.

3. Set the EFT of this activity as its EST plus its activity time.

The addition of the START node guarantees that the algorithm always has a way to begin and that Step 1 can commence. Step 2 simply says that an activity can start no sooner than all activities that must precede it have been completed. Step 3 says that the earliest an activity can finish is the sum of its earliest start time and its duration. We then repeat these three steps until all activities have been considered. When we reach one or more activities that are not immediate predecessors of any other activities, we connect them to the dummy node labeled END. Since END has no duration, its EST and EFT are equal.

2.6.2 *Latest Finish, Latest Start, and the Backward Pass*

We now have a network with a START and an END. Once we finish the forward pass we can start figuring out the LFT and LST values. The LST of END is the same as its EST. Given this value as a starting point we complete the Backward Pass as follows:

1. Find an activity such that the LST of all its immediate successors have been computed.

2. Set the LFT of the activity as the minimum of the LST values of its immediate successors.

3. Set the LST of the activity as its LFT minus its activity time.

The addition of the END node guarantees a starting point for this pass. Step 2 simply states that the latest completion time for an activity that does not increase Makespan is the time its successor activity must begin. In order to finish by this time, the activity must start no later than the LST computed in step 3.

We repeat steps 1 to 3 until all activities have been considered. At the conclusion of the backward pass the calculated LFT of START should equal 0. If it is any other value, a mistake has been made.

2.7 Putting the Pieces Together: Appointment Scheduling at Eastern Hospital Outpatient Clinic

We wish to apply the ideas behind CPM to address a hard problem in health care management - namely, the scheduling of appointments in outpatient settings. To keep the problem manageable let us focus on a clinic session with only three appointments to be scheduled. To make the problem a bit more realistic we will assume that each of these 3 visits will have a slightly different process flow. Data on the sequencing, precedence relationships, and durations are provided in Table 3. The network diagram built with this information is shown in Figure 2.8.

Note that CI1 refers to the **Check-In** time for the first patient on the schedule. V1 refers to the **Vitals** activity, R1 refers to the resident's face time with the first patient, T1 refers to the teaching activity and also involves the attending. A1 refers to the Attending's face time with this patient, and CO1 refers to the **Check-Out** time for patient 1. The precedence relationships relate to the sequence of events for each individual patient. For each activity we need to include its immediate predecessors. Note that these relationships may involve multiple flow units. For example, R3 cannot occur before A1 because the Resident is involved in step A1 during which both

Table 2.3 Activity Data for Made-Up Clinic

Activity	Predecessor	Duration
CI1	– –	10
V1	CI1	4
R1	V1	15
T1	R1	4
A1	T1	10
CO1	A1	4
CI2	CI1	4
V2	CI2,V1	4
A2	V2,A1	12
CO2	A2	4
CI3	CI2	10
V3	CI3,V2	4
R3	V3,A1	18
CO3	R3	4

the Attending and Resident interact with the patient.

In this example three distinct process flows are depicted. For Patient 1 both the resident and the attending are involved. This process matches the Process Map shown in Figure 2.1. For Patient 2 we omit the resident and use the Process Map from Figure 2.2. For Patient 3 we omit the attending. We have seen this type of arrangement when clinics include NEW patients, RETURN patients and FOLLOW-UP visits for simple checks. A NEW patient is one visiting the clinic for the first time for this particular condition. A RETURN visit is most often scheduled at the end of a NEW visit and tends to be much shorter. Some clinics will also have some visits for very quick things like prescription refills. These visits can often be handled by a physician's assistant or the resident. Thus, clinics often meld three types of visits on a single schedule.

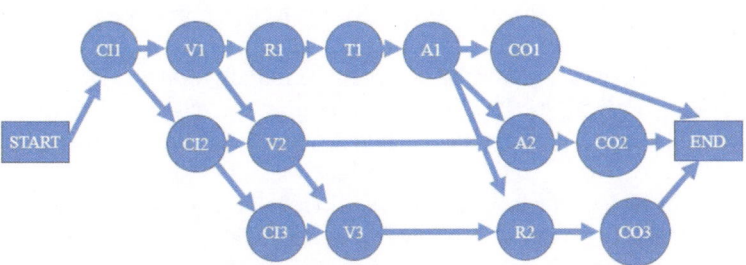

Fig. 2.8 Network Diagram for E-HOC Clinic Schedule. CI, check-in; V, vitals; R, resident; T, teaching; A, attending; CO, check-out.

In this context, a path is simply a route from START to END. Notice that even in this simple diagram we have multiple paths. The length of each path is the sum of the activity times for nodes along that path. With this in mind we list all path lengths in Table 2.4.

Table 2.4 Path Lengths for Three-Patient Schedule . CI, check-in; V, vitals; R, resident; T, teaching; A, attending; CO, check-out.

Path	Durations (min)	Length (min)
CI1-V1-R1-T1-A1-CO1	10 + 4 + 15 + 4 + 8 + 4	45
CI1-CI2-V2-A2-CO2	10 + 10 + 4 + 12 + 4	40
CI1-CI2-CI3-V3-R3-CO3	10 + 10 + 10 + 4 + 18 + 4	56
CI1-V1-V2-A2-CO2	10 + 4 + 4 + 12 + 4	34
CI1-V1-R1-T1-A1-A2-CO2	10 + 4 + 15 + 4 + 10 + 12 + 4	59
CI1-V1-R1-T1-A1-R3-CO3	10 + 4 + 15 + 4 + 8 + 18 + 4	63
CI1-V1-V2-V3-R3-CO3	10 + 4 + 4 + 4 + 18 + 4	44

The table shows that the critical path has a length of 63 minutes. So far we have implicitly assumed that all three patients arrive at the start of the session. However, it is clear that patients 2 and 3 do not need to be present at time 0 and their appointment times can be greater than 0 without increasing Makespan. We can use CPM to determine how much greater these arrival times can be without increasing the completion time for the entire schedule.

We work forward through the network to find the EST and EFT for each node. For START these values are set by default to 0 and 0. If we include START and END we have 16 nodes with EST and EFT values shown in Table 2.5.

When an activity has multiple immediate predecessors the EST is the maximum of the EFT for those predecessors. Thus, we have multiple points in this example at which the EST is the maximum of two values. For example, the EST for V2 is the maximum of the EFT for V1 and the EFT for CI2 or max(14, 20) = 20. Given EST and EFT values we can work backward to look for the LFT and LST for each job. We begin with the END node and assign it a duration of 0 and LFT(END) = LST(END) = 63. We fill in the remaining values to get those shown in Table 6.

We have added the calculation of slack in Table 2.6, which is the difference between the LFT and the EFT. Equivalently, we could use the difference between the LST and the EST. For CI2 we have an EST of 10 and an LST of 17. Thus, this activity can begin any time between times 10 and 17 without increasing Makespan. We would expect this to be operationalized by setting the appointment time for the second patient on the schedule as 15 minutes after the appointment time for the first. The 7-minute slack time also implies that if this patient arrives 5 minutes early or

Table 2.5 Results of Forward Pass

Activity	EST	Duration	EFT
START	0	0	0
CI1	0	10	10
V1	10	4	14
R1	14	15	29
T1	29	4	33
A1	33	8	41
CO1	43	4	45
CI2	10	10	20
V2	20	4	24
A2	41	12	53
CO2	53	4	57
CI3	20	10	30
V3	30	4	34
R3	41	18	59
CO3	59	4	63
END	63	0	63

Table 2.6 Results of Backward Pass

Activity	LST	Duration	LFT	Slack
START	0	0	0	0
CI1	0	10	10	0
V1	10	4	14	0
R1	14	15	29	0
T1	29	4	33	0
A1	33	8	41	0
CO1	59	4	63	18
CI2	17	10	27	7
V2	43	4	47	23
A2	47	12	59	6
CO2	59	4	63	6
CI3	27	10	37	7
V3	37	4	41	7
R3	41	18	59	0
CO3	59	4	63	0
END	63	0	63	0

2 minutes late, the Makespan will be unaffected. With a larger schedule we could work through the same steps and identify the LST for each appointment and use these values to help develop a complete appointment schedule.

2.8 Key Take-Aways

In this chapter we have discussed two tools that can be used for the analysis and presentation of processes of interest: Gantt Charts and the CPM. As motivating examples we focused on simple clinic visits. However, the same tools could be applied to many other types of processes including scheduling of operating rooms, sterilizing equipment, fulfilling prescriptions, and a myriad of other tasks. Important points related to the CPM and its application for our purposes include:

1. We can translate information from the Process Map to depict process flow using nodes to represent activities and arrows to indicate precedence relationships. A START node can be added to precede any node that does not have another immediate predecessor. An END node can be added after any node that has no immediate successor.

2. The CPM was originally designed to deal with a single project. However, the same logic can be applied to any sequence of jobs such as patient visits, procedures in an operating room, etc.

3. Given this node-based representation we can calculate the earliest start times that are feasible moving from START to END. EFTvalues are the ESTplus the duration of each activity

4. LFT values can be calculated by moving from END back to START. LST values are LFT minus the duration of each activity.

5. With these values, we can calculate LFT - EFT for each activity to determine how much the beginning of an activity can be moved without increasing Makespan. This tool enables us to analyze and present information in a way that leads to a workable schedule.

2.9 Review Material and Prior Works

Many of the examples discussed above are stylized versions of settings that we have studied in detail. Names are changed as a courtesy to all parties involved. Of particular relevance for this chapter are works that we conducted in the Blaustein Pain Treatment Clinic within the Johns Hopkins Outpatient Clinic (JHOC) . To consider supporting data and analysis in more detail consult Chambers and Williams (2017b), Chambers and Williams (2017a), Williams et al (2012), and Williams et al (2015). Much of our study concerning Parallel Processing is discussed in Chambers et al (2016), and Conley et al (2016).

To ensure that you understand the material covered here, consider analyzing the following scenario.

2.9.1 Surgeon Using Two Rooms: Normal Cases

Recall the scenario described in the Prologue (Section 0.1.3) that details the surgical procedure for Frank Caldwell. Assume that the times provided there are good estimates of actual activity times and respond to the following:

1. Draw a map of the procedure process for a single case described in Section 0.1.3.

2. Create a Gantt Chart showing the activity times and resource use for a total of four cases that use rooms 1 and 2.

3. Provide the earliest possible start times for the four cases.

4. What is the surgeon's utilization rate calculated from the start of the surgeon's activities until the end of those activities?

5. What is the room utilization rate calculated from the start of its use until the end of its use? (Note that two rooms are involved).

6. If a room costs $1,000 per hour and the surgeon cost $250 per hour, is it more costly to assign the surgeon two rooms or to assign only one?

2.9.2 Surgeon Using Two Rooms Double Cases

Recall the scenario described in the Prologue (Section 0.1.3) that details the surgical procedure for Frank Caldwell. Assume that the times provided there are good estimates of actual activity times. It turns out that some patients require a procedure on both wrists, instead of only one. The surgeon's operating time is 25 minutes for one wrist, but 45 minutes for the "Double" cases. For a session that includes two single cases and two double cases, the hospital wants to identify start times for each case that minimizes Makespan. One viable proposal is to alternate case types (Single - Double - Single - Double) placing the single cases in one room and the double cases in the other. Under these assumptions, complete the following tasks.

1. Create a network flow diagram for this scenario of four cases.

2. Find the critical path for this schedule.

3. Identify the latest start times for cases 2, 3, and 4 that minimize Makespan.

4. Find the utilization levels for the rooms, and the surgeon based on total Makespan.

Chapter 3
Special Issues in Process Analysis for Health Care: Shared Resources and Cycles

Abstract The essential logic of process analysis is that work flows through a process along some Route in which Resources engage in Activities directed to modify the Flow Unit. This sequence intuitively suggests that we can narrowly focus on the resources and individual activities to understand the limitations of a process. In many instances this narrow focus is adequate. However, in health care settings we often find that complexities in defining the Route, Resources, and Activities require additional consideration. In this chapter we focus on three such complexities: job configuration, or how multiple resources must be combined for one or more activities; parallel processing where multiple flow units are worked on simultaneously; and resource pooling in which a resource is shared among providers. Understanding the logic of each of these elements will position a manager to better measure, monitor, and improve process flow.

3.1 Introduction

The central theme of this text is that we focus on a Process in which Flow Units proceed along some Route over which Resources engage in Activities with the larger objective to transform the Flow Units involved. This rather generic definition is being used deliberately because we want to use the same ideas to consider a wide variety of types of processes and settings. In many instances the most significant problems involving a process will have simple solutions. Some critical Resource is in short supply, or some Activity is being repeated without a good reason. In these cases process mapping, measurement, and the related simple calculations are sufficient to see the means to improve performance. A plethora of texts and readings on Operations Management explain how to handle these situations (Anupindi et al (1999), Hopp and Lovejoy (2012), Karuppan et al (2021)).

On the other hand, many health care settings add factors that greatly complicate the analysis. For example, many hospitals double as teaching institutions and have

© The Author(s), under exclusive license to Springer Nature Switzerland AG 2022
C. Chambers et al., *Improving Processes for Health Care Delivery*,
https://doi.org/10.1007/978-3-031-19043-8_3

residents (as well as interns, and fellows) who play critical roles in many process flows. Their involvement increases the number of steps, processing times, and costs. Health care is also characterized by a great deal of specialization of labor. Various levels of nurses, technicians, trainees, and other medical specialists are brought to bear and are often barred from engaging in an activity assigned to another resource. This level of specialization results in the need to coordinate the actions of multiple resources for one or more activities. In some cases, steps involving a specific combination of specialized resources may be sequential but may also be done in parallel or revisited later in the route. Consequently, the set of resources needed changes from one case to the next but can also evolve from step to step within a single case.

At the same time, many resources including specialists, rooms, and equipment are shared among some number of more general care providers. In many situations a specialized resource is needed more than once over a session but is not needed for each case by each provider. In such settings resources may be shared and will float from one case to another on an as needed basis. This floating may occur according to a set schedule or may happen randomly. This factor is yet another element that complicates the calculation of process metrics.

Each of these complicating factors adds nuances to system performance that can be misunderstood without the use of formal tools for visualization and analysis. With this in mind we explore several elements by considering of a set of canonical problems. These problems will be presented in an order of increasing complexity to help the reader develop insight into how they influence a system and can be accounted for in process analysis. We loosely tie each problem to a health care setting that we have studied but note that no single problem is a complete description of any real setting. Complex systems blend elements of these stylized problems. The study of simplified problems is meant to expose essential trade offs in a way that arms the analyst with a collection of insights and tools to address real settings in practice.

Along the way we will focus on key process performance metrics including Cycle Time which is the duration from the entrance of a Flow Unit to a process until its exit; Makespan, which is the duration from the start of the first job on a schedule to the completion of the last job; Utilization of key resources which we calculate as the cumulative duration of resource activity divided by the Makespan; and Throughput which is the rate at which Flow Units enter or leave a stable system. In particular, we are interested in how these metrics are affected by process structure. At several points we will consider cost in a rather generic way, as we will return to this topic later. For the moment it is sufficient to calculate costs by multiplying some cost per minute for a resource by its busy time. Finally, we will close with a more complete description of a highly complex setting that includes many of the elements laid out here and walk through a scheduling process in more detail to provide additional insights.

3.2 Process Mapping

To this point, we have taken an ad hoc approach to the process mapping step. This is quite sufficient when considering single-step processes or processes with few exceptions that run in a simple serial fashion. To expand our consideration to more complex settings it is useful to establish a few guidelines on how a process map should be presented. We can summarize these guidelines as a short list.

1. Activities will be represented as rectangles and will include information on the Resources involved and Activity duration.

2. Waiting between steps will often be treated as an Activity, and the number waiting or average time spent will be presented when known.

3. Decision points will be represented as a circle with multiple departure points, and criteria for selection of the departure point will be provided.

4. Arrows will indicate precedence relationships with the event at the tail of the arrow being an immediate predecessor of the event at the head of the arrow.

3.3 Parallel Processing

Let us begin with the simplest process construction of interest. This process involves a single Activity that we will simply label **Exam** and a single costly resource that we will label as Attending. Each iteration of this activity takes 60 minutes and is performed by the attending physician. This is akin to a very small clinic in which an attending works solo for a 4 hour clinic session. We will refer to this construct as Process α. Figure 3.1 uses a simple Gantt Chart to illustrate a single clinic session. (Note that we truncate the display from the left to fit on the page with the understanding that time is measured from 0.) Each row shows the **Exam** time for the attending serving each patient. Since this process includes only one activity and only one resource, each row reflects the Cycle Time for one visit. Thus, it is clear that each Cycle Time is 60 minutes. Since we are tracking only one resource, and that resource cannot be in two places at once, a job (patient visit) must be completed before service on the next one can begin. In other words, a patient must leave the system before the next can be seen. In this arrangement completion of the appointment schedule will occupy 4 hours - 1 hour for each of the 4 patients. Scanning Figure 3.1 immediately shows that the Makespan will be simply 4 * 60 = 240 minutes, attending Utilization will be 100%, and Throughput will be 4 patients over 4 hours or 1 patient per hour.

Fig. 3.1 Schedule of Four Visits with Single Step - Single Worker Process

While this construct is elegant in its simplicity, it is rarely seen in practice. A clinic visit will involve a variety of tasks that are not purely medical in nature. Other tasks include collection of payment information, location of patient records, leading a patient into an examination room, scheduling a follow-up appointment, etc. Consequently, let us add a second resource that can perform such activities.

As a more concrete example, envision one attending handling clinic visits. The attending could handle the visit alone if need be. However, it is far more common to use another resource such as a Clinical Assistant (CA) to handle the first part of the visit. Let us assume that the CA is with the patient for 15 minutes and label this Activity as **Check-In**. Then part of what the attending had been doing is taken care of before the attending is required. As a result the attending may only need 50 minutes with the patient instead of 60. We note that the total processing time has risen from 60 minutes to 15 + 50 = 65 minutes. Let us refer to this arrangement as Process β.

One might ask why Process β would be used if Process α is simpler, faster, and involves fewer resources. We now note two key facts. First, the CA is likely to be a less expensive resource than the attending. Second, the clinic is likely to have access to more than one examination room. Using Process β, each patient has a Cycle Time of 65 minutes. However, **Check-In** for the second patient can take place while **Exam** is still ongoing for the first patient. This scenario is called parallel processing. It can be coordinated in such a way that the attending can move directly from the first patient to the second with no delay, just as was assumed for Process α. Figure 3.2 displays a Gantt chart associated with an implementation of this process for the same four patients. The chart shows that the completion time of each subsequent patient is 50 minutes after the first. Under this arrangement Makespan becomes 65 + 50 + 50 + 50 = 215 minutes instead of 240. Utilization of the attending falls to (50 * 4) / 215 = 93%. Throughput becomes four patients over 215 minutes or 1.17 patients per hour.

In all likelihood, the attending is the most expensive resource in this system making it attractive to maximize utilization of this resource. However, this example highlights the fact that maximizing attending utilization is not synonymous with maximizing throughput. Recall that in Process α attending utilization was 100%. In

Process β attending utilization is reduced because **Check-In** must be done before the first engagement with the attending. However, given this new arrangement attending utilization is as high as possible. This is evidenced by the fact that once the attending enters the process, every vertical column includes exactly one instance of a cell indicating that the attending is in use. Adding the CA as a resource increases process complexity and Cycle Time while reducing attending utilization, but also reduces Makespan, and increases Throughput. The latter is key because revenue is most likely maximized by maximizing Throughput. Whether the addition of the CA is attractive will depend on how much each resource costs, the collections related to each patient visit, and whether demand is high enough to take advantage of the possible increase in capacity.

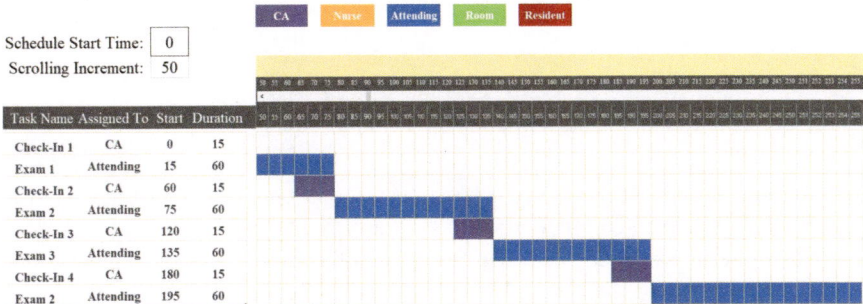

Fig. 3.2 Schedule of Four Visits with Two Steps - Two Resource Process. CA, Clinical Assistant

The ubiquity of this arrangement strongly suggests that the increased throughput is more than enough to offset the increase in cost. This brings up another facet of health care settings that is highly unusual. When viewed on a cost per minute basis it is not unusual for the fully loaded cost of one category of direct labor to be 10 times higher than another. Cost gaps of this magnitude are almost unheard of in most production settings. It is not so unusual for senior management to be 10 or 100 or even 1000 times as costly as direct labor in many firms, but it is very unusual for direct laborers to have such a large cost gap. In hospitals, both a CA and an attending have direct medical contact with patients over a single episode of care. If the attending costs $200 per hour and the CA costs $20 per hour then saving 25 minutes of the attending's time over a clinic session is an implicit savings of $200 * 25/60 = $83. At the same time, the added cost of the CA for the entire session is $20 * 215/60 = $71.67. Thus the savings on one resource exceeds the added cost of the other. These kinds of trade offs often justify the added complexity of turning a one-step process into a two step process. Of course we are ignoring the fact that the CA is certainly performing other value-adding activities between these 15 minute encounters with patients. If we can assign some value to those activities then this arrangement makes even more sense. The key message is that the use of multiple resources can facilitate parallel processing, and when the changes to the process metrics are properly accounted for, this can be a reasonable approach.

3.4 Combining Resources

Building on the previous section, we will consider a process that consists of three steps, and involves three resources. We generically label the steps 1, 2, and 3. Similarly we label the resources A, B, and C. In the most straight forward arrangement we have one resource for each step and one step for each resource. Thus A is involved alone for **Step 1**, B is involved alone for **Step 2**, and C is involved alone for **Step 3**. For ease of understanding let us assume that each step requires its associated resource for 20 minutes. We will refer to this as Process γ. In this arrangement completion of the job (Cycle Time) takes 20 * 3 = 60 minutes. In addition, it is clear that each resource is used for 20/60 minutes or 1/3, and Throughput is 1 job per hour. As a very rough example, these resources could refer to a nurse, a resident, and an attending dealing with a single clinic visit.

Now consider an alternate arrangement. If resources are able to operate together, it may be possible to complete each step more quickly. Let us assume that if resource A, and B work together, then **Step 1** can be completed in 15 minutes. If B and C work together, then **Step 2** can be done in 15 minutes. Finally, if A and C work together, then **Step 3** can be done in 15 minutes. We will label this arrangement Process δ. With this process, it is apparent that Cycle Time is reduced to 15 * 3 = 45 minutes; Throughput rises to 1 job every 45 minutes or 1.33 patients per hour; and Utilization of each resource rises to (15 * 2)/45 = 2/3. Figure 3.3 shows a Gantt Chart linked to a single visit under both arrangements. The first 3 rows depict the simpler Process γ, and the next 6 rows depict Process δ. The chart documents that Makespan is reduced, and utilization improved with no additional resources.

If cost is accounted for on a dollar per minute basis, it is clear that the cost per minute using Process δ is greater than the cost of Process γ. However, it is likely that this increase can be offset by the increase in Throughput. Selection of one arrangement over the other can be made once all of these data are accounted for.

Consideration of a single Flow Unit is illustrative but can also be misleading. Let us extend this example to look at a schedule with two patients. Under Process γ resource A is used for 20 minutes and is available for the next job immediately thereafter. Thus, we can begin with the first patient at time 0 and begin the second at time 20. After this initial delay for the second patient no further interaction between these flow units takes place. The first patient is completed at time 60 just as before and the second is completed at 60 + 20 = 80 minutes from the start of the session. This is the same type of parallel processing that we saw earlier. Each resource is used for 2 * 20 = 40 minutes and utilization is 40/80 = 50%. Moving from a sched-

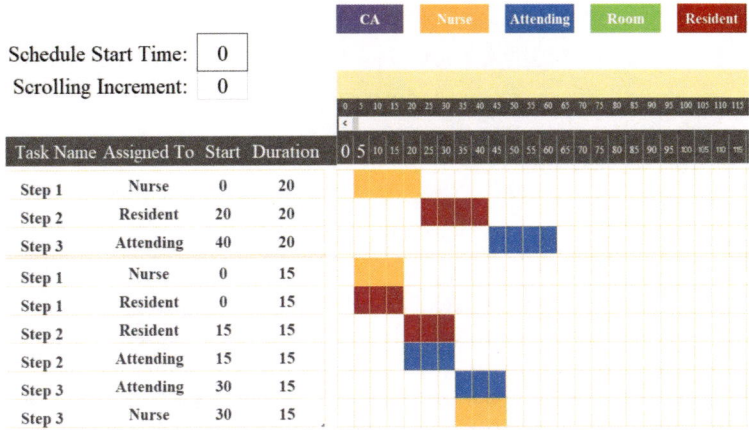

Fig. 3.3 Two Versions of Three Step Process: Without and With Resource Sharing

ule of only 1 job to a schedule of 2 jobs increases Makespan but does not double it because activity times have not changed and utilization is increased from 1/3 to 1/2.

Next, consider a schedule with two patients under Process δ. The first patient can start at time 0 and will take 45 minutes just as before. The key question is, when can the second patient begin? Note that Activities 1 and 2 cannot be carried out at the same time because they each involve the resident. Similarly Activities 2 and 3 cannot overlap because of the involvement of the attending. Activities 1 and 3 cannot overlap because of the involvement of the nurse. Consequently, the second job cannot begin until the first job is completed. Thus the Makespan for a schedule of 2 jobs is twice that for a schedule of 1 job because no parallel processing is possible. Makespan for 2 jobs under this arrangement becomes simply 45 * 2 = 90 minutes, and Utilization becomes (20 * 2) / 90 = 4/9. An effort to improve performance appears to be effective if we only look at one job at a time, but it is counter-productive as soon as we consider multiple jobs. This finding highlights the fact that the configuration of work can produce unintended consequences.

Sharing resources for a single step is quite common in health care settings because of the degree of specialization involved. Sometimes this is medically essential. The surgeon and anesthesiologist must both be involved simultaneously and the level of attention to detail needed by each party means that we do not want a system that has one party doing both jobs. However, in other settings double-duty occurs owing to a lack of training, regulatory constraints, or even simply tradition. In these cases, breaking the need to have resources co-located can produce gains in utilization and efficiency. Notice that in the example above, splitting the tasks to allow each resource to work alone makes each step longer, but the increased time is offset by the ability to have steps take place in parallel if multiple jobs are on the schedule. The key lesson is that the trade offs involved in combining resources or combining steps must be thought through carefully in light of a schedule to gauge whether a change is worthwhile.

3.5 Sharing Resources

In health care settings it is routine for attendings to share resources such as a CA or examination rooms. Thus far we have ignored the cost of the rooms because we have treated this cost as fixed. However, in settings where a practice is renting rooms, that cost should be explicitly accounted for. In Process α we had one attending and presumably one room and both had utilization rates of 100%. On the other hand, when we considered Process β we calculated the utilization of the attending at roughly 93%. However, we have yet to account for utilization of the 2 examination rooms needed to facilitate the parallel processing involved. Under Process α room utilization was a non issue. Using Process β we reduce Makespan and increase Throughput, but part of the cost of doing so is that room utilization falls to $215 / (2 * 215) = 50\%$, and utilization of the CA is only $(15 * 4) / 215 = 28\%$. Even though the CA and the room are each likely to be less expensive than the attending, these utilization levels are still quite low.

One way to address this issue is to have multiple attendings in a clinic space at the same time and to have resources available that can work with more than one attending. Attendings could share rooms and a CA. Such arrangements are quite common in larger clinics.

Consider a setting in which two attendings share 3 examination rooms, and one CA. Each attending deals with a distinct set of 4 patients. Notice that we are adding one attending as a resource, while reducing the duplication of other resources. Figure 3.4 shows a Gantt chart for this scenario.

In this arrangement each patient's Cycle Time is unchanged. Makespan becomes 250 minutes. Utilization of the CA becomes $(8 * 15) / 250 = 48\%$, and since we have three rooms to account for, room utilization becomes $(8 * 65) / (3 * 250) = 35\%$. We note a subtle trade off that is being made here. To manage room utilization we are asking one attending to start roughly 1 hour after the first. We are assuming that this is a simple adjustment, even though we have found in practice that it is surprisingly difficult to bring about. Sharing resources works best when the agents involved are willing to provide some accommodation to the process structure.

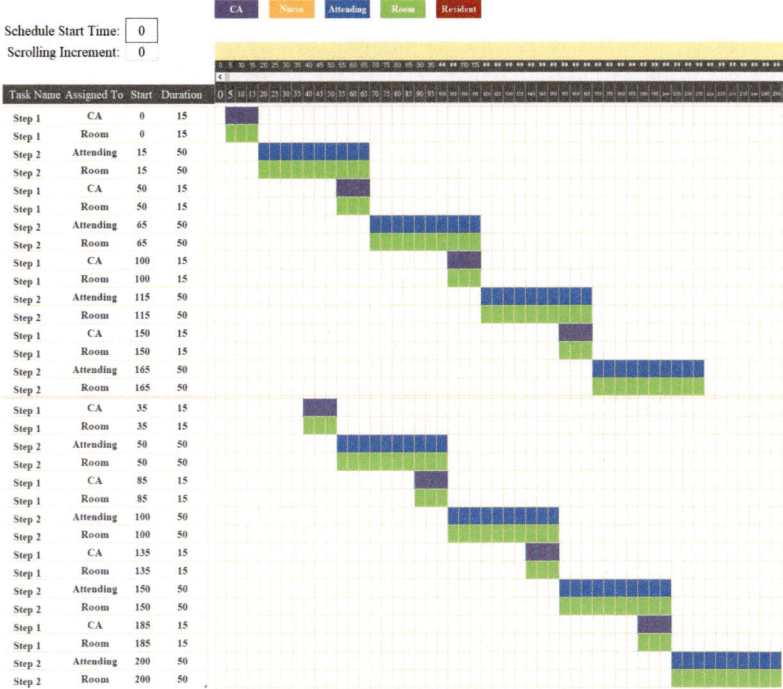

Fig. 3.4 Two Attendings Sharing a CA and 3 Rooms

3.6 Scheduling Jobs with Variable Activity Times

Thus far we have worked with Process Maps, Gantt Charts, and Critical Paths for work flows when we knew the activity times. The obvious limitation of this approach is that in health care settings, we do not know actual activity times. There are at least three distinct approaches to handle this issue: 1) Optimization, 2) Simulation, and 3) Heuristics. Optimization refers to finding an optimal schedule using advanced mathematical techniques. These approaches require accurate descriptions of the random variables involved, and a deep understanding of mathematical tools (Begen and Queyranne (2012), Bevan (2006), Cayirli et al (2006)). Unfortunately, staff and physicians do not have the time or interest to master this material in addition to the massive amounts of information and techniques that they have already spent years accumulating. In addition, even if these techniques were mastered by hospital staff, the fact is that every scheduling problem changes from day to day and from setting to setting. In addition, patients expect to be assigned appointment times far in advance. The use of daily optimization is simply impractical for facilities working in real time.

Simulation, refers to the idea of creating models that are mathematical abstractions of a real setting and using some form of experimentation or trial and error method to find a good schedule for the work to be done. In many ways simulation is relatively easy to master and is commonly used by consultants in the health care industry (Laguna and Marklund (2005), Karuppan et al (2021)). However, many of the same issues arise as with the use of optimization. The time involved in the creation of good simulation models for a specific setting makes them good tools to learn lessons from, and excellent resources for consulting and longer term improvement projects. However, managers will need a quicker approach for day to day problems until such models can be built.

Fortunately, Economics and Industrial Engineering share a lengthy history of a much more practical approach that can be implemented in real time - namely the use of heuristics for problem solving. A heuristic is a decision rule or analytical approach designed to get near an optimal policy when more elaborate methods are not fast enough. For the problems that we are dealing with here, one heuristic is to adjust the blocks of time in a way that takes into account the variability of Activity times. Once this is done, we can use tools like Gantt Charts or the Critical Path Method to lay out how work is to proceed. This approach is useful in many endeavors including process design, and appointment scheduling (Chambers and Dada (2014), Dada and Chambers (2019), Kolker (2010a), Kolker (2010b)).

To suggest a good heuristic we will need three things. First we need data on real settings to work with. Second, we need a way to find an optimal policy so that we can compare a heuristic to it. Finally, we need some logic to motivate and explain the decision rule and how to apply it. In our work we have collected a great deal of data from functioning medical units that can be used. Researchers in the fields of Operations Research and Industrial Engineering have developed sophisticated ways to optimally solve the related problems. Given these tools, we will work to explain the rationale behind some heuristics that we have found useful.

In particular we are going to focus on a problem of devising an appointment schedule for an outpatient clinic. A very long list of complicating factors exist for this problem, but we will consider a few factors that are common in hospital settings. We will consider patients who do not arrive for an appointment, a mix of NEW and RETURN patients, variable activity times, and a teaching mission that has to be accommodated. Though this problem is still more complex than that seen in many settings, any lessons that we can reach here will be helpful in other cases.

3.7 A Cyclic Approach to Appointment Scheduling

We have generated multiple data sets via direct observation of a Physical Medicine and Rehabilitation (PM&R) clinic, and we use the underlying data as the foundation for this extended discussion (Chambers et al (2018)). The goal of these projects was to improve patient flow. In this context, improvement meant "treating more patients, on schedule, and completing the clinic session on time without compromising quality of care or the hospital's teaching mission". Some managerial goals can be easily translated into metrics such as Makespan, Throughput, and Cycle Times. However, most clinic managers will not state their concerns this way. They are much more likely to focus on clinic sessions that run beyond the scheduled 4 hour block, and patient waiting times. However, it should be clear that overtime operations is just clinic sessions that have a Makespan beyond the targeted 4 hours. In addition, if the processing times are going to be the same regardless of the schedule, then reducing waiting times is the same as cutting Cycle Times.

When working on this class of problems our analysis centers on accounting for the fundamental trade off that must be optimized; namely, waiting times versus overtime or Cycle Times versus Makespan. For example, if we only want to minimize Makespan we would simply schedule all visits at the start of the session. This approach is likely to ensure that the bottleneck resource is always occupied because the clinic never has to wait for patients to arrive. Of course, waiting times would be very long and the realized Cycle Times for some patients would be extremely large. On the other hand, we could put large gaps between all appointment times. This approach would allow earlier cases to exit before the next case arrives, minimizing each patient's waiting time and Cycle Time. However, the Makespan would be very large and the end of the clinic session would be greatly delayed. Any time used after the scheduled session end time will be referred to as overtime.

We must find a balance between these two types of outcomes. The most common way to approach these problems is to assign some cost to a minute of patient waiting time, and a higher cost to a minute of overtime operations. One then works to minimize the sum of the accumulated waiting and overtime costs. This is an incredibly difficult problem for a host of reasons; chief of which are the high levels of variability linked to the arrival and activity times, inclusion of a teaching mission into the process flow, and strategic behavior of agents in the system.

When studying this particular clinic the raw performance data revealed several additional issues. The clinic experienced a no-show rate of roughly 25%. In other words, on average one out of every four patients on the schedule did not show up. This rate is not unusual in outpatient settings. Other research has found no-show rates as high as 40% (Dantas et al (2018).) Consideration of no-shows makes scheduling quite difficult because it means that we need to schedule more cases than we ideally have capacity for. A similar practice takes place when airlines overbook flights. If everyone who purchased a ticket arrives at the gate, the airline must make some arrangement for the extra passengers.

One way that this is operationalized in a clinic is the use of double-booking, which is the practice of having multiple appointments scheduled for the same appointment slot. Part of the rationale for this practice is that if two appointments are set for a time and one does not come, the clinic does not sit idle awaiting the next arrival. Of course one big difference is that the airline can provide an incentive for any "extra" passengers to take a later flight, whereas the clinic must treat all of the patients who arrive, even if this means running over the planned completion time. Double booking is one reason that it is common for a planned 4-hour clinic session to take more than 240 minutes. In fact, in this particular clinic the session exceeded the 240 minute target roughly half of the time.

Medical appointment scheduling is made more complex by the teaching mission of the hospital. Teaching hospitals are often referred to as academic medical centers (AMCs). The process flow for clinics in an AMC has added elements when the role of a trainee such as a resident must be merged into the patient visit. This unique combination of high no-show rates, double booking, and a teaching mission creates a high level of complexity. In addition, resources are shared if multiple attendings are in the clinic simultaneously, and a CA, and/or resident, and/or an attending are combined for some process steps on multiple jobs. On the other hand, the presence of multiple resources might facilitate parallel processing. One CA, a resident, and an attending may be involved in up to three different stages of a process for up to three different patients at the same time.

3.7.1 Problem Setting and Identification

Historically, this clinic scheduled an average of 7 patients per session for an attending. Rising demand led clinic management to seek a schedule to handle 9 patients per session. In teaching settings the patient encounter routinely requires three activities for the physicians. The patient is examined by a resident. Later, the resident discusses the case with the attending, and finally, the resident/attending dyad examines the patient. We refer to this sequence of steps as Process 1 and depict it in Figure 3.5 . However, in practice one additional element must also be accounted for. In periods of high congestion the attending has the option of treating one or more patients without the involvement of the resident. If the attending does this, then care is provided in a streamlined approach which we will refer to as Process 2, depicted in Figure 3.6. Direct observation taught us that Process 2 is used frequently when the system falls behind schedule or physicians approach the end of the clinic session.

Adding to the complexity of the problem, a schedule for 9 patients needs to include 3 NEW patients and 6 RETURN patients. Activity times for both the resident and the attending are greater for NEW patients than they are for RETURN patients. Patients were seen by a team of one attending and one resident. Historically, patients were scheduled in 20-minute time slots with NEW patients given two concurrent slots. The 25% no-show rate was believed to be stable and clinic management accommodated it through the use of double-booking. Though this practice was routine, the clinic had no formal policy regarding which slots would be double-booked

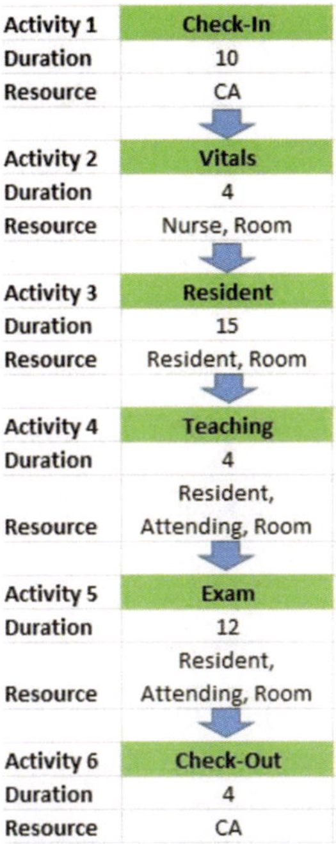

Activity 1	Check-In
Duration	10
Resource	CA

Activity 2	Vitals
Duration	4
Resource	Nurse, Room

Activity 3	Resident
Duration	15
Resource	Resident, Room

Activity 4	Teaching
Duration	4
Resource	Resident, Attending, Room

Activity 5	Exam
Duration	12
Resource	Resident, Attending, Room

Activity 6	Check-Out
Duration	4
Resource	CA

Fig. 3.5 Process Map of Office Visit: Academic Medical Center

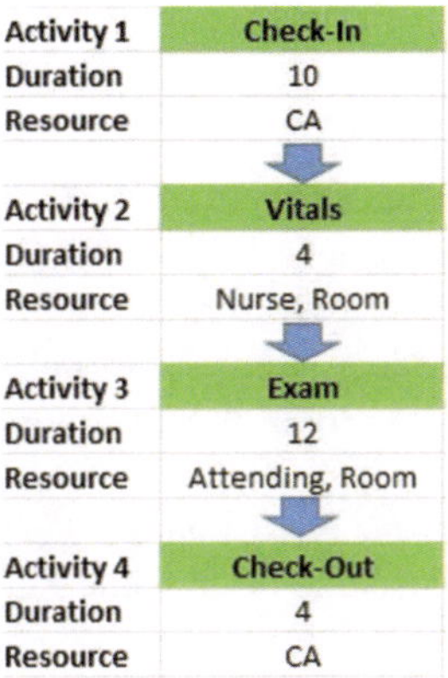

Activity 1	Check-In
Duration	10
Resource	CA

Activity 2	Vitals
Duration	4
Resource	Nurse, Room

Activity 3	Exam
Duration	12
Resource	Attending, Room

Activity 4	Check-Out
Duration	4
Resource	CA

Fig. 3.6 Process Map of Office Visit: Private Practice

and what types of patients would be loaded into such slots.

In dealing with hard problems that involve multiple stages like this one it is often better to solve a series of easier problems and then put the solutions back together to achieve a final product. This approach is sometimes called "decomposition" because it relies on decomposing something into smaller parts that can be more easily digested. In addition, it is often counter-productive to get lost in details that cannot be implemented. For example, if we propose a schedule in which patients should arrive at 8:00, 8:13, 8:36, and 8:57, it would never be implemented. It would be far more useful to advocate for a schedule with arrivals every 15 minutes.

With these ideas in mind, we chose to address the problem by looking at groups of patients in Cycles, where one cycle consists of 3 appointments that are a mix of 1 NEW and 2 RETURN patients. Thus, we decompose the problem of scheduling 9 patients into three smaller ones that each find a schedule for 3 patients. The idea of a cycle is important because the plan for 1 cycle would be repeated over the larger schedule. When viewed in this way the problem of selecting 9 appointment times becomes one of picking start times for 3 cycles and then solving a smaller problem for the 3 times within that cycle. We will sidestep some of the more complex mathematical analysis needed to find the optimal schedule but try to convey enough details to allow the reader to understand how it was done. In the optimized schedule, appointments are not equally spaced within a cycle and the cycles are not equally spaced within the clinic session. Since the cost incurred from exceeding the scheduled session length is not fully relevant until the end of the session is reached; therefore, to create a schedule that works to minimize cost, it is prudent to assign more visits early in the session and leave some slack near the end.

We can describe the problem setting a bit more formally as follows. We use L to represent the number of patients to be scheduled. In this example, we have a total of $L = 9$ patients and we index the patients using the variable ℓ. We group the 9 patients into sets of 3. Each set or cycle will include one NEW patient and two RETURN patients.[1] Each cycle will begin with a double-booking to include one NEW patient and one RETURN patient. If both of these patients arrive we will use the process from Figure 3.5 for the NEW patient and use the process from Figure 3.6 for the RETURN patient. This way we have a formal policy on the use of double-booking and we guarantee that the resident is involved in all NEW cases. The second RE-TURN patient in each cycle will arrive sometime after the first one. Hence, we have three cycles and each cycle can be thought of as having two jobs. The first job is a "composite" job composed of one NEW and one RETURN patient. The second job in the cycle is a simple job consisting of only one RETURN patient.

Any job delayed after its appointment time will be assigned a waiting time cost per minute of ($w = \$1$). Our session is meant to end at time $T = 240$. Therefore, we will calculate the related costs as though we have an appointment (job $L + 1$) arriving at that time and the per minute cost of its delay is the cost of overtime operations, which we will label as W. Since we have three cycles, we must decide what times the second and third cycles start and how long after the start of each cycle the second RETURN patient in that group should arrive.

---

[1] The logic of using cycles as an approach to scheduling parallels that used in Schmidt et al (2001).

Note how this decomposition has significantly simplified the problem. Instead of looking for nine appointment times, we are really only looking for five. We know up front that Patients 1 and 2 will arrive at time 0. The first decision will be the appointment time for Patient 3. The next decision will be the shared appointment time for Patients 4, and 5. We also need an appointment time for Patient 6, a time for Patients 7, and 8, and finally a time for Patient 9. We will add time $T = 240$ as the appointment time for our virtual Patient 10. Thus we have five values to uncover.

3.7.2 Finding an Optimal Schedule

While we discuss this specific problem, our larger objective is to help the reader think through approaches that yield good policies for similar settings. In most cases, it will not be possible to identify an optimal policy - meaning one that minimizes expected cost accounting for all of the problem's complexity. For these settings, it is far more practical to search for "good" policies that get close to the best that could be done if we had infinite time and resources to study the problem. These "good" rules are often referred to as heuristics. A heuristic is a rule of thumb that can be applied in the real world with full knowledge that though it may not be perfect, it is based on good analysis and a solid understanding of what is meant by "optimal".

Of course, the only way to prove that a recommended heuristic is reasonable is to compare its performance to that of an optimal policy. The search for such a policy depends on calculating waiting times and overtime using real data and thinking through how the costs will change with changes in appointment times. We will walk through a way to find the optimal solution for this particular setting.

In short we seek appointment times for each job, A_ℓ. Consider what happens if we increase A_ℓ for one patient, but leave all of the other appointment times unchanged. Doing so will have at least two effects. First, the expected waiting time for job ℓ must be reduced. If all other appointment times are held fixed and we make one appointment later, then that appointment is less likely to be delayed because more time is allotted to complete jobs 1 through $\ell - 1$. On the other hand, if the appointment time for job ℓ is increased, then the expected waiting time for jobs $\ell + 1$ to L can only increase. Recall that job $L + 1$ has an appointment time $A_{\ell+1} = 240$. Any delay for job $L + 1$ will be treated as overtime and involves a cost of W per minute. Since the waiting time for job $L + 1$ is synonymous with overtime we look for a schedule that minimizes the total of expected waiting times.

Stating things a bit more formally, when we increase an appointment time (A_ℓ) the marginal expected delay for job ℓ decreases. We can weigh this value by the probability that the server is busy when job ℓ arrives. We do this because a waiting cost is only incurred if the server is busy upon patient arrival. On the other hand increasing A_ℓ means that we increase the expected waiting costs for job $\ell + 1$, $\ell + 2$

and so on. This cost is weighed by the probability that the server is busy when each of these later jobs arrive. For each job, look for a value A_ℓ that balances these costs.

Consider a simple case that has only two jobs on the schedule. In effect, we have to find three appointment times. However, we know that the appointment time for the first job will be at time $A_1 = 0$ and we have our imaginary job at the end of the clinic session so $A_{L+1} = T$. Therefore, devising a schedule really requires only one decision; namely the appointment time for the second job, A_2. This problem has two uncertain values. These are the processing times for jobs 1 and 2. Let us refer to these values as τ_1 and τ_2. Each of these values comes from some Activity time distribution.

We label the Cumulative Distribution Function (CDF) of these random variables as F_1 and F_2. For example, $F_1(A_2)$ is the probability that job 1 is completed by the time that the second job arrives and the second job will not have to wait. Thus, $1 - F_1(A_2)$ is the probability that job 1 is not yet completed when the second job arrives and it does have to wait. Increasing the value of A_2 reduces the probability that the second job has to wait, but it increases the probability that the third job has to wait. This is why the selection of A_2 must balance the expected costs of these possible events. Mathematically this can be expressed as,

$$(W_{L+1}G_{L-1}(A_L^*)) * \bar{F}_L(T - A_L^*) = w_L \bar{G}_{L-1}(A_L^*) \tag{3.1}$$

Notice that this equation includes a new term, G_{L-1}, which refers to the CDF of the completion time for job $L-1$. In this case, since we set $L = 2$, $L-1$ is simply 1 and G_{L-1} is simply F_1. However, we write the function this way in anticipation of more complex problems where L can be greater than 2. It is convenient to rearrange the terms of this equation to yield,

$$\bar{F}_L(T - A_L^*) = \frac{w_L \bar{G}_{L-1}(A_L^*)}{W_{L+1}G_{L-1}(A_L^*)} \tag{3.2}$$

This equation looks pretty hairy so let's examine what it really says. Since the schedule has two jobs, L is simply 2. A_L^* is the best time for job 2. When looking at job L we know that G_{L-1} is the CDF of the completion time for the previous job. Thus, $G_{L-1}(A_L^*)$ is the CDF of the completion time for the first job, evaluated at the appointment time for the next job. In other words, it is the probability that the first job is finished when the second job arrives. Likewise, $\bar{G}_{L-1}(A_L^*)$ is the probability that the second job on the schedule has to wait. w_L is the cost per minute linked to waiting time for job L. Also recall that job $L+1$ is really the scheduled end of the session at time T. Thus W_{L+1} is just the per minute cost of overtime. The right hand side of the equation balances the cost of waiting for the last real job on the schedule with the cost of waiting for our imaginary job at the planned end of the session.

On the left hand side of the equation we have $\bar{F}_L$. This is 1 minus the CDF of the activity time for the last job. Therefore, $\bar{F}_L(T - A_L^*)$ is the probability that the completion time for the last job is greater than the alloted time, which is $T - A_L^*$. Using the equation is a little tricky because A_L^* appears on both sides. However, it should be easy to see that we can simply try every reasonable value of A_L to find the one that works. Though this approach can be a bit tedious for larger problems it can be applied to a schedule for any number of appointments to find the optimal policy. Fortunately, computers are ideally suited for such tedious tasks, making it possible to find an optimal schedule. To apply this reasoning to real-world problems we only need to collect enough data on activity times to construct a distribution for each job's completion time.

3.7.3 Composite Jobs

Direct observation can be used to collect data on how long an Activity takes. Figure 3.7 displays histograms for our four possible settings. If a RETURN patient arrives at the start of the cycle and the NEW patient is a no-show then we use Process 1 for this patient. Panel A shows the histogram of completion times for this scenario. If the NEW patient arrives but the RETURN patient does not, we treat that patient using Process 1 (histogram shown in Panel B). If the second RETURN patient in the cycle arrives, that patient is treated using Process 2 (histogram shown in Panel C). Finally, if both the NEW and RETURN patients arrive at the start of the cycle we treat this composite job using a combination of Process 1 for the NEW patient and Process 2 for the RETURN patient (histogram shown in Panel D). Using these data we can construct the CDF of the durations for the processing time for each job F_ℓ. If we combine this information with a set of appointment times we can construct the CDF of the completion time for each job on the schedule as well (G_ℓ).

Almost all researchers in this field prefer to assume that these activity times come from an exponential distribution. This is done because it makes the math much easier, and eliminates the need to "try every reasonable value" to find A_ℓ^*. However, it seems safe to say that the histograms shown in Figure 3.7 are not from such a distribution. This is one reason direct observation is key to improving these systems. Second, the logic that we introduced above makes no assumptions about the shapes of these distributions. Each appointment time decision is made to balance waiting and overtime costs. As long as this is the problem being dealt with, the fact that our distributions do not look "pretty" is of no real concern.

3.7.4 Application in the AMC

With a bit of background about how to find an optimal schedule, let us return to our specific setting. Given three cycles a composite job arrives at appointment times A_1, A_3 and A_5. By construction, we also have a dummy job at $A_7 = 240$ minutes. We

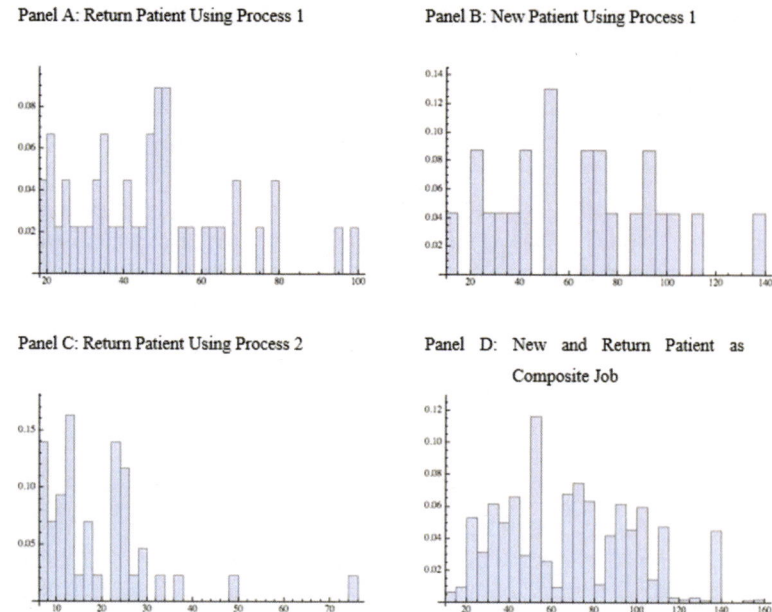

Fig. 3.7 Histograms of Processing Times

know that $A_1^* = 0$. Thus, the three Cycle Length values are $A_3 - A_1 = A_3$, $A_5 - A_3$, and $240 - A_5$. The second RETURN patient arrives at A_2, A_4 and A_6.

To find a cost minimizing schedule we need to assume some values for the per minute cost of waiting and overtime. To keep things simple we assign a value of $1 per minute for waiting. This does not need to be literally true, because we can scale all other costs to be multiples of this one. We will display results given per minute overtime costs of $10, $20, $30, and $40. Table 1 presents the lowest cost cyclic schedule given these 4 levels of overtime cost.

TABLE 1: OPTIMAL SCHEDULES WITH OT COST = $10, $20, $30, $40

OT Cost	A2	A3	A4	A5	A6	Pr OT	Exp Wait	Exp OT	Tot Cost
$10	40	62	121	143	213	50.3	128.1	20.3	$331.8
$20	33	52	110	132	206	43.8	154.4	18.5	$524.0
$30	30	47	104	126	203	41.2	169.8	17.9	$705.1
$40	27	44	100	122	193	40.2	184.5	17.4	$881.1

We refer to the spans from the start of one cycle to the start of the next as the Cycle-Length. From the first row of Table 3.2, we see that when overtime cost is $10 per minute the Cycle-Lengths are 62, 143 - 62 = 81, and 240 - 143 = 97 minutes. Similarly we refer to the spans from the start of a cycle to the arrival time for the second RETURN visit within each cycle as the Cycle-Gap. Thus we have Cycle-Gaps of 40, 121 - 62 = 59, and 213 - 143 = 70 minutes respectively. Optimal Cycle-Lengths and Cycle-Gaps are unequal across cycles and are increasing. In other words, as we approach the end of the schedule the gaps between appointments gets larger. This evidence supports the argument that a reasonable way to develop a schedule would be to act as though appointments later in the session are simply longer than those at the start of the session.

In addition, for an optimal schedule, as overtime becomes more costly, the amount of expected overtime decreases. The decrease in overtime cost comes at the expense of an increase in patient delays. Thus, if W_7 is increased, it is clear that optimal values for other appointment times will fall, meaning that they will be moved earlier in the session to reduce the probability of running beyond the intended session length. Looking at Table 2 we see that as W_7 rises from $10 to $40 per minute, overtime drops by 2.9 minutes to 17.4 minutes. In contrast the expected total of patient delays rises by 56.4 minutes to 184.5. In addition to cost data, the Table also reports the probability that a session will involve overtime operations. We note that when $W_7 = $10 this probability is roughly 50%. Recall that direct observation revealed that this clinic scheduled an average of 7 patients for a 4-hour session and experienced overtime operations in 50% of the observed sessions. Thus, we have increased the number of patients on the session schedule from 7 to 9 with no increase in the likelihood that the session completion time exceeds 240 minutes.

3.7.5 Heuristics for Appointment Scheduling

In some sense, the simplest policies are those that are fully defined by a single value. Since clinic staff were comfortable with making slots for NEW patients twice as long as those for RETURN patients we hypothesized that fixing the ratio of the Cycle-Gap to the Cycle-Length to 2:3 would produce an intuitive and practical heuristic. When this ratio is fixed, we can fully define a scheduling rule by specifying a single Cycle-Length. We label the resulting rule the *LR* (Length-Ratio) policy. Table 2 presents results for a variety of policies when $W_7 = $20. (Parallel results hold when $W_7 = $10, $30, and $40 are tested.) We can compare these cost levels to the cost linked to the optimal policy defined earlier. Note that the cost minimizing Cycle-Length in this approach is 66 minutes.

Adding the constraint that the Cycle-Gap must be a fixed proportion of the Cycle-Length greatly simplifies the problem. But we know that we can do better because the optimal schedule allows these gaps to grow as we approach the end of the session. We relax this constraint by making the Cycle-Gap a decision variable as well. Thus for each Cycle-Gap, we find the best Cycle-Length and identify the Cycle-Gap, Cycle-Length pair that yields the lowest cost in the third line of the table. We label this the LG (Length-Gap) policy. When we make the Gap a decision variable

TABLE 3.2: COST UNDER SEVERAL CYCLIC SCHEDULING RULES

Policy	A2	A3	A4	A5	A6	Pr OT	Exp Wait	Exp OT	Tot Cost	Variables
Optimal	33	52	110	132	206	43.8	154.4	18.5	$524.0	5
LR	44	66	110	132	176	44.8	158.4	19.4	$547.5	1
LG	45	66	111	132	177	44.9	158.5	19.5	$547.5	2
LR+	42	63	105	126	206	44.3	153.7	19.0	$534.6	2
LG+	41	63	104	126	206	44.2	154.4	19.0	$534.4	3
LG++	30	55	105	130	205	43.5	158.1	18.3	$526.1	3

performance has to improve because we are implicitly considering more options. However, for this particular problem the improvement is negligible (more precisely $547.52 - 547.50$). This suggests that for this setting, our simple Length-Ratio policy is not too bad.

When we compare the Optimal, LR, and LG policies the most dramatic difference is in the selected value of A_6. This implies that there is a strong end of session effect, meaning that moving the time of the last appointment has an outsized effect on total cost. With this in mind, we modify the LR policy to allow an adjustment of the last appointment time. The resulting policy is labeled LR+ and is presented in Row 4 of the Table. For the sake of comparison we also make a parallel modification to the LG policy and label it LG+. Just as the LG policy is only marginally better than the LR policy, despite having one additional variable, we see here that the LG+ policy is only marginally better than the LR+ policy which is easier to compute.

Comparing the LR+ policy with the optimal policy suggests an additional direction for finding a better heuristic. If we consider sets of two consecutive jobs in the lowest cost policy we have lengths of $A_3 - A_1 = 52$, $A_4 - A_2 = 77$, $A_5 - A_3 = 80$ and $A_6 - A_4 = 96$. Notice that the first gap is quite short, the next two are of almost equal intermediate length, and the last gap is quite long. Thus, in the optimal policy just as the end-of-session effect lengthens the last cycle, it appears that the beginning-of-session effect shortens the first cycle. Therefore, we modify the LG+ policy to reflect a beginning-of-session effect by making both A_2 and A_6 decision variables; while enforcing a rule that the two middle cycles be of the same length. This modification yields the LG++ rule presented in the last row of Table 3.2. LG++ offers a marked improvement and the total cost is within 0.4% of the optimal value. We can explain this near-optimal performance by noting that each of the four values of $A_i - A_{i-2}$ (when $i = 4, 5, 6, 7$) are quite close to those in the optimal policy: 55, 75, 75, and 100 versus 52, 77, 80, and 96.

Figure 3.8 shows the increase in cost above the optimal policy of selected scheduling rules. The LR rule increases costs by between 4% and 6%. The LR+ rule reduces this error to between 1.7% and 3.4%. Finally, the LG++ rule cuts the error to between 0.3% and 0.4%. In addition, we see that the performances of the LR and LR+ rules degrade relative to the optimal policy as OT cost is increased. On the other hand, the performance of the LR++ rule actually improves as OT cost is increased.

FIGURE 3.8: INCREASE IN COST ABOVE OPTIMAL POLICY

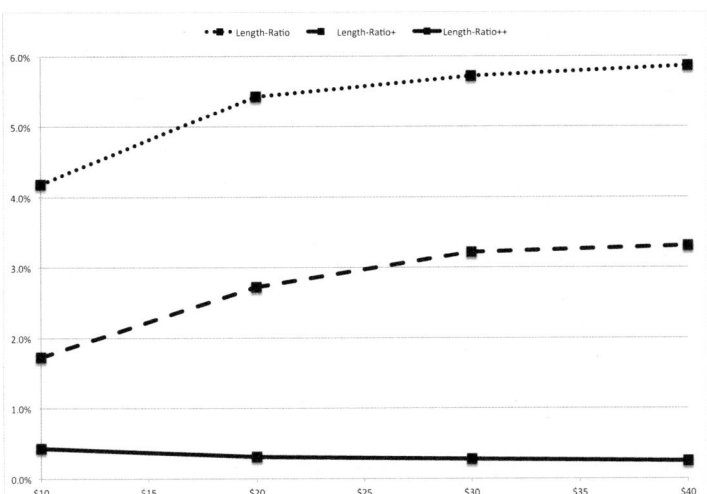

Fig. 3.8 OT Cost in Dollars

We recognize that the effort taken here to find the optimal policy and use it as a gauge for the quality of our heuristics is not likely to be practical for most clinics, and we would not expect clinic management to undertake it. Our main objective was to explain how we know that our recommended policies are reasonable to use in practice. We now turn to the explanation of a simple rule based on our analysis that is easier to explain and implement.

3.7.6 Gantt Chart of Simple Heuristic

After having identified an optimal policy and explored a collection of decision rules, we are in a better position to think through a good rule of thumb for the problem at hand. Let us summarize a few key points here.

1. To find a good schedule we look for appointment times that balance waiting and overtime costs.

2. The best appointment slots are closer together at the beginning of the session and become more spaced out as the schedule unfolds.

3. Some extra slack is needed after the last appointment because overtime cost per minute is much greater than waiting time cost per minute.

With these factors in mind we can devise a much more practical approach. We can find the average job length and its standard deviation based on direct observation. This data collection should accommodate key nuances of the problem structure. For example, with double booking which is very common in clinic settings, we have a composite job to start each cycle that includes the planned arrival of a NEW and RETURN patient along with a strategy to handle them if they both arrive. It turns out that the average time for these composite jobs is 70 minutes with a standard deviation of 30 minutes. For the second return visit, these values turn out to be 45 and 25 minutes respectively.

We have three cycles in our problem. Experience suggests that when we look at appointments per attending this schedule is a reasonable decomposition for many clinics. In such cases we suggest the following scheduling rule.

1. Schedule the jobs as though we know the activity times but subtract 1 standard deviation for each average time to create spaces between appointments for the first cycle.

2. To schedule appointments for the middle cycle(s) work as though we know the activity times but subtract 0.5 standard deviation from the average times.

3. To schedule appointments for the last cycle work as though we know the activity times but add 0.5 standard deviation to the average times.

4. In all cases round the appointment times down so that we are using reasonable time breaks.

Using this approach, we find that if the clinic session starts at 8:00 AM, the resulting appointment times are 8:00, 8:20, 9:00, 10:00, 10:30, and 11:20. Use of this schedule given the data collected for this clinic results in an expected cost within 2% of the optimal value. The schedule is shown in the form of a Gantt chart in Figure 3.9.

The AMC setting we considered here is a very complex environment for appointment scheduling, and is likely to be much more complex than most settings of interest. The factors making this a very hard problem include mixing patient types, mixing types of providers, double-booking, no-shows, highly variable activity times, blending delivery processes, and decisions about which process to use based on patient arrivals. One valuable approach to handling such difficult problems is to break down the hard problem into a set of easier problems. The resulting decomposition

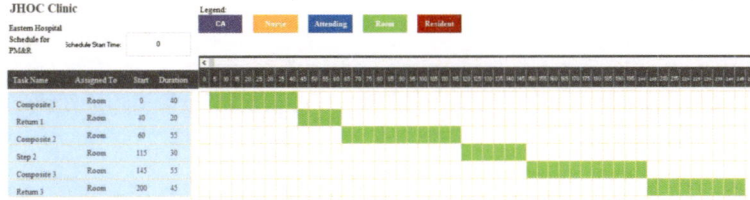

Fig. 3.9 Gantt Chart of Proposed Schedule

presents a collection of problems that are easier to understand. We combine this idea with a set of managerial decisions including the fact that the resident must be involved in all NEW cases, and double booking can be used at the start of each cycle to fit our approach to the setting under consideration.

The fundamental trade-off involved is that putting appointments close together will increase waiting times and spreading them apart will cause them to end closer to the end of the session increasing the use of overtime. This is the underlying logic of most scheduling systems. We can develop a simple scheduling rule that incorporates this logic and accounts for the amount of variability in the underlying Activity times by adjusting blocks based on the variability present.

3.8 Key Take-Aways

Realistic systems that deliver health care services include a wide array of characteristics that make their analysis more complex. One way to develop an understanding of these problems is to consider stylized examples and draw lessons from each one. If the example is understood, then many hard problems can be decomposed into some combination of these examples. Then it becomes easier to solve the smaller problems to optimality or to find some reasonable heuristic that quickly allows us to suggest a solution or policy. This process is not a perfect substitute for a more detailed analysis, but it can be very helpful for managing day to day patient flows. We gather a few related insights here:

1. The performance of a process that we wish to improve can be described using standard metrics such as Cycle Time, Makespan, Utilization and Throughput, but these terms must be applied carefully in health care because a number of complicating factors may be present.

2. Many processes in health care involve activities that can be performed in parallel. Performing activities in parallel may require adding steps and resources. However, if we coordinate them properly we can still cut Makespan, and increase

Utilization, and Throughput.

3. High levels of specialization can result in having multiple resources involved on one or more process steps. When multiple resources are used, we must account for overlapping times and inserted idle times when we seek to measure process performance.

4. When considering a change to process structure, we may need to account for the costs of the resources involved. Therefore, it is often convenient to look at resources on a cost-per-minute basis when comparing proposed process structures.

5. The combination of costly resources and specialization can mean that the most cost effective way to improve performance is to have resources shared across activities or providers.

6. Finding an optimal policy is probably not a realistic goal in real time. However, if the underlying logic needed to find an optimal policy is understood and the basic nature of the problem setting is described, then simple tools can be very helpful to improve process performance.

3.9 Review Material

To ensure that the material covered here can be applicable to your settings develop responses to the scenarios laid out below.

3.9.1 Cyclic Scheduling Template with NEW and RETURN Patients

Recall the appointment template described in the Prologue that details the patient visit to the specialty clinic. Assume that the average times and standard deviation for NEW patients are 70 and 30 minutes respectively. Also, assume that for RETURN patients these values are 45 and 25 minutes.

1. Under these assumptions, draw a Gantt chart for the posted schedule.

2. Calculate the idle time for the key resources based on the chart that you develop.

3. Create a Gantt chart assuming that the actual times for patients in the first cycle are equal to the average time minus 0.5 times the standard deviation and times

for patients in the last cycle are the average plus 0.5 times the standard deviation.

4. Calculate the cost associated with this schedule if overtime operations are $40 per minute.

5. Calculate the cost associated with Frank's suggested schedule given the same activity times.

3.9.2 Cyclic Scheduling Template with only RETURN Patients

Recall the appointment template described in the Prologue that details the patient visit to the specialty clinic. Assume that the average times and standard deviation for both NEW and RETURN patients are 45 and 25 minutes.

1. Under these assumptions, draw a Gantt chart for the posted schedule.

2. Calculate the idle time for the key resources based on the chart that you develop.

3. Create a Gantt chart assuming that the actual times for patients in the first cycle are equal to the average time minus 0.5 times the standard deviation, and times for patients in the last cycle are the average plus 0.5 times the standard deviation.

4. Calculate the cost associated with this schedule if overtime operations cost $40 per minute.

5. Calculate the cost associated with Frank's suggested schedule given the same activity times.

Chapter 4
Management of Queues

Abstract The most common complaint from patients regarding the delivery of health care services is that waiting times are too long. Several tools from industrial engineering and Operations Research have evolved explicitly to consider waiting times in systems with random times between arrivals and random service times. The most common mathematical approach to this topic is known as queuing theory. While this approach has several limitations that make it an incomplete depiction of the systems that we consider here, it does provide a collection of extremely useful insights that system managers would be wise to internalize. In this chapter we introduce the basic elements of the theory and use a collection of simple examples to highlight the conclusions that we have found to be most useful.

4.1 Introduction

In the early 1950's researchers in the UK became interested in the management of waiting times in the National Health System (Bailey (1952), Bailey (1954), Welch and Bailey (1952)). These scholars were asked to consider ways to measure, manage, and improve on the times patients spent waiting for service within various parts of the system including outpatient clinics. Research has consistently shown that the most common complaints related to outpatient services involve waiting times, and longer waiting times degrade a patient's evaluation of care quality (Dexter (1999), Feddock et al (2010), Huang (1994), Seals et al (2005), and Thomas et al (1997)). In addition, working in areas with longer waiting times increases the stress felt by doctors and other staff, reducing their satisfaction as well (Mawardi (1979), and Zandbelt et al (2004)). In some medical settings waiting times are directly correlated with mortality, and many other negative outcomes. For example, long waits in emergency departments can be disastrous and must be avoided if at all possible (Guttmann et al (2011), Prentice and Pizer (2007)).

A great place to start in our effort to improve the behavior of systems that deliver care is with process mapping. Creating the process map will provide a sense of system structure, the resources involved, and any constraints likely to cause problems. Data collection and the presentation of information created in the process mapping exercise will facilitate the calculation of several useful metrics that will help us to identify and quantify these problems. In particular, a good process map equips us to calculate Throughput, the average rate at which Flow Units move through the process; Inventory or Census, the average number of flow units within the process boundaries; and Cycle Time, the average duration that a Flow Unit spends within the process boundaries. Although these metrics are extremely useful, they are limited in that they do not fully account for variability in the activity times and/or patient arrival times involved. Consequently, early researchers on waiting times in health care settings saw the need to expand the tool set to include rigorous theory meant to capture the linkages between variability and waiting times. This body of knowledge became known as queueing theory. The word "queue" is a British term for what most Americans call a waiting line.

For our purposes, waiting occurs when the flow unit is ready for the next activity in a process but that activity has yet to begin. The activity may not have begun because some needed resource is unavailable or because some other proceeding activity has not been completed. Recall that we define a Process to include a Route along which Resources perform Activities designed to alter the state of a Flow Unit. Within this definition the Route can be depicted as a process map, which shows precedence relationships among process steps and the resources involved. For example, a clinic visit, may include steps like **Check-In**, **Exam**, and **Check-Out**. The resources may include staff, equipment, and space; and the Flow Unit is most often (but not always) the patient.

In short, any time the patient is ready for something to happen and it cannot happen at that time, the patient experiences waiting time. For example, the patient has checked in at a clinic and would like to move to an examination room, but all rooms are currently full. However, waiting may also take place because the patient is not directly involved in all process steps. For example, a patient may need an x-ray or some other image to be evaluated. The physician may wish to evaluate the image before facing the patient. This time spent is not "wasted" in the sense that productive work is being done. However, the patient still experiences this as waiting time and is likely to perceive it as a waste.

Given the infinite variety, and complexity of processes involved in health care delivery it is not surprising that waits will occur at various steps. It is easy to get lost in the nuances of such process designs or realized experiences. With this in mind our approach here will be to simplify the discussion as much as possible. We will focus on questions regarding simple, proto-typical processes and models to convey several key insights that the manager needs to internalize.

It is impossible to cover the topic of queue management in a useful way without a good bit of rigor. With that being said, our approach will develop a taste of the mathematical background needed to analyze and discuss our examples in a way that highlights the insights that we have found to be the most useful. For detailed coverage of the underlying theory see Shortle et al (2018) and Klienrock (1975).

After we identify some key examples and cover the necessary theory, we will deal with questions about these systems in a rigorous way. Our narrative will involve direct calculations as well as a discussion of the insights generated. Once we have these foundations in place, we will step back and highlight both the usefulness and limitations of this approach. As always we close with a gathering of take-aways and review material.

4.2 Problem Setting

To build intuition on the topic let us anchor our discussion using a short narrative. Consider a simple process in which patients arrive for an injection to protect them from some nasty virus. To facilitate rapid deployment of the vaccines, the state has decided to make use of pharmacies inside a national chain of drug stores. The drug stores deliver the shots on a first-come-first-served basis and customers/patients walk-in for the service. The patients arrive one at a time and the arrivals are separated by some random time. Fortunately, this pharmacy is near a prestigious university that houses a Health Care Management program, and a student from that program has been hired to gather data on patient flow. By direct observation the student noticed that, 54 patients arrive in a typical hour. This number implies that the average time between arrivals, or the "average inter-arrival time" is (60 min) / (54 pat) = 1.11 min, or 66.67 sec.[1] (A parallel discussion of a setting using roughly the same parameters appears in Kolker (2010a).)

Given no additional information about the underlying population we see no reason to believe that these arrivals are coordinated in any way. In other words, no patient alters their behavior based on what other patients do or are likely to do. We also note that if we take a snapshot of the line of people waiting for service, we gain no evidence about how long anyone has been standing in it. If these conditions hold then our best description of this is to say that it is a "memoryless" process. In other words when we first observe the system, our expectation is that the next patient will arrive 1.11 minutes from now. Saying that the arrival process is memoryless, is equivalent to saying that the best guess about the next arrival is simply the average inter-arrival time. This is, by far the most common assumption in the analysis of queueing systems and has been validated in a myriad of studies in health

---

[1] We typically use pat, hr, min, and sec as abbreviations for patients, hours, minutes, and seconds respectively.

care, banking, call centers, and other service settings.

When we focus on one of the pharmacies administering the shots, we note that the pharmacy manager has responsibilities that include this process. However, the activities associated with these vaccinations are a small part of what the pharmacy does overall, and this activity is assigned to a small space. Due to concerns related to the virus involved it has been set up with a dedicated entrance and exit that does not cross the flow of patients in other parts of the system. After running this process for a few weeks management has decided that it is a reasonable time to see how the process is running and make some decisions about possible improvements. At this stage the process manager has specific interest in a number of simple questions.

1. What is the capacity of this process in patients per hour?

2. How long do patients spend in the assigned space?

3. What is the average number of patients within the space at a time?

4. How long do patients spend waiting in the line?

In thinking about the process, management recognizes that the public health situation is rather volatile and that changes may be needed if capacity needs to be expanded rapidly. On the other hand, regulators may require that additional steps be added to the process. In that case some resources involved may need to be stretched to cover other tasks. As a result, we would like to consider a number of speculative questions including:

1. What happens if we change the number of servers?

2. What happens if we split patients into groups?

3. Is it cost effective to use slower servers if they are less expensive?

Intuition suggests that, in practice this process must have at least three steps. In Step 1 (**Check-In**) patients will check-in, provide some required data, and verity their identity. On completing this step, they move on to Step 2 (**Vaccination**). Step 3 (**Check-Out**) may include payment processing or questions about any immediate reactions. In this discussion we will assume that the patients were able to check-in and handle data management tasks using some sort of virtual or on-line mechanism. In other words, not all steps in the care delivery process have to take place in the facility, and management of those steps may involve different mechanisms and decision makers. Consequently, our direct observation highlights Steps 2 and 3. Step 2, **Vaccination** is a very standard procedure and the duration of this step will be quite short in most cases. We will model these activity times as draws from an Exponential distribution with a mean of 120 seconds (2 minutes). Direct observation leads to the simple process map shown in Figure 4.1.

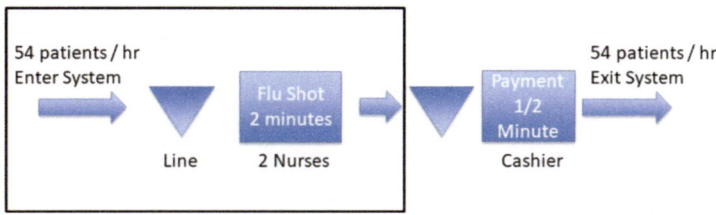

Fig. 4.1 Process Map for Vaccination Delivery

We see that the process currently includes two nurses who administer the shots. Given no additional information, we will assume that these two providers are identical, meaning that the service time comes from the same distribution for each nurse. The process map indicates key resources involved in each step or activity including the nurses at the **Vaccination** step and the cashier at the **Check-Out** step. It also shows basic information including the average arrival rate, and the average time for each activity.

For each patient the exit time minus the entry time is the patient's Cycle Time (CT). Since the process is assigned to a specific space with a single point of entry and exit it is easy to position an observer outside this point to record entry and exit times. Owing to privacy concerns our student does not observe the actual service or waiting time within the clinic walls, but we are willing to assume that the average service time is 2 minutes because the Nurses involved are experienced with the task and we have measured similar activities many times before. A sample of the data with a randomly selected starting point is shown in Table 4.1.

TABLE 1: TIME STAMPS FOR A SET OF PATIENTS

Patient	Entry	Exit	Cycle Time
Patient 1	3	14	11
Patient 2	3	13	10
Patient 3	4	11	7
Patient 4	5	16	11
Patient 5	7	16	9
Patient 6	7	21	14
Patient 7	8	14	6
Patient 8	9	27	18
Patient 9	11	19	8
Patient 10	12	23	11

Several observations can be made here. First, since two nurses are working, up to two patients can either start or end at the same time. Second, the CT values of 11, 10, 7, 11, 9, 14, 6, 18, 8, and 11 minutes yield an average CT of 10.5 minutes. Recall, that for this step the expected activity time was only 2 minutes. Hence, the average waiting time must be 10.5 - 2 = 8.5 minutes. Although this dataset is informative, it does not explain why the waiting time was over 4 times as long as the service time.

4.3 Analysis of Waiting Times

Given actual service times it would be easy to schedule patients in a way that eliminates waiting. However, doing so is not feasible when arrival times are random. If both the arrival times and service times are known it is easy to identify waiting timesfrom any data set after the fact and assess whether these values are acceptable. However, decision makers need insights into what these values will be before patients arrive to make decisions about staffing levels, and the size of the waiting area.

Let us consider how we would go about describing the waiting time distribution for a patient. To make the problem more concrete let us consider a setting with one server and look at the waiting time for the 10th customer that arrives. First, we need to know about the arrival time for this customer. Let us call this value A_{10}. From the perspective of the system manager, we know nothing about Patient 10. In all likelihood the best we can do is to work with the distribution of the time between patient arrivals. If the time between arrivals is t we may use historical data to describe the distribution F_t. We can think of the arrival time A_{10} as $A_1 + t_1 + t_2 \ldots + t_9$. As long as we assume that the time between arrivals is from a stationary process - meaning that the distribution does not change, we should be able to determine the distribution of A_{10} as the convolution of 10 variables. This calculation is a bit tedious but doable.

When Patient 10 arrives, the server may be busy with Patient 9. If Patient 9 did not have to wait, then Patient 10 will have to wait if $A_9 + t_9 > A_{10}$. However, if Patient 9 had to wait then we really need to know the completion time for Patient 8. Similarly, we need to know the distribution of completion times for Patient 1, Patient 2, Patient 3, and so on. This problem can be solved, but it is extremely cumbersome unless we make some strong assumptions about the distributions involved.

Notice that we have omitted a few things here. First, we have two servers instead of one. This makes the problem more complex. Second, we have an estimate of 54 patient arrivals per hour. If this system runs for 8 hours per day, we may be looking at more than 400 patients. Determining the waiting time distribution for patient 400 will be extremely difficult for the general case.

When considering hard problems for which an optimal solution is impossible or impractical to find, we advocate for using some heuristic in lieu of a perfect solution. A heuristic is a "rule of thumb" or an approximation designed to generate a "good" solution when a perfect solution is unavailable. Fortunately, researchers have already put much work into this type of problem and the field of queueing theory includes a collection of standard results that we can use. If we can describe the inter-arrival time distribution, the service time distribution and the Utilization of resources involved heuristics are readily available for this type of problem.

4.3.1 Resource Utilization

When a process accommodates random arrivals, it is not always possible to designate a first and last patient on the schedule, therefore we have to be a little clever to describe the portion of time that resources sit idle. In queueing systems it is customary to analyze the process as though it has no fixed starting or ending time point. One simple way to think about utilization is to think in terms of the ratio of time a resource is busy divided by the time that has elapsed. For example if patients arrive every 2.2 minutes and the server is busy for 2 minutes for each patient, intuition suggests that utilization for that resource would be 2 / 2.2 = 90%. Thus, the average utilization level can be calculated as a ratio of two values. The numerator will be the average busy time per patient multiplied by the expected number of patients. The denominator will be the average inter-arrival time for patients multiplied by the expected number of patients. In this ratio the expected number of patients falls out of the equation leaving the ratio of the average busy time for each patient divided by the average inter-arrival time.

When there is only one unit of a resource we can write this as, $\rho = \lambda/\mu$ where ρ is the utilization level of the resource under consideration. Here λ is the arrival rate for work reaching that resource, and μ is the service rate. This arrival rate is simply the inverse of the average inter-arrival time written as $1/\lambda$ and service rate is the inverse of the average service time written as $1/\mu$. For this setting, the average service time is 2 minutes. Thus, the service rate is 1 patient every 2 minutes or, μ = 0.5 pat / min = 30 pat / hr. Similarly, since the average time between arrivals is 60 / 54 = 1.11 min, the arrival rate is λ = 1 / 1.11 = 0.9 pat / min = 54 pat / hr. (Calculations based on flow units per minute or based on flow units per hour will yield the same results, but we must always be careful to specify our units or scales.)

In practice, utilization should always be calculated based on the total work to be done divided by the total capacity to do that work. With two nurses giving the shots we would say that Nurse utilization is $\rho_N = 54/(2*30) = 0.9 = 90\%$. (In this case the subscript N simply indicates that we are focusing on the nurses as a resource.) We will write $\rho = \lambda/\mu$ and $\rho_i = \lambda_i/(s*\mu_i)$ for resource i where s is the number of units of that resource available.

Assuming that we have only one cashier we can calculate the utilization for this resource as, $\rho_C = \lambda / \mu_C$ where μ_C refers to the service rate for the cashier. Since the average service time at this step is 1/2 minute we can say that the service rate is 2 pat/min = 120 pat/hr. Thus, utilization for the cashier becomes $\rho_C = 54/120 = 45\%$.

We make one final observation about the utilization of the cashier. When we stated that the arrival rate of flow units to this step was the same as the arrival rate to the process, we are implicitly assuming that we have a stable process. For now it is sufficient to state that a stable process is one in which capacity is great enough to meet demand on average. In other words no resource has a planned utilization level above 100%. As long as this is true, the arrival rate for a downstream resource will balance with the arrival rate at the upstream resource. We say that these rates balance, as opposed to saying that they are identical because we may have to account for differences in the number of servers. For example, the process sees 54 patients per hour, and each of the two nurses faces 27 patients per hour. Since utilization of the nurses is below 100% we can say that the arrival rate at the cashier is the sum of these values. In other words 27 + 27 = 54 patients reach the cashier per hour. This number balances with the arrival process and the upstream activities.

Given that we have only two resources to consider and utilization for the nurses is much higher than that for the cashier, it is natural to focus on this resource when analyzing the system. This focus is reasonable, because the nurses are clearly the bottleneck resource. In this discussion, we will say that the resource with the highest utilization level is the bottleneck resource.

We now have a more complete picture of the process at hand. Patients line up in a queue prior to **Vaccination**. They wait an average of 8.5 minutes, before moving to the first available nurse. The nurses are identical in terms of the service time distribution. The patients receive the key service over 2 minutes, make a payment and leave. In this particular case, we immediately notice that we have an average waiting time in practice that is over 4 times as long as the service time, for a stable system, even though it appears that the server is idle roughly 10% of the time. This observation highlights a limitation of the process analysis done so far. If the only concerns are direct costs and utilization, this analysis may be sufficient for decision making. However, if we are also interested in managing waiting times, then it seems clear that something is missing from the discussion.

Imagine a setting in which the times between arrivals were always exactly 1.11 minutes, and the service time was always exactly 2 minutes. The two servers would each see a patient every 2.22 minutes and would then be busy for 2 minutes with 0.22 minutes of idle time before the arrival of the next patient. In this idealized world, utilization would still be 90% but waiting time would be 0. In other words, the absence of variability implies that we should have no waiting time, and the presence of variability means we have positive waiting times. In this sense we can say that variability causes waiting, or that the cause of waiting in this system is simply variability. Consequently, it becomes clear that we need a different approach to thinking about how to manage this system

4.4 Theoretical Foundations for the Study of Queues

The fact that waiting times can be much greater than would be seen in a deterministic world indicates that we must create a different way to approach the analysis of these systems that explicitly accounts for the variability. We will need to cover four topics to facilitate the analysis. First, we need to be more explicit about what defines the system of interest. What are the parts and defining characteristics of these systems that matter in the analysis? Second, it turns out that the assumption that we have a memoryless process is a key to facilitating the needed analysis. We need to understand more about what this means. Third, we need to understand a collection of key mathematical findings about a special family of processes that make the analysis work. Fourth, we need to understand a formal relationship between the number of flow units in a system, the total time in that system, and the rate of flow through the system. With this background in place we will be able to quantify expected results for systems with one or more servers at a process step.

4.4.1 Anatomy of a Queueing System

The mathematical study of waiting times in settings with variable inter-arrival and service times is known as queueing theory. To fully describe the queueing system we will need to include six key pieces of information.

1. The source population of the flow units: For most settings of interest here the Population will be a potential patient pool. As a practical matter, we will treat this population as a group of infinite size as all people eventually need health care.

2. How the flow units arrive to the system: This is often referred to as the arrival process. For our cases we will almost always assume that arrivals are fully defined by the distribution of inter-arrival times. However, we note that this assumption is not quite true for all appointment based systems. Clearly, in such settings intuition suggests that the appointment schedule has some effect on the times between arrivals.

3. The physical line itself: This is often referred to as the Queue Configuration. Configuration simply means how the line connects the flow units to the service mechanism. Consider a clinic with two attendings who see patients. If the next person

to be seen simply goes to the first available server, we call this a multi-server, single-channel queue. Alternatively, we may have a setting in which patients line up for a specific server, even if both servers are identical in their activity time distribution. If we do not allow customers to change lines once they enter one, we have a multi-channel queue. The number of channels used is the key aspect of the configuration that matters.

4. The way flow units are selected from the line: This is often labeled the Queue Discipline, and is the rule that explains which flow unit will be served next when a server becomes available. In the vast majority of queues, the flow unit served next is simply the one that waited the longest. However, this rule is modified in many health care settings. For example, a patient experiencing severe bleeding or shortness of breath will be "bumped" to the head of the line in virtually every health care setting.

5. Characteristics of the service provider(s): When we describe the Service Mechanism, at the very least we must indicate the number of servers, whether they are identical in terms of expected activity time, and whether they may be interrupted during the work-flow. In most settings we will assume that servers are identical, and once they start a job, they work on it until it is completed. However, in some settings these assumptions have to be relaxed.

6. Conditions of the flow units when they exist the system: We will typically assume that upon exiting the system the flow units can be viewed as completed jobs.

4.4.2 Exponential Time Distributions

When we introduced the description of the arrival process, we argued that it is a "memoryless" process because our best guess about the time to the next arrival is simply the average inter-arrival time. It turns out that this assumption brings with it a rather precise corollary. If this assumption holds, only one type of distribution is consistent with it - namely an exponential distribution. In other words, when we state that the arrivals are memoryless, we are implicitly assuming that the time between arrivals is exponentially distributed.

Let us pause here and consider this assumption for a moment. Arrivals are only observable when they occur, and seeing patients waiting in line is not informative about how long they have been there. As a result we argued that this was a memoryless process and that exponential distribution fit that setting. On the other hand, the service delivery is observable from start to finish. If I walk into the area where the shots are being administered it would not be too difficult to tell the difference between a patient who has just walked in and another who is about to walk out. Therefore, it is hard to argue that the service delivery process is truly "memoryless" in the sense that the remaining service time should always be drawn from the same distribution. Thus, we may ask whether an exponential activity time is a good mental model for these durations.

Figure 4.2 shows the probability density function for an exponentially distributed random variable. More formally, it is the assumption that the probability density function for the time involved can be written as $f(t|\lambda) = \lambda e^{-\lambda t}$. In this statement the random variable is time t and the parameter of the underlying distribution is λ. Perhaps the most obvious characteristics for this function are that; 1) it is at its maximum at $t = 0$; 2) it is monotonically decreasing for all $t > 0$; and 3) time (t) has no upper bound. When a variable is bound from below by 0 but not from above, the very high values skew the average. In other words, when we calculate the expected value of this variable, we must assign positive probabilities to some very high values. Therefore, the only way to have a finite average is if most of the realizations are close to 0. In fact, for an exponential variable roughly 62% of all of the observations will be below the mean. We can ask if this makes sense.

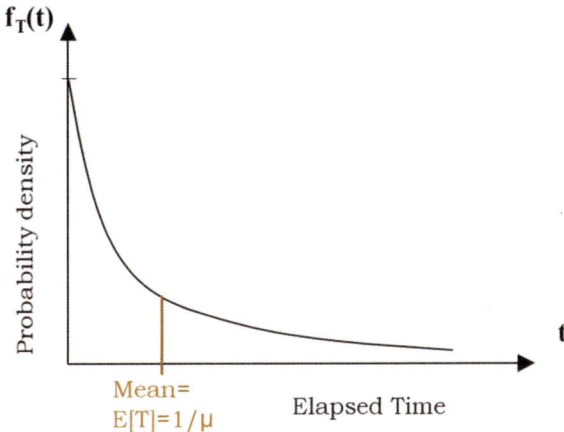

Fig. 4.2 Probability Density Function for Exponential Random Variable

We must recognize that no theoretical distribution will ever be a perfect fit to a collection of direct observations. However, in many service settings most of the customers, patients, etc. have fairly routine needs or present common jobs. As a result most of the activity times will be below the average. A much smaller set of patients will have much more complex needs and require a much longer service time. In any health care delivery process there is some small chance that things will not go as planned. For example, some patients will literally faint at the sight of a needle. When these rare events take place, the needed response is much more intense and complex than it is for the typical case. These rare, but long processing times are part of the data set of activity times. The exponential distribution presents a reasonable fit for settings in which most cases are routine but a few become very long. This is one reason it is so commonly used when describing activity times in health care settings.

Without getting too bogged down in statistical theory, it turns out that the exponential distribution also brings a few other very nice properties that simplify the analysis. We list a few of these below:

1. $f(t)$ is strictly decreasing in t

2. $Pr(T > t + \Delta t \mid T > t) = Pr(T > \Delta t)$

3. Both the expected value and standard deviation of t are $1/\lambda$

4. Given n exponentially distributed variables, $T_1 \ldots T_n$ the minimum of these values is exponentially distributed with a mean of $1/(\sum_{k=1}^{n} \lambda_k)$

For the sake of clarity let's translate these statements into simple language. The first property more formally states that the probability distribution function (PDF) always moves lower as time (t) passes. This property follows from the negative exponent in the PDF, and is important because it causes the summations of key terms such as the mean number of flow units in the system to converge to a finite value. The second statement is a more formal way of saying that the process is memoryless. If we are at any time t and look at the PDF as it moves forward from this point it always has the same shape regardless of t.

The third property states that the standard deviation of t and the mean have the same value. This odd sounding property can be understood as a consequence of the fact that the derivative of e^u is always $e^u \partial u$ where ∂u is the partial derivative of u. Note that e is a constant and that the only parameter that we need to estimate is λ. We can easily estimate λ by counting the number of occurrences over some period of time. For example, if we see 54 patients arrive in an hour, our estimate of the arrival rate is simply 54 patients per hour.

Property 3 allows us to also state that the standard deviation has that same value. This principal is particularly useful because we do not have to do extra work to find this value. Direct observation can be used to completely describe the distribution in question. It is easy to under-appreciate the significance of this fact. Observers working within a system or viewing it from the outside find it rather easy to think in terms of averages. It is also easy to count occurrences in a data set or record keeping system. Virtually all human beings find it much more difficult to think about variances. Property 3 allows us to work around this issue entirely. If we have time stamps related to arrivals we can easily get a good estimate of the arrival rate, λ. This estimate is sufficient to completely describe the arrival process. Not only does this make life much easier, it avoids disagreements over what the variability actually is.

The fourth property is a bit more subtle. It states that when considering a collection of exponentially distributed random variables that may have different means, it is easy to state the expected value of the minimum of those values. We determine the minimum value by simply adding the rates. For example, if we serve two different patient groups and patients in one group arrive at a rate of 5 per hour and those in the other group arrive at a rate of 4 per hour - the arrival process will look exactly the same as one serving a single group with an arrival rate of 5 + 4 = 9 patients per hour. This fact makes it very easy to think about what happens when we combine populations into a single pool or split that pool into smaller parts.

4.4.3 Contributions of Markov

To develop an understanding of queueing systems we repeatedly use a collection of insights that are commonly attributed to a Russian mathematician named Andrey Markov (Basharin et al (2004)). Among his many areas of research, Markov studied a particular type of process known as a Birth-Death Process. Figure 4.3 depicts the type of system in question.

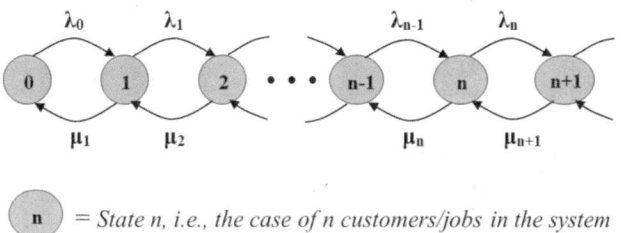

n = State n, i.e., the case of n customers/jobs in the system

Fig. 4.3 State Changes in Birth - Death Processes

In this diagram the nodes (depicted as circles) refer to the number of items in the system. If the system is empty this value is 0. In the context of our current discussion, the node values represent the number of patients waiting for the shot or currently receiving one. If the system is empty and a patient arrives, the number in the system increases from 0 to 1. In a Birth-Death process this arrival is referred to as a "Birth". When a job is completed, the number of flow units in the system falls. For example it may drop from 1 back to 0. This exit from the system is referred to as a "Death." The rate of birth is the rate at which we would move from 0 to 1 and the rate of death is the rate at which we would move from 1 to 0. As the diagram implies, it is possible for these rates to be dependent on the number of flow units in the system. In other words, it is theoretically possible for λ_1 to be different from λ_2

and so on. These differences can occur with multiple servers or if servers accelerate when the system is busy. We have observed clinics in which such rate changes occur. However, for now we will assume that $\lambda_0 = \lambda_1 = \ldots = \lambda$ and that $\mu_0 = \mu_1 = \ldots = \mu$.

One observation that Markov formalized is known as the Rate-In/Rate-Out prin-cipal. This idea is that if the system is stable, meaning it does not simply grow to infinity, then the rate at which the system enters any state must equal the rate at which it leaves it. Consider State 0, meaning the system is empty. How do we get to this state and how can we leave it? The only way a system can reach State $n = 0$ is for it to be in State $n = 1$ and have a death that takes place at rate $\mu_1 = \mu$. The probability of being in State $n = 1$ can be written as P_1. The only way for a system to leave State $n = 0$ is for a system in State $n = 0$ to experience a birth at rate $\lambda_0 = \lambda$. If the rate into State $n = 0$ must equal the rate out, then we will have a balance that can be expressed as $\mu_1 P_1 = \lambda_0 P_0$. If we define P_0 as the probability that the system is empty, we will get $P_1 = \lambda/\mu P_0$. Thus, if we know the probability that the system is empty, along with the arrival rate and service rate, we can calculate P_1.

Now consider State $n = 1$. Note that this state can be entered in two ways. We can be at $n = 0$ and have a birth at rate λ or we can be at $n = 2$ and have a death at rate μ. In addition we have two ways to exit the state. We can move up to $n = 2$ or move down to $n = 0$. The Rate-in/Rate-out principal tells us that, $\lambda P_0 + \mu P_2 = \lambda P_1 + \mu P_1$. We can rearrange these terms to see that $P_2 = \lambda/\mu P_1$. In other words, once we know P_1 the arrival rate and the service rate we can find P_2. We can generalize this result and write $P_n = \lambda/\mu P_{n-1}$.

The next observation that we can use is that when we have a single server sys-tem, the only way for the server to be idle is for the system to be empty. In other words, the utilization of the server is also $1 - P_0$, or equivalently $P_0 = 1 - \rho$. If we know utilization, we immediately know P_0. Knowing P_0 is enough to determine P_1. Knowing P_1 lets us calculate P_2 and so on. The iterative nature of these calculations ultimately allows us to state that $P_n = \rho^n(1 - \rho)$.

With this insight in hand we can turn our attention to figuring out the expected number of flow units in the system. In general terms the expected value of a discrete random variable (X) that has a range from 0 to infinity must be $E[X] = \sum_x^\infty x P_x$. In other words, the expected value of a variable X must be the sum of all possible realizations of X multiplied by the probability of each realization. For the special case of the system under consideration we get:

$$L = \sum_n^\infty n\rho^n(1 - \rho) \tag{4.1}$$

We can think of L as the length of the line including the flow unit(s) being served. Fortunately, as long as $\rho < 1$ this series will converge and ultimately yield, $L = \rho/(1 - \rho)$. Thus, knowing the arrival rate and service rate allows us to find P_0, but it also allows us to calculate directly the expected number of jobs in the system L.

When we think about the number of customers in the queue, we can say that this value is simply the expected number of customers in the system, with some adjustment made for the periods of time that the server is busy but no additional customers are in the system. Stated differently, the expected number of customers waiting in line is the same as L times the probability that a customer has to wait in the line. Thus, $L_q = \rho L = \rho^2(1 - \rho)$.

Finally, we note one additional result about these systems that is commonly attributed to Markov. This result is often abbreviated as PASTA, which stands for "Poisson Arrivals See Time Averages". The term "Poisson Arrivals" refers to settings in which the times between arrivals are described by an exponential distribution. One corollary of this idea is that when a new job arrives the likelihood that the server is busy at that time is the same as the likelihood that the server is busy on average. Though this result may seem intuitively obvious, it can actually be proven by using the properties of the exponential distribution. One implication is that for a single server queue, the probability that an incoming job will be forced to wait is the same as the utilization level of the server. This fact is often written as $P_W = \rho$, which means the probability of waiting is simply ρ.

4.4.4 Little's Law & Queues

One final building block needed to analyze these systems is known as Little's Law. This law attributed to John Little (Little (2011)) states that for any stable system the average number of flow units in that system must equal the rate at which units enter that system times the average time that flow units spend within that system. This statement is analogous to the idea that "Rate * Time = Distance". For stable systems the rate that work enters the queue will equal the arrival rate (λ), L is the total number of units in the queue, and the total time in the queue can be referred to as a CT. In general, we will write this CT as W when it includes the time being served and as W_q when it refers only to time spent in the queue waiting for service.

The utility of Little's Law stems from the fact that if we know an arrival rate (λ) and have a way to find the average number of units in the system (either L or L_q) then we can find the average time spent in the system (either W or W_q). More formally, for single server systems we will have $L = \lambda W$ and $L_q = \lambda W_q$ or equivalently, $W = L/\lambda$ and $W_q = L_q/\lambda$.

4.4.5 M|M|1 Queues

Once we have a complete description in place we can suggest a number of performance measures related to waiting times that are likely to be useful. We include
some of these as a short list below.

1. ρ = Utilization level for a resource such as a server

2. P_0 = Probability that there are no flow units in the queueing system when a new
    Flow Unit arrives

3. P_n = Probability that there are exactly n flow units in the system when a new unit
    arrives

4. L = Average number of jobs in the system including those in line and those being
    served.

5. L_q = Average number of flow units in the queue, excluding any units currently
    being served

6. W = Average time a flow unit spends in the system including the service time

7. W_q = Average amount of time a flow unit spends in the queue excluding the ser-
    vice time

8. P_w = Probability that an arriving flow unit will have to wait for service.

We have discussed the definition of ρ previously. For the special case of having
only one server, $\rho = \lambda/\mu$. We apply the implications of the idea known as PASTA
to deduce that $P_W = 1 - \rho$. Using the Rate in/Rate Out principal we found that
$P_n = \rho^n(1 - \rho)$. Using the definition of expected values for discrete random variables we found that $L = \rho/1 - \rho$. We can think of L_q as an adjustment to L that
accounts for how often the server is busy to get $L_q = L\rho$. Using Little's Law we can
compute W and W_q as L/λ and L_q/λ respectively. Therefore, in the special case of
the single server queue under consideration we can collect these results in a simple
table (Table 4.2).

It is customary to refer to single server queues with exponentially distributed
inter-arrival times and service times as M|M|1 queues, where the M pays homage to
Markov.

TABLE 4.2: RESULTS FOR THE M|M|1 QUEUE

ρ	λ/μ
P_0	$1-\rho$
P_w	ρ
P_n	$\rho^n(1-\rho)$
L	$\rho/(1-\rho)$
L_q	$\rho^2/(1-\rho)$
W	$1/(\mu-\lambda)$
W_q	$\rho/(\mu-\lambda)$

4.4.5.1 Two Small Examples

Consider a small, walk-in clinic in a county hospital that has one attending physician. Let us focus only on the role of the attending for the moment. Direct observation reveals that patients arrive at a rate of 2 per hour ($\lambda = 2$), and when working continuously the attending can complete service for 3 patients in an hour ($\mu = 3$). The results shown in Table 4.2 are applied to this setting and gathered in Table 4.3.

TABLE 4.3: RESULTS FOR THE M|M|1 QUEUE WHEN $\rho = 2/3$

ρ	$\lambda/\mu = 2/3$
P_0	$1-\rho = 1/3$
P_w	$\rho = 2/3$
P_n	$\rho^n(1-\rho) = 2/3(1/3)^n$
L	$\rho/(1-\rho) = (2/3)/(1/3) = 2$
L_q	$\rho^2/(1-\rho) = (2/3)^2/(1/3) = 4/3$
W	$1/(\mu-\lambda) = 1/(3-2) = 1$
W_q	$\rho/(\mu-\lambda) = W * \rho = 2/3$

Table 4.3 displays physician utilization at 2/3, implying that the attending will be idle 1/3 of the time. It seems safe to say that this idle time is not likely to be attractive from a financial perspective. If the most expensive resource is idle 1/3 of the time and margins are small, financial difficulty is around the corner.

Second, on average this system will have two patients in the clinic at a time; one being served and one waiting. In addition, the average time for a patient in the system is 1 hour, even though each sees the physician for only 20 minutes. In short the attending is idle for 1/3 of the time and the typical patient must wait 40 minutes to see the doctor. If we think about the perspectives of the patient, the attending, and an administrator, it is quite likely that none of the three is very happy. The patient waits (on average) twice as long as the visit with the doctor. The doctor is idle 1/3 of the time, and the administrator is paying for this idle time. Recall that all of these issues disappear if variability is absent. Without variability, the doctor could treat 3 patients per hour (increasing revenue), the system is not paying for any idle time, and no patients has to wait. Variability is the root cause of all of these negative outcomes.

We can also consider a modified version of our setting for the vaccinations. If we imagine that one nurse could handle 60 patients per hour ($\mu = 1$ pat/min) and patients arrive at a rate of 54 per hour ($\lambda = 0.9$ pat/min), then nurse utilization $\rho_N = 0.9/1 = 90\%$. This value matches what we saw in the setup with two nurses. The formulas from Table 4.2 yield the results gathered in Table 4.4.

TABLE 4.4: RESULTS FOR THE M|M|1 QUEUE WHEN $\rho = 9/10$

ρ	$\lambda/\mu = 0.9$
P_0	$1 - \rho = 0.1$
P_w	$\rho = 0.9$
P_n	$\rho^n(1 - \rho) = (0.9)^n(0.1)$
L	$\rho/(1 - \rho) = (0.9)/0.1 = 9$
L_q	$\rho^2/(1 - \rho) = (0.9)^2/(0.1) = 8.1$
W	$1/(\mu - \lambda) = 1/(1 - 0.9) = 10$ min
W_q	$\rho/(\mu - \lambda) = 0.9/(1 - 0.9) = 9$ min

We highlight two observations here. First, based on the functional form of the equation for L we find that L is very sensitive to small changes in ρ when utilization is high. For example if ρ were to rise to 91%, 92%, 93%, 94%, and 95%, L rises to 10.1, 11.5, 13.3, 15.7, and 19 respectively. Thus, a rise in utilization of 5% doubles the length of the line. In the prior example, when ρ was roughly 67% a rise to 72% increases L from 2, to 2.6. In other words, small changes to the utilization of the busiest resource have a dramatic effect, whereas similar changes in utilization for moderately used resources have almost no effect. We routinely refer to the resource with the greatest utilization as the bottleneck resource and argue that the only way to meaningfully improve average waiting times is to change the utilization of that resource.

4.4.6 M|M|s Queues

We have discussed the setting with a single line of customers leading to a single server. However, in the pharmacy's vaccination process, we have two nurses who administer the shots, thus we have a two server system. Let s represent the number of servers. In this case $s = 2$. Note that no one waits unless at least two patients are in the system when a new patient arrives. This situation makes it a bit more complicated to determine how likely the system is to be empty, because P_0 is not simply ρ. We omit the details of the derivation, but it turns out that for multi-server queues P_0 can be written as:

$$P_0 = \left(\sum_{n=0}^{s-1} \frac{(\lambda/\mu)^n}{n!} + \frac{(\lambda/\mu)^s}{s!(1 - \lambda/(s\mu))} \right)^{-1} \tag{4.2}$$

For the case with $s = 2$ we get;

$$P_0 = \left(1 + \lambda/\mu + \frac{(\lambda/\mu)^2}{2(1 - \lambda/2\mu)}\right)^{-1} \tag{4.3}$$

Note that λ can be greater than μ as long as it is less than $s * \mu$. Otherwise, the system is not stable. The probability that the system is empty has to account for the proportion of time that some servers (but not all) are busy. The first term in equation 4.2 deals with these instances. It must also account for the times when all of the servers are busy. The latter situation is dealt with by the second term. This term makes P_0 a much more complex expression, however, it is still only a function of λ, μ, and s. Fortunately, once P_0 is calculated, the analysis proceeds much like it did for the single server case. Specifically we can write L_q as:

$$P_n = \left\{ \begin{array}{l} P_0 \frac{(\lambda/\mu)^n}{n!} \ for \ n = 1, 2, ..., s \\ P_0 \frac{(\lambda/\mu)^n}{s! s^{n-s} P_0} \ for \ n > s \end{array} \right\} \tag{4.4}$$

With this definition in place we can construct the expected number of flow units waiting in the line in a multi-channel queue as,

$$L_q = \sum_{n=s}^{\infty} (n - s) P_n = P_0 \frac{\lambda \mu (\rho)^s}{(s-1!)(s\mu - \lambda)^2} \tag{4.5}$$

By application of Little's Law we get $W_q = L_q/\lambda$. Thus we have,

$$W_q = P_0 \frac{\rho^s}{\mu s s! (1 - \rho/s)^2} \tag{4.6}$$

Since W is simply the time spent in the queue plus the service time we know that $W = W_q + 1/\mu$. Similarly, we see that $L = L_q + \rho$. These results are collected in Table 4.5:

TABLE 5: RESULTS FOR THE M|M|S QUEUE

ρ	λ/μ
P_0	$\left(\sum_{n=0}^{s-1} \frac{(\rho)^n}{n!} + \frac{(\rho)^s}{s!(1 - (\lambda/s\mu))}\right)^{-1}$
P_w	$\frac{P_0 \rho^s}{s!(1 - \lambda/(s\mu))}$
L_q	$P_0 \left(\frac{\lambda \mu \rho^s}{(s-1)!(s\mu - \lambda)^2}\right)$
L	$L_q + \rho$
W_q	$P_0 \frac{\rho^s}{\mu s s!(1 - \lambda/(\mu s)^2)}$
W	L/λ

The complex appearance of these results can be quite off-putting. This complexity results largely from the need to account for the combinatoric nature of the setting. For example, given three servers (A, B, and C) there are actually three situations in which two servers are busy; A and B, A and C, and B and C. Having to account for this range of scenarios is ultimately what leads to these more complex formulas. However, the key point is that the only terms involved are simply the arrival rate, service rate, and number of servers.

4.5 Examination of Vaccine Delivery Process

Now that we have a full system description in place, and the mathematical results needed to depict system behavior, we are in a position to return to the questions raised in section 4.2.

4.5.1 System Capacity

What is the capacity of this process in patients per hour?

We now understand that the capacity of a queueing system is the same as the capacity of the bottleneck resource. In this process we only considered two resources; nurses with a utilization of 90%, and the cashier with a utilization of 45%. Clearly, the nurses are the bottleneck resource. Because they have a capacity of 60 patients per hour, this rate is also the theoretical capacity of the process. We use the phrase Theoretical Capacity here because this calculation comes with a major caveat.

Recall that for a single server queue $L = \rho/(1 - \rho)$. This equation implies that as ρ approaches 100% L approaches infinity because L becomes 1/0. Clearly this is impossible in practice, so no system will be run at this level. Thus, this theoretical capacity will never actually be realized. Often, it is better to ask: What is the capacity of the system if utilization is held below some acceptable level?

4.5.2 Average Cycle Time and Census

How long do patients spend in the assigned space?
What is the average number of patients in the space at a time?

We can easily answer these questions together. Since $\lambda/\rho < 1$, we have a stable system. Consequently, the throughput rate will match the arrival rate, and Little's

Law will apply. We also have data from our direct observations that tell us that the average CT is 10.5 minutes. Thus, Little's Law tells us that the average number of flow units in the system is Ave CT $* \lambda = 10.5$ min $*0.9$ pat / min $= 9.45$ patients.

We note that this general approach is useful as long as we have reliable time stamps for arrivals and departures. With this information we can calculate inter-arrival times and CT. Many settings in health care will produce reliable time stamps for patients who enter and exit a system. For example, many clinics use a kiosk at which patients can check in and handle payments or make follow-up appointments right before they leave.

4.5.3 Average Waiting Time

How long do patients spend waiting in line?

Thus far we have not required queueing theory to answer the questions of interest. However, when we turn explicitly to questions about waiting times, simple process analysis is insufficient. Fortunately, the results shown in Table 4.5 can easily be applied to this two-server case and yield $L_q = 7.66$ pat, $L = L - Q + \rho - 7.66 + 1.8 = 9.46$, $W_q = 8.5$ min, and $W = W_q + 1/\mu = 8.5 + 2 = 10.5$.

Note that these values are entirely consistent with both our observations and the results shown for our single server approximation that had one nurse with the capacity of these two nurses combined.

4.5.4 Process B: Two Servers with a 50/50 Split

What happens if we split the patients into groups?

In thinking about this question it may be useful to envision a motivation for it. Consider a setting in which management has decided that it wishes to split the population into two segments. An example might be those above and below the age of 55. Let us consider a setting in which historical data have shown that roughly half of the arriving patients will fall into each of these two groups. In this setting we really have two, single-server queues and the arrival rate for each server is 1/2 of the total. Intuition may suggest that this system will perform just like the original system since arrival rates, service rates, and resource levels are unchanged. However, we must note one additional fact. If patients are only allowed to see a particular server, then we will have instances in which a line forms waiting for one server, even though the other server is idle. Thus, the average waiting time will rise - though it is unclear by how much.

For an M|M|1 queue with $\lambda = 0.45$, and $\mu = 0.50$ we can use the equations in Table 4.2 to get the results shown in Table 4.6.

TABLE 6: RESULTS FOR THE M|M|1 QUEUE

ρ	$\lambda/\mu = 0.9$
P_0	$1 - \rho = 0.1$
P_w	$\rho = 0.9$
P_n	$\rho^n(1-\rho) = (0.9)^n(0.1)$
L	$\rho/(1-\rho) = (0.9)/0.1 = 9$
L_q	$\rho^2/(1-\rho) = (0.9)^2/(0.1) = 8.1$
W	$1/(\mu - \lambda) = 1/(0.5 - 0.45) = 1/6\,\text{hr} = 20$
W_q	$\rho/(\mu - \lambda) = 0.9/(0.05) = 18\,\text{min}$

Using the equations derived earlier, we see that L and L_q are unchanged. However, since the service time is 2 minutes, W and W_q rise to 20 and 18 minutes respectively. In other words the average waiting time in the system doubles, even though the load on the system has not changed.

This result highlights a major point about management of queueing systems, namely that specialization increases waiting times. The only difference between the two scenarios was the inclusion of specialized servers, meaning that they each serve only a specific patient type. If specialization increases the processing rate of each server because they are more focused, then this trade-off might reduce waiting times. However, if specialization does not significantly increase the processing rate, then this new configuration will dramatically increase waiting times. This issue is particularly important in health care because the degree of specialization is often very high.

4.5.5 Process C: Two Less Experienced Servers with Reduced Speed

Is it cost effective to use slower servers if they are less expensive?

As fate would have it tremendous growth in the demand for this service led to an increase in the number of providers and locations. Consequently, the more experienced servers were reassigned to another location with greater demand and were replaced with two servers who have an average service time that is 15 seconds longer. Thus, the average service time rose from 120 to 135 seconds. Because speed decreased by roughly 12.5% the manager suspects that waiting times may rise proportionately. Waiting times were considered to be acceptable in the first scenario, and it is assumed that this small change should pose no real problem.

If the average service time rises from 120 seconds to 135 seconds, the service rate falls from 0.5 pat/min to 0.45 pat/min. When we calculate the utilization under this scenario we see that $\lambda/(2\mu) = 0.9/(120/135) = 1.01$. We are now violating the basic assumption that we needed to have a stable system. This result suggests that queueing theory is not very useful for describing what will happen in this case. This limitation is disappointing because the change in system structure was relatively small. For settings like these, it appears that some other tool and/or approach to the analysis will be needed.

4.6 Key Take-Aways

Though our presentation of queueing theory is quite brief and omits several valuable extensions and adjustments necessary to model more complex settings, it does suggest a number of conclusions that should be helpful.

1. For M|M|1 queues the critical measurement of interest is the level of server utilization. Since waiting times are convex in this measurement and approach infinity as utilization approaches 100%.

2. Given the convex nature of the linkage between utilization and waiting times, small changes in arrival rates or service rates can have dramatic effects if utilization is initially high. On the other hand the same change may have a negligible effect when utilization is low.

3. When using queueing theory to gain insights into system behavior, we must view any steady-state results cautiously because it may take a very long time for system averages to converge to these long term averages.

4. For multi-server queues the key issue is the configuration of the system. If we increase from one to two servers, and all servers work on the next job, regardless of type, it is like doubling the speed of the system. If the servers can work only on a specific type of job, then it is like creating multiple systems that are not coordinated.

5. Changes in the structure of a queueing system can have unexpected consequences. Therefore, formal models of such systems are valuable because they can help us to see when intuition is most useful, and when it can get us into trouble.

It is particularly important to note that all of the results presented so far implicitly assume that the system has no pre-defined starting or ending time. The formulas
that we have for L_q involve the summation of an infinite number of terms. Such
terms can only exist given an infinite time horizon. That is why we say that these
are "steady state" results. This phrase means that these are the average values that
we would see if we observed the system over an infinite span of time. Obviously,
there is no such thing in a literal sense. The question becomes whether these results
are useful in practice. To explore this question we return to our base case in which
the average waiting time would be roughly 8.5 minutes. This duration was entirely
consistent with the data collected. Nevertheless, we should not expect to see this
average waiting time value over every 1-hour period or every day that the service is
provided.

Figure 4.4 shows the evolution of average waiting time for a simulated process
based on the setting discussed here.[2] Given our simple process structure, we can
simulate random arrivals and service times. We do this over 10,000 minutes in this
figure. Within the simulation we can recalculate average waiting time up to that
point upon every customer exit. This new average becomes a point on the plot. (We
provide a more detailed discussion of such simulation models in Chapter 7.) We note
that Figure 4.4 shows only one realization of average waiting times. If we simulate
this process 100 times, every simulation will have its own unique plot. However, in
all instances the average waiting time will eventually match the calculated value.
The key observation is that it can take quite a while for the average seen in a system to match the steady state results that queueing theory allows us to calculate.
As such, steady state results are good guideposts and "rules of thumb" but are not
precise depictions for any clinic over a single session or shift.

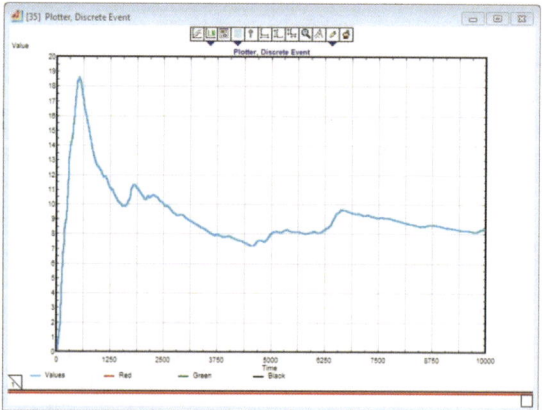

Fig. 4.4 Evolution of Average Waiting Time

---

[2] ExtendSim blocks copyright © 1987-2022 Imagine That Inc. All rights reserved.

The figure highlights several key points. First, the average waiting time does work out to be roughly 8.5 minutes. In this sense the steady state results are informative about what we should expect over the long term. Second, the horizontal axis of the figure which shows time in minutes indicates that we reach an average waiting time of about 8.5 minutes beginning at approximately 5000 minutes and maintain that value. In other words, if this system runs continuously, with no significant changes in service rates or arrival rates for 80 hours or so, our model holds up quite well.

Unfortunately, a process is almost never going to reach this kind of steady state in practice. Third, we note that the path toward this average value is not monotonic. In other words, it does not start at 0 and move smoothly up to 8.5 minutes. In fact it starts at 0 because the first couple of arrivals will have no waiting time. It then moves up dramatically, before settling down towards the predicted value. Our findings suggest that queueing theory is informative about long-term average behavior, but must be taken with a very large "grain of salt" if we want to speak authoritatively about waiting times over some shorter interval such as a clinic session or a worker's shift. With these facts in mind, we will aim to expand the collection of tools at our disposal when we consider such systems in the coming chapters.

4.7 Review Material

Our discussion of queueing systems is quite general and relates to virtually any service systems. More details on the related material are available in a plethora of sources. However, we find ourselves repeatedly using introductory presentations on the topic including Kolker (2011), Karuppan et al (2021), and Moore and Weatherford (2001).

We can consider additional data and apply the results stated above to gain a deeper understanding of the behavior of several queueing systems.

4.7.1 Large Scale Vaccination Site: Process A

Consider a large drive-through facility for vaccinations. In this system the vaccination recipients have appointment times, that are 1 minute apart. This process has three major steps that we can label **Check-In**, **Vaccination**, and **Holding**. In holding, recipients are instructed to wait 15 minutes before exiting in case they experience some sort of allergic reaction to the vaccine. Reactions are rare, but when they do happen, they take a good bit of time to handle.

1. Assuming that inter-arrival times are fixed at 1 minute, and service times are fixed at 2 minutes, how many identical servers does the system need to keep utilization of each server below 80%? Assume that the answer must be an integer.

2. Given your answer to the prior question, what is the capacity of this system if another worker handles check-in and that step takes exactly 1 minute.

3. Because space is limited, the site can accommodate only 100 cars at a time being served or in line. How much space does the site need in this area to be sure that all of those who arrive will be served? This is the space for the line, the service, and the holding area.

4. How do your answers change if the service time for the vaccination step is 90 seconds (instead of 60)?

4.7.2 Large Scale Vaccination Site: Process B

Consider a large drive-through facility for the same vaccination service. In this system the vaccination recipients have appointment times, but the actual arrival pattern is not distinguishable from random arrivals because so many people arrive much earlier than the appointed time. This process has three major steps that we can label **Check-In**, **Vaccination**, and **Holding**. In Holding, recipients are instructed to wait 15 minutes before exiting in case they have some sort of allergic reaction to the vaccine. Reactions are rare, but when they do happen, they take a good bit of time to handle.

1. A paid observer records times between arrivals. A sample of this data shows values in minutes of 1,1,2,1,1,2,5,1,2,1,1,2,1 and 4. If we model these times as draws from an exponential distribution, what is your estimate of the mean and standard deviation? (Round up to the nearest integer.)

2. Sample vaccination times in minutes are 1,2,3,1,1,2,1,4,1,6,1,2,2,1, and 2. Assuming that these times are also from an exponential distribution, how many identical servers does the system need to keep utilization of each server below 80%? When you state the service time round the mean up to the nearest integer.

3. Because space is limited, the site can accommodate only 100 cars at a time served or in line. How much space does the site need to have in this area to be sure that 99% of those that arrive will be served? (To answer this question consider making a spreadsheet where you calculate P_n values. You can sum these values to find the number n that will be exceeded only 1% of the time.)

4. After receiving the vaccination, patients wait in cars in a parking area for 15 minutes. Assuming that this value is always exactly 15 minutes, how many spaces does the site need to have to be 99% sure that the number of parking spaces does not cause a back-up in the process?)

5. Reconsider the size of the parking area if the time for the Holding step is exponentially distributed with a mean of 15 minutes. In other words, how many spaces will the site need to ensure that the number of cars in this part of the system can handle the load 99% of the time?

Chapter 5
Cost Estimation and Process Improvement

Abstract The limitless variety of medical conditions and processes involved in the management of those conditions makes it virtually impossible to develop a rigid approach to cost calculations that will be a perfect fit across all settings. However, the existential threat of reimbursements that are rising slower than costs means that administrators must have some useful approach to the calculation of costs that allows them to see whether one process is more cost effective than another. We focus on Processes in which Flow Units follow some Route through a network in which Resources perform Activities to deliver care. With this definition in place, we decompose the cost estimation problem into a collection of problems to estimate the cost of each activity. This is done using a heuristic approach based on busy times for costly resources. We combine these activity costs to estimate process costs. This can serve as a valuable input when making decisions about potential process changes. We discuss several stylized examples to explore the issues involved and illustrate our approach.

5.1 Introduction

According to the Organization for Economic Co-operation and Development (OECD) the United States spent 16.9% of its gross domestic product (GDP) on health care in 2018. This works out to roughly $10,600 per capita. (Much more than $10,600 per patient!) This spending is about 45% higher than the second highest level by country and is more than twice the average (OECD, 2019). While we are not going into all of the issues driving this extraordinary level of spending, it is commonly understood that this is not sustainable over the long term and costs must be reduced. While this spending level is unprecedented, it exists in a setting in which most large hospitals in the United States lose money on a typical episode of in-patient care (Bai and Anderson (2016)). This is only possible if payments are below costs (after overhead is included). The largest class of payers of these costs is Government at state and federal levels. Growing deficits and the political need to claim to be "driving down health care costs" create an environment in which it is safe to say that reimbursements from government are not going to grow rapidly beyond current levels. The combination of a setting in which revenue cannot grow much higher and costs already exceed revenues presents an existential problem for most hospitals and providers. No organization that constantly has costs exceeding revenues will survive forever.

To make the setting more concrete, consider the conglomerate of businesses and units that define the Johns Hopkins Health Care System. This network includes an international collection of hospitals, hospital management companies, laboratories, outpatient clinics, schools of Medicine, Nursing, and Public Health, insurance companies, and an intricate supporting structure of staff, equipment, and facilities. Given this level of complexity and a challenging economic environment it is imperative that those attempting to manage this system be able to evaluate, communicate, and understand its economic performance. This is only possible if all parties involved can agree on a common vocabulary and a collection of rules which explain how relevant data will be collected, reported, and interpreted. Fortunately, accounting practices have evolved to include tools to accomplish such tasks. In particular, cost accounting has a long history of explaining the cost to produce items based on the calculation of direct costs including materials and labor, along with some allocation of indirect costs including management, equipment, and facilities.

The record of success for these approaches is well documented (Baker (1998), Cooper and Kaplan (1992)). Virtually every plant manager that we have ever worked with in manufacturing settings was able to answer the question "what does it cost to produce one unit?" of the most common items that the plant produces, and everyone involved understood that if we could figure out a way to produce that same item at a lower cost, profits would rise and the competitive position of the enterprise would be enhanced. On the other hand, almost no provider or administrator that we have worked with in a hospital can answer the question, "what does a patient visit cost?"

If we ask something like "how can you manage a process without knowing the cost to deliver its output" we get responses that highlight three key factors. First, each job is unique. If we think of a patient as an input to the process then it is literally true that every flow unit is unique. Furthermore, patients differ along multiple dimensions that are not medically relevant simultaneously including reimbursement rates from the payer, and attitudes. In addition to being unique cases medically, each patient has a different set of expectations, willingness to cooperate, and definition of quality.

Second, decision makers at the most advanced hospitals frequently argue that experience at other institutions is less informative than one might think. We have had several physicians explain that "We are the hospital of last resort," meaning that many of the patients that come here are those who have already been told at other institutions that nothing more can be done. As a result, many of these patients will bring needs and associated costs that are not commonly dealt with at other places. Consequently, the approach to cost estimation used at one facility may not fit as well at another.

Finally, in some organizational structures, each unit such as a clinic or department is treated as a profit center, but the true costs of patient care includes some allocation of multiple layers of overhead that are virtually impossible for a unit manager to see. Consequently, we have a situation in which costing systems must be clearly and rigidly defined to be useful for communication after the fact, being used to describe patient care that can never be rigidly defined before the fact.

5.1.1 Cost are Just a Percentage of Charges - Right?

Invariably, if we push administrators to wrestle with questions about the cost to deliver care, what we hear is some version of "I know what we charge." The implicit assumption is that charges are fair predictors of costs (Kaplan and Porter (2011).) Several aspects of the health care industry motivate administrators to embrace this idea. The major payers demand a consistent and rigid approach to the statement of charges. Such logic is consistent with the goals of most cost accounting systems. When charges are an accurate predictor of costs this is a great place to start. For many years Medicare, which is the largest single payer in the US, used a cost-plus system that required hospital departments to prepare an annual Medicare Cost Report (MCR). These reports would detail costs at the department level, as opposed to looking at costs at a patient level.

This type of aggregation makes it almost impossible to back out costs for any specific patient unless it is done by assuming that each patient represents some fixed portion of cost. Payers are using aggregated data to come up with payments. This motivates hospitals to use aggregated payments to estimate costs. Thus, an internally consistent system can be built. Unfortunately, it is clear that the resulting system is consistently wrong. Total hospital expenditures per patient typically exceed revenues per patient. This occurs even though the assumptions about costs and charges imply that each patient must be profitable because our estimated costs (which are some percentage of charges) will always be below our estimated revenues. Thus, administrators find themselves in a position where they lose money on each patient but the cost accounting system motivates them to make it up in volume - an obviously fatal strategy.

To make matters worse, not only are charges not a good predictor of costs, charges are not even good predictors of payments. Most payers have a schedule defining how much they are going to disperse for a case based on some pre-defined

code that may be for a Diagnosis Related Group (DRG) [1] or an International Classification of Diseases (ICD) [2]. This code-based approach allows payers to develop a
menu of payment amounts that is easy to codify and apply consistently across different states or countries. This approach to payments supports a tightly defined cost
accounting system for the payers. Complex algorithms are built to generate these
payment levels and the end result is that once a case is coded for a specific ailment,
payment is effectively fixed. In other words, from the payer's perspective the cost
is entirely known. The hospital can state whatever charge they like, but the revenue
will be the same. As a result, we have a large network of voices including governments and insurance companies who all fully understand cost, as "what we pay."
This reinforces the notion that hospitals should think of costs, as "what we charge."

While all of this is going on hospitals hold onto one glaring exception to these
rules. Some patients, particularly those from outside the country, are expected to pay
the stated fee. In other words, some customers do pay the "sticker price" while almost no government agency or insurance company comes close to it. Consequently,
the hospital has a strong incentive to increase this price year over year even though
the vast majority of patients are never going to pay that amount. These prices become the basis for claims about how health care costs always rise faster than in-
flation. The stated charges rise faster because of the small minority of people who
actual pay those amounts. The growth rate of the actual reimbursements for the great
majority of patients is an entirely different matter.

The assumption that charges are fully informative about costs can only be valid
if treatments and cases can be standardized in a way that parallels the way the payments can be standardized. As long as the work being done can run lockstep with
the payment system we have no problems. This works wonderfully well in many
manufacturing environments, but falls apart rather quickly in most health care settings. A variety of approaches have been taken to estimate costs for classes of cases
or ailments. It is then assumed that this amount should be charged for each case
in that group. This mimics the way that payments are made and simplifies billing
and projections of both costs and revenues, but the uniqueness of each case guarantees that it is never precise. One can hope that the instances in which costs are
under-estimated will balance against instances in which they are over-estimated,
but there is really no good reason to think that this will be true for any particular patient, clinic, procedure, or hospital. Consequently, this approach, which might
makes sense for most of the world, and is very useful for planning at a high level,
has little value when considering changes to a singular process at a specific location.

The result is a flood of data on charges, which are costs for the payers, that are
assumed to be proxies for costs incurred by the providers. This data sits along side

---

[1] This is a classification system that typically specifies a lump sum payment to cover all charges
from admission to discharge based on which group is designated by the main diagnosis.

[2] ICD codes are useful in allowing comparison of mortality rates across countries. The list has
been revised 10 times and thus, produces ICD-10 codes.

actual expenditures and revenues at the provider level. Consequently, the clinic or hospital administrator is swamped with numbers that do not add up, are not particularly informative, and simultaneously paint a dire picture of un-sustainability. Attempts to improve system performance in this setting will always be hamstrung because it is rarely clear whether such efforts will make the financial situation any better. If we cannot explain how a change in operational metrics translates into an enhanced ability to keep the doors open, why would anyone go through the effort needed to make such changes happen? In addition, having providers invest a great deal of time into such efforts is problematic. No patient wants a doctor whose primary concern is the hospital's financial statement, and no doctor wants cost considerations to be foremost in the thought processes linked to the delivery of care.

With these factors in mind we offer a small idea. A perfect depiction of the cost of a patient visit is neither possible, nor the most important objective. But, if we can identify a straight-forward way to talk about costs that doctors and staff can relate to, which provides insights about whether a process change will be worthwhile on a financial level, we will have a useful tool. We do not need to claim that this approach is exhaustive or the best possible rubric. We only look to present a simple framework that allows the calculation of cost for an event or encounter that tells us which direction constitutes improvement. One might say that we need enough insight to know "which way is up" even if we might haggle over how far up the proposed change will take us. As long as we can look at two processes and reasonably argue that one is better in terms of cost, we need not be so concerned about how much better it will finally appear to be in the hospital's accounting system.

5.2 Cost Measurement at a Prototypical Outpatient Clinic: Process 1

To make it easier to relate to the remaining discussion, let us focus on a stylized example. Eastern University Hospital offers a variety of clinical, in-patient, and ancillary services. While some of its funding comes from philanthropy, funded research, and endowment income, most of its operating revenue comes as a result of direct contact with patients. To deliver its services, Eastern is divided into departments that are managed as profit centers. Each department, in turn recruits physicians along with other health care providers and support staff.

To serve patients efficiently, many departments contract with the Eastern Hospital Outpatient Center (E-HOC) and rent examination rooms (Rooms) in one of its many multi-specialty suites. These Rooms are rented for 4-hour sessions and the rent payment also covers some support services, including Clinical Assistants (CA), and front-desk staff. Given the incentive structure, each Attending physician (Attending) decides how many Rooms to rent. For the purpose of illustration, let us consider a prototypical physician, Dr. Prince who currently rents two Rooms to see patients. Dr. Prince has two types of patients which we will label as NEW and RETURN. The appointment schedule creates 30 minute slots for each NEW patient and 15 minute slots for each RETURN patient. In parallel, the billing system generates a charge of $300 for a visit from a NEW patient and a charge of $150 for a visit from a RETURN patient.

Currently, for each hour, the clinic seeks to schedule 1 NEW and 1 RETURN patient. The hourly rent for a Room is $60, thus two Rooms will cost $120 per hour. In addition, an hour of time for the Attending Physician is $180. A typical patient needs one (NEW) visit for an issue along with one follow-up (RETURN). Consequently, for a typical patient, the total Charge will ultimately be $450; $300 for a visit as a NEW patient and $150 for a visit as a RETURN patient.

In actuality, reimbursement rates are negotiated with the various payers. Thus, the amount received for any particular visit depends on which payer is involved. Some payers will view this as two separate bills, while others view it as a single bill for $450. Thus, hospitals with a different mix of payers will have different revenue streams even if they handle an identical set of cases. Each hospital will have historical data on the mix of payers they are dealing with. Using this information, they come up with a standardized collection rate for planning and budgeting purposes. Exactly how this rate is determined is treated as proprietary information. For this example let us use a value of 70%. In other words when bills are generated for $300 and $150, payments received average $210, and $105 respectively.

Given this data we can say that the cost of running the clinic (including the cost of the Attending and the clinic space) is $180 + $120 = $300 per hour. Analogously the patients are charged $300 + $150 = $450 dollars over the same block of time. From these numbers we can calculate a Cost to Charge ratio (CCR) of $300 / $450 = 2/3 or 66.7%. The CCR is a standard accounting value that is reported regularly and is publicly available from a variety of government agencies. Given these figures, intuition suggests that the gross margin is 1 - 2/3 = 1/3 or roughly 33%. However, as noted above, the payments expected for one hour of clinic time are actually $210 + $105 = $315. After paying the expenses noted here, Dr. Prince's department nets $315 - $300 = $15 per hour, which is a contribution margin of roughly 5%.

Many readers will consider a 5% margin to be rather paltry. This value is on par with traditionally low margin businesses such as grocery and discount stores. Why an essential industry, with arguably the most highly trained workforce on the planet is unable to generate larger margins is a complex question. However, this economic reality cannot be avoided in the short run and must be managed accordingly. Additionally, management in this environment is made more difficult by the fact that, as a general rule physicians might keep track of the charges they generate, or the Relative Value Units (RVU) involved, but it is quite rare to find one that keeps track of the collection rate or contribution margin. On the other hand, a department chair, who is required to track these operating statistics, will often conclude that clinicians simply need to see more patients because the margin is small, but clearly positive.[3]

Given this setup, we see that Dr. Prince is working for 45 standard minutes per hour for a utilization of 75%. If there is a sufficient backlog Dr. Prince has an incentive to add one more RETURN patient to the schedule every hour. However, there are at least two complicating factors here. First, the number of RETURN patients is actually a function of the number of NEW patients recently treated. Thus, marketing efforts to find more RETURN patients to put on the schedule cannot make sense. In addition, many payers deliver a fixed payment for patients with a coded condition. In these instances revenue is fixed once the NEW patient is associated with a particular ailment. The payer may agree to pay for 1 RETURN visit, but any additional visits will have a reimbursement rate of $0. As a result, providing such patients with more RETURN visits increases costs but does not increase revenue. Second, even if 1 RETURN patient with a positive reimbursement rate could be added to the schedule, this would drive the expected value of utilization for Dr. Prince to 100%. In theoretical settings in which processing times are known with certainty, this might be feasible. However, in settings with large variances in processing times, such as health care, this is logically impossible. Patients are not always punctual, staff get delayed by unexpected events, and some patients require extra attention. As a result, Dr. Prince will feel pressure to reduce face time with patients to manage the stress placed on the system, and this has an adverse affect on both patient and provider satisfaction.

Fortunately, Dr. Prince has other alternatives to increase the contribution margin. He may notice that, while in the original schedule his utilization is 75%, since he is renting two Rooms, each Room is utilized at a little over half his rate, or about 37.5%. If Dr. Prince were to only rent one Room instead of two, he could save $60 per hour. Such a strategy would increase the contribution by a factor of 5, going from $15 to $75 per hour. While Dr. Prince and his department may find this attractive, the clinic director would probably be unhappy since E-HOC would have to recruit another physician to fill the un-rented Room. When each entity within the same organization is treated as a profit center, such transfer payments lead to a zero sum game dissuading managers from working together to lower overall costs. Reducing the number of Rooms improves the apparent operating efficiency for a single practice. However, it does not create additional revenue or enhanced margins for the system.

While adding one more RETURN patient may not be feasible, when considering a 4-hour session Dr. Prince may notice that one more NEW and one more RETURN patient can be added to each four-hour session. This would add revenue of 70% * $450 = $315 dollars per session or $78.75 per hour. In this scenario, Dr. Prince's workload would go up by 30 + 15 = 45 minutes during the session or by 11.25 min-

---

[3] The Relative Value Unit is a basis for reimbursement levels used by Medicare.

utes per hour. His utilization would become 93.75%. If only one Room is available, its utilization will also be 93.75%. If two Rooms are used, each Room would be utilized roughly 47% of the time. In some settings, a 93.75% utilization level for one resource might be manageable if there is excess capacity for each of the other supporting resources. However, having such a high utilization level for both the Attending and Rooms will be very difficult to work with. As a result, using 2 Rooms adds additional cost, but using 1 Room may be infeasible. This occurs because of the assumed "indivisibility" of the Room. In other words we have implicitly assumed that Dr. Prince must pay for full use of either 1 or 2 Rooms, even if the most attractive level of this resource is someplace in between.

An alternative strategy might be to find another physician whose workload complements that of Dr. Prince. If the two can coordinate their appointment schedules, they may benefit from sharing 3 Rooms during the same session. It would be as though there was a resource pool of Rooms that both Attendings draw from. Using this structure, each Attending would have a utilization level of 93.75% while each of the three Rooms would have utilization of around 60%. This arrangement saves each practice a rental fee of $60/2 = $30 dollars per hour.

We have collected data in several clinics where Rooms are pooled in this manner. However, we routinely notice that the more common practice is one in which each clinician rents at least two dedicated Rooms. As this simple example illustrates, the way we have accounted for costs does not always make it clear how some operational changes help the system. Effective operations management can significantly improve efficiency and profitability, but this will only take place if the decision makers involved have a shared understanding of revenues and costs. The classic costing method that we used earlier to present an informal operating audit does not make the connections between process changes and improved margins immediately clear. A slightly more sophisticated technique that prices resources by time, and not just by unit volumes may be more instructive. We will ultimately argue, that such an approach gets us closer to the goal of having a shared understanding more likely to facilitate improvement efforts.

Let us pause for a moment at this point and collect some of what we have uncovered.

1: The hourly cost of running the clinic = $180 + $120 = $300.

2: The ratio of Cost to Charges = $300 / ($300 + $150 = $450) = $300/$450 = 67.%

3: The reimbursement rate per hour = 70% * $450 = $315.

4: The contribution per hour = ($315 - $300)/$315 = 4.75%.

These values are easy to calculate using the approach to cost measurement that we began with. However, as a unit manager concerned about efficiency and the contribution from clinic operations we can envision a number of additional questions that might like to address. For example;

1. What is the contribution for each NEW and RETURN patient?

2. Which patient type is more profitable?

3. If RETURN patients take 13 minutes instead of 15, what happens to contribution?

4. If NEW patients take 31 minutes instead of 30 what happens to contribution?

5. How can the unit not be profitable is the CCR is less than 1?

If we have some way to allocate costs to NEW and RETURN patients we may be able to state some estimate of contribution. This allocation would drive any discussions about contribution by patient type. Unfortunately, given our current structure small changes in processing times cause no change in realized costs or revenues so it is not clear how to address questions about linkages between processing times and contribution. Finally, intuition suggests that if the CCR is below 1, then more volume must result in greater contribution, but how much is enough to cover costs depends on how those costs are allocated. If these are some of the types of questions that a manager needs to wrestle with, then perhaps we need a different way to think about costs for this setting.

5.3 Time-Driven, Activity-Based Costing

When considering problems of high complexity one is forced to utilize some methodology to make the analysis manageable. Two common approaches are, 1) some form of decomposition, and 2) the use of heuristics. The term "decomposition" refers to the idea of decomposing or splitting a larger problem into a collection of smaller ones that are easier to solve. We then find some way to put the solutions back together to come up with a policy or measurement for the larger problem.

A heuristic is akin to the notion of a "rule of thumb." It is a simple rubric that it is reasonable to believe will generate answers that are "in the ballpark" of the optimal response or exact value. As an example, one famous heuristic is known as "the rule of 72." This is the idea that to find out how many periods it takes for a value to double when it grows at a fixed percentage rate per period, we simply divide that value into 72. For example, if an account grows at 6% per year, we would expect the initial account value to double after 72/6 = 12 years. Such approaches are generally taken to be imperfect, but much better than nothing.

For the most difficult problems, we often find that we need to employ a combination of these methods. In the cases of interest here, we will decompose the processed involved into a set of activities. We then use a heuristic to estimate the cost of each activity that focuses on how long each resource is involved in an activity. We can combine these activity costs to estimate a total cost for a process such as a clinic visit. Such an approach is fully consistent with our focus on the analysis of a <u>Process</u> in which <u>Flow Units</u> proceed along some <u>Route</u> over which <u>Resources</u> engage in <u>Activities</u> with the larger objective to transform the Flow Units involved.

The approach of decomposing a costing problem and using a heuristic for each part is not a new idea. One name for this approach is Time-Driven, Activity-Based Costing or TDABC. In the example of a clinic visit the Flow Unit is a patient, the Route is simply the sequence of steps involved in the clinic visit, the Resources might include Clinical Assistants (CA), Residents, Attending Physicians, Examination Rooms, Equipment and the like. Within this construct we can calculate, or better yet, observe how much time each resource spends on each activity. These time values become the main inputs to our cost estimation process.

As outside observers the easiest things for us to measure are the passage of time and the number of resource units employed. Once this data is collected, it can be sorted in many different ways. We can use the same logic to find the cost per patient visit, cost per procedure, cost per clinic session, cost for the entire schedule for a given day, etc. We can look across multiple episodes of care to consider the cost associated with a patient from first visit to the resolution of the underlying problem. This end-to-end costing is consistent with the desire of payers to specify a payment up front based on the DRG or ICD code. These costs can be compared to reimbursement rates to search for any mis-matches that occur. In other words we can look at patients, groups of patients, providers, groups of providers, or medical conditions using the same logic and better inform a host of critical decisions and negotiations.

The ability to come up with a large sample of case or patient-specific costs for a condition enables decision makers to work from an understanding of the distribution of these costs. When we compare this to the estimate of costs based on the Cost-to-Charge ratio it is like moving from a setting in which only expected values are given to one in which the entire distribution is described. This better equips decision makers to negotiate contracts, assess financial risks, and explain system performance in a more robust way. As we evolve from fee-for-service models to fee-for-diagnosis models to capitation models this understanding becomes critical.[4]

---

[4] In a capitated model the provider receives a lump sum to treat some population of patients, regardless of how many patients present during that period. This approach is favored by some governments because it provides cost certainty for the development of annual budgets.

5.3.1 Cost Measurement at Eastern Hospital Outpatient Center: Process 2

Let us expand the clinic visit example used earlier to make it a bit more realistic. A simple Process Map for this modified scenario (Process 2A) is shown in Figure 1.

Activity 1	Check-In
Duration	10
Resource	CA

Activity 2	Vitals
Duration	4
Resource	Nurse, Room

Activity 3	Exam
Duration	12
Resource	Attending, Room

Activity 4	Check-Out
Duration	4
Resource	CA

Fig. 5.1 Process Map of Office Visit: Private Practice

In this more common structure, we have four Activities labeled **Check-In**, **Vitals**, **Exam**, and **Check-Out**. We see that a CA is involved in both **Check-In** and **Check-Out**. A Nurse is involved in **Vitals** and an Attending is involved in **Exam**. We will also assume that a Room is involved in both the **Vitals**, and **Exam** activities. For the sake of illustration let us assume that **Check-In** takes 10 minutes, **Vitals** takes 4 minutes, **Exam** tasks 12 minutes, and **Check-Out** takes 4 minutes. Note that the time for the Attending has been reduced from our earlier depiction. This is reasonable if the added resources of the CA and Nurse facilitates specialization in that they perform much of the work that our Attending was doing in the earlier version.

Figure 2 presents a simple Gantt chart for this process. This representation makes it immediately clear when multiple resources are involved in an Activity. Columns are linked to intervals of time (minutes in this example), and colors are assigned to each resource. If we look down any column and see two or more different colors, we know that multiple resources must be coordinated for an activity. For example, the Nurse and Room are both in use at the same time for **Vitals**. If we see two or more instances of the same color in any column, we know that a resource is being over-committed for that minute. In general, the number of instances for any color in a column must be less than or equal to the number of units of that resource on hand.

We can see immediately from either figure that we have 4 Resources involved in this visit and 4 estimates of busy times; the CA is busy for 10 + 4 = 14 minutes,

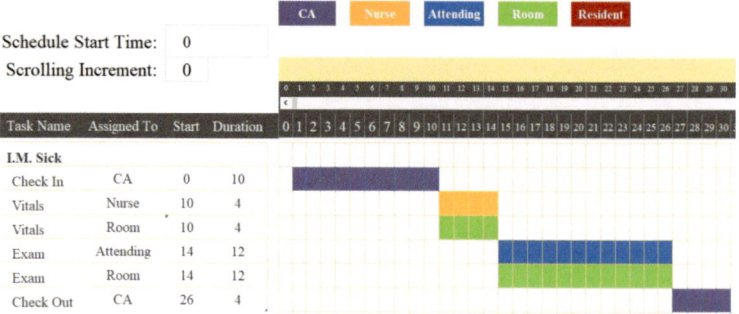

Fig. 5.2 Gantt Chart for Single Office Visit in Private Practice

the Nurse is busy for 4 minutes, the Room is busy for 4 + 12 = 16 minutes, and the Attending is busy for 12 minutes.

For most processes, coming up with the relevant list of resources and busy times for direct labor and the space that they rent is relatively easy. Our approach is to multiply these times by some cost rate per minute for each resource. This part of the approach can become a bit more complex. A general recipe for finding a cost rate can be summarized as:

1. Find annual cost for the resource whose primary role is patient care.

2. Find minutes per year that this resource is involved in patient care.

3. The ratio of these values is our estimate of the cost rate per minute spent in the activity of interest.

For additional details, a great deal of published work on the application of TD-ABC in health care settings has been done, including (Cooper and Kaplan (1992)), (Kaplan and Anderson (2003)) and (Kaplan (2014)). The underlying logic is to define this rate as the (Expenses Attributable to a Resource) divided by the (Available Capacity of that Resource). For example, suppose we pay a laborer $80K per year, and expect 2000 working hours. One may argue that we have a cost rate of roughly $80,000 / (2000 * 60) = $0.67 per minute. However, we note two complicating factors. First, additional money will be spent on benefits such as retirement fund contributions, tax payments, insurance etc. Thus, the actual expenditure may be closer to $100K. Second, not all of this 2000 hours will be spent on patient care. Some of it will be spent on vacations, sick leave, training, breaks, or even research time. If we are paying this total expense for patient care, then we want to assign all of these costs to the minutes spent on that care. If the time spent on patient care turns out to be roughly 5/6 of the total possible time, then we have a cost per minute of $100,000 / (2000 * 60 * 5/6) = $1 per minute. Using a parallel logic we might conclude that a total cost for Dr. Prince is closer to $4 per minute.

Many applications of TDABC will take this a step further, by adding costs of additional resources that are needed to support the function of the direct labor. This may include some share of the costs of supervision, space, equipment, and even Information Technology. This can be a tricky exercise for several reasons. For example, if an organizational chart places a supervisor over 10 other people, one can argue that 1/10 of this cost is allocated to each of those 10 workers. However, the supervisor's time may not be distributed in a uniform fashion across these workers. New workers may use a disproportionate share of that time. The allocation of the cost of IT services to individual care-givers can be even more complex.

In this sense, our approach to costing is less inclusive than many applications of TDABC. For our purposes the nuances of these calculations are less important than the relative values. If we are willing to assume that these elements of overhead are proportional to salaries of the personnel and cost for the spaces directly involved, then we can get started on a costing exercise simply based on relative salary and rent levels. For example, if the Attending makes roughly twice as much as the Nurse, and 4 times as much as the CA, and we assume that the costs of supporting resources that we do not see directly are proportional to those salary levels, then we have enough to make progress in seeking improvement.

Let us assume that we are willing to scale costs such that the Room and the CA cost 1 unit of cost per minute. This implies the the Nurse costs 2 units and the Attending costs 4 units. If these values hold then we can come up with a cost estimate for this patient visit of:

1. 14 Minutes * $1 = $14 for the CA

2. 4 Minutes * $2 = $8 for the Nurse

3. 12 Minutes * $4 = $48 for the Attending

4. 16 minutes * $1 = $16 for the Room

This suggests a total cost of 14 + 8 + 48 + 16 = $86 for this patient visit. This information can be included in a comparison to some alternate arrangement to get an idea on whether an improvement (in terms of cost) has occurred. For example, let us speculate that we could have the Nurse perform some additional task that the Attending had been performing. Realistically speaking, this is likely to generate some redundancy of effort. Consequently, we might see the time for the Nurse in the process rise by 6 minutes to a total of 10, while the time for the Attending falls by 4 minutes to a total of 8. We label this slightly modified arrangement Process 2B.

Under this structure the cost estimate becomes:

1. 14 Minutes * $1 = $14 for the CA

2. 10 Minutes * $2 = $20 for the Nurse

3. 8 Minutes * $4 = $32 for the Attending

4. 18 minutes * $1 = $18 for the Room

This suggests a total cost of 14 + 20 + 32 + 18 = $84. This small improvement in estimated cost becomes one metric that is useful in comparing these two processes.

5.3.2 Process Metrics Using Process 1

It is instructive at this juncture to revisit the approach to cost estimation that we presented earlier (Section 5.2). That approach used an hourly cost for the labor and space to calculate a total cost per hour. There was no need to assume anything about the number of patients served to find this cost. If Dr. Prince uses 2 Rooms at a cost of $1 per minute per Room, and his direct cost is another $180 / 60 = $3 per minute, we have a total cost incurred over an hour of (2 Rooms * 60 minutes * $1 = $120) for the Room and another $180 for the Attending yielding the total of $300 for the hour, or $5 per minute.

However, both Dr. Prince and the Rooms are only busy for 45 of those minutes. Thus, there is 15 minutes of idle time for the Attending and 75 minutes of idle time for the Rooms. It is as though operating the clinic costs $2 + $3 = $5 per minute, but that operation is only connected to revenue for 45 of every 60 minutes. This suggests that for NEW patients we get a contribution margin of 70% * $300 - (30 * $5) = $60. Similarly, a RETURN patient yields a margin of 70% * $150 - (15 * $5) = $30. If a patient visit takes a minute longer, this suggests that the contribution drops by $5. On the other hand, if it takes a minute less, it rises by $5. This is somewhat confusing because, from a cash flow standpoint, if there is no change to the schedule or resource levels, neither the cash flows linked to activities nor the revenue linked to cases has actually changed. Therefore, there is no real change in the contribution that stems from 1 hour of clinic time.

We suggest that a useful way to handle this, which is consistent with the TD-ABC framework is to create a virtual job which we typically label UNUSED. Thus, instead of 2 patient types, we now have three: NEW, RETURN, and UNUSED. In this example, the cost of UNUSED is 15 minutes * $3 = $45 for Dr. Prince, and 75 minutes * $1 = $75 for the Room. Thus the total cost incurred is $120 for the

NEW patient, $60 for the RETURN patient, and $120 for UNUSED. The total cost for these 3 jobs is ($120 + $60 + $120 = $300). Note that the $120 connected to the UNUSED patient cannot be connected to a particular charge, and therefore is not linked to revenue. This explains why we can have attractive CCR values and still lose money. One of the advantages of an Activity based approach to costing is that it allows us to quantify the cost of the unused capacity and focus on it as a key to improving the margins of a practice, clinic, hospital or other economic unit.

5.3.3 Process Metrics Using Process 2

One sticky issue with a TDABC approach is that we need to assume some patient load to come up with the cost rate. This occurs because we use the number of minutes dedicated to patient care to come up with those values. If the amount of time actually spent on patient care differs from this initial estimate, we have a mismatch between an assumed rate and a realized rate. In effect we are allocating costs to jobs and the realized volume of jobs changes the allocation. This is one reason, that we should not use costs based on TDABC (or any other method) as the sole criteria for a process change. In addition, any comparison of processes has to include additional dimensions such as:

Cycle Time: The time measured from the beginning to the end of a process for one flow unit.

Throughput: The rate at which flow units actually move through the process. This may be expressed as units per hour, patients per clinic session, operations per day, cases per shift, etc.

Makespan: The span of time from the start of the first job to the completion of the last job on the schedule.

Utilization: Ratio of the amount of a resource actually used over the amount of that resource available. Labor utilization is most commonly expressed as actual time spent processing flow units divided by the associated Makespan.

A process with a lower cost but a much greater Cycle Time may be impractical because the work needs to fit into some reasonable session lengths. If reducing cost reduces throughput more, then the system may be worse off. If a process change seems to cut costs but greatly increases Makespan we run into problems related to working overtime that has to paid for somehow. If utilization of some resource approaches 100% we have an infeasible schedule because waiting times will explode. Changes in costs are clearly important, but never sufficient to justify a major process change. Consider Processes 2A, and 2B if we have a clinic schedule with 2 patients (instead of just one). Using Process 2A we would like to have the 2nd patient arrive

14 minutes after the first to minimize waiting time. We need this time lag because the CA is involved for 14 minutes in the process. (Note that the Room is used for 16 minutes, but we have 2 of these so they are not a bottleneck.) In this arrangement we get:

1. Makespan = $(10 + 4 + 12 + 4) + (14) = 44$ Min

2. Throughput = 2 patients / (44/60 Hours) = 2.73 patients/hour

3. Cycle Time = $10 + 4 + 12 + 4 = 30$ Min

4. CA Utilization = $(14 *2)/44 = 64\%$

5. Nurse Utilization = $(4 * 2)/44 = 18\%$

6. Attending Utilization = $(2 * 12)/44 = 55\%$)

7. Room Utilization = $(16 * 2)/(44 * 2) = 36\%$

8. Cost = \$86 * 2 = \$172

If we utilize Process 2B instead, we have parallel performance metrics of:

1. Makespan = $(10 + 10 + 8 + 4) + (14) = 46$ Min

2. Throughput = 2 patients / 46 Min = 2.61 patients/hour

3. Cycle Time = $10 + 10 + 8 + 4 = 32$ Min

4. CA Utilization = $(14 *2)/46 = 61\%$

5. Nurse Utilization = $(4 * 2)/46 = 17\%$

6. Attending Utilization = $(2 * 8)/46 = 35\%$)

7. Room Utilization = $(18 * 2)/(46 * 2) = 39\%$

8. Cost = \$84 * 2 = \$168

Thus we see that even though these 2 processes are quite similar, we have differences along multiple dimensions. Process 2A has a shorter Makespan, greater Throughput, and lower Cycle Time. Utilization is higher for the CA, Nurse, and Attending, but lower for the Room. This difference is subtle because the change in

Makespan makes interpretation of changes in utilization a bit tricky. It does seem clear that Process 2A has slightly greater cost per patient. Taking all of this into account, which of these processes is preferred cannot be settled based on costs alone because the other dimensions need to be accounted for.

Additionally, we argue that this decision cannot be made on cost alone for another reason as well. The approach to costing that we looked at with Process 1 was actually a more traditional one. We looked at costs per hour for personnel and space and came up with a total. This could be compared to revenue to look for any inconsistencies and to come up with an estimate of profitability. When we moved toward a TDABC approach we made a rather strong assumption that must be discussed. More specifically, claiming that Process 2B was better in terms of costs implicitly assumes that the time savings for the Attending is a cost savings for the system. If this time is simply reassigned to the virtual patient labeled, UNUSED then the savings is not material. We cannot assume that the Attending will not be paid when not facing a patient.

Process 2B can only be better in terms of costs if we think of time for the Attending not as a cash flow, but as an opportunity cost. In other words, we can argue that Process 2B is better in terms of cost because the Attending has an opportunity to do some other work with the time saved. This is a subtle, but important point. If the time saved cannot be leveraged in a useful way, then we have simply shifted cost from a NEW or RETURN job to the UNUSED one, and the second process is actually worse on almost all metrics. At the end of the day, whether this process is better or worse becomes a judgment call. However, making that judgment in the absence of a coherent costing approach is next to impossible. Our main point is that cost can be included on the list of measurements being accounted for, and becomes an important part of the evaluation of alternate processes.

5.4 Key Take Aways

To facilitate the more general application of these terms and ideas, let us collect many of the insights involved into a short list.

1. Health care costs appear to be rising faster than reimbursement rates, and managing in this environment requires a credible estimate of costs.

2. Estimating costs based on charges introduces several problems including the disconnect between charges and payments, and the disconnect between average values and any specific patient.

3. We can use a variant of Activity Based Costing by multiplying busy times for identifiable resources and cost rates for those resources.

4. A perfect statement of resource costs is less important than relative levels of costs for the resources involved.

5. The cost of handling any job is a function of the job itself, as well as how the work is organized to complete the activities involved.

6. Cost is but one of a collection of metrics that need to be considered when comparing one process to another. A holistic view must be taken to drive choices about process structure.

5.5 Review Material & Prior Works

We have documented several issues related to the collection of data needed to facilitate in Conley et al (2016). To ensure that the material covered here can be applicable to your settings consider your responses to the scenarios described below.

5.5.1 Cost for Blood Test with Attending Follow-Up

A clinic schedule handles cases in which a patient is seen using the process described in Figure 1 with one addition. The Nurse collects a blood sample from each patient during **Vitals** and conducts a test using that sample. This test can be done in parallel with the **Exam** and takes 12 minutes. If the test comes back negative, no additional steps are needed. If the test comes back positive, the patient needs an additional 5 minutes with the Attending for follow up. We will label this added step **Consult**. Historically, the test is positive 50% of the time. Find the performance metrics for this process assuming a schedule of 2 patients, by calculating Cycle Times, Throughput Rates, Makespan, and Utilization of the four key resources. Assume cost rates of $1 for each of two Rooms and the CA, $2 for the Nurse and $4 for the Attending. Discuss how the performance metrics change if this test is included as a part of the patient visit.

5.5.2 Cost for Blood Test with Nurse Follow-Up

A clinic schedule handles cases in which a patient is seen using the process described in Figure 1 with one addition. The Nurse collects a blood sample from each patient during **Vitals** and conducts a test. The patient is sent back to the waiting

room until the results are in, and this takes 12 minutes. If the test comes back negative, no additional steps are needed. If the test comes back positive, the patient needs
an additional 10 minutes with the Nurse for follow up, (label this step **Consult**) before being seen by the Attending. Historically, the test is positive 50% of the time.
Find the performance metrics for this process. Assume cost rates of $1 for each of
two Rooms and the CA, $2 for the Nurse and $4 for the Attending. Discuss how the
performance metrics change if this test is included as a regular part of the patient
visit.

Chapter 6
A Process Improvement Process

Abstract Demands for increased capacity and reduced costs in health care settings create a need for a coherent strategy regarding how to collect, analyze, and use data to facilitate and lead to process improvements. Specifically we are interested in system performance related to patient flows in care units in Academic Medical Centers that schedule patients by appointments. We describe ways to organize information about patient care as we map delivery processes, collect data to formally describe the system, create discrete event simulations of these systems, use simulation as a virtual lab to explore possible system improvements, and identify proposals as candidates for implementation. We close with a discussion of several projects in which we have used our approach to understand and improve these complex systems.[1]

6.1 Introduction

With passage of the Affordable Care Act (ACA) an increased proportion of Americans gained access to health care insurance. By some estimates, the ACA extended access to health insurance coverage to roughly 30 million previously uninsured people and that coverage expansion is likely to lead to between 15, and 26 million additional primary care visits annually. (Glied and Ma (2015); Beronio et al (2014)) In addition, according to the US Census Bureau the number of people 65 and older will grow from 43.1 million in 2012 to 83.7 million by 2050. (Ortman et al (2014)) This rapid growth in the size of the population above the age of 65 will correlate with additional demand for health care services.

At the same time, Medicare and other payers are moving away from older "fee for service" models towards "bundled payment" schemes. Under these arrangements providers are paid a lump sum to treat a patient or population of patients. One clear

---

[1] This chapter repeats much of our prior publication Dada and Chambers (2019) and is used with permission. It has been reformatted and edited to be consistent with the rest of the text.

© The Author(s), under exclusive license to Springer Nature Switzerland AG 2022
C. Chambers et al., *Improving Processes for Health Care Delivery*,
https://doi.org/10.1007/978-3-031-19043-8_6

result of this trend is the gradual move away from inpatient care to the delivery of care through outpatient settings. Consequently, a disproportionate share of the growth in demand will be processed through outpatient clinics, as opposed to hospital beds. This approach is also seen as one of the key strategies needed to help get health care cost in the US down closer to the costs experienced in other developed countries (Lorenzoni et al (2014).)

An additional complicating factor is that health care delivery is often interspersed with teaching and training of the next generation of care providers. In the US, roughly 40 million outpatient visits per year are made to teaching hospitals known as Academic Medical Centers (AMC) (Hing et al (2010)). Inclusion of the teaching component within the care process increases the complexity of each patient visit. The classic model of an outpatient visit where the patient is led to an examination room (ROOM), seen by a single physician and then leaves the clinic is not a sufficient description of the visit process in the AMC. Adding a medical trainee (Resident) into the process introduces new steps for the interaction between the Resident and the patient as well as interactions between the Resident and the Attending Physician (Attending). These added steps increase Cycle Times, the number and levels of resources deployed, and system congestion (Boex et al (2000); Franzini and Berry (1999); Hosek and Palmer (1983); Hwang et al (2010)). The delays added are easy to understand when one considers the fact that the Resident typically takes longer then the Attending to complete the same task, and many teaching settings demand that both the Resident and the Attending spend time with each patient (Williams et al (2007); Taylor et al (1999); Sloan et al (1983)).

The additional mission of Resident education is not simply adding steps to a well managed process. The added teaching mission is akin to changing from a single server queueing system to a hybrid system (Williams et al (2012, 2015)). Multiple options exist regarding the role of the Resident in these systems, and how these options are exercised creates both dramatic and subtle reactions, which are reflected in various process metrics. The Resident may function as a parallel (but slower) server, the the Resident and Attending may function as serial servers such that a one step process becomes a two step process, or decisions on how the Resident is intertwined in the process may be made dynamically, meaning that the Resident's role may change depending on system status.

In short we are asking our current health care system to improve access to care to a rapidly growing and aging population as demand is shifted from inpatient to outpatient services in teaching hospitals using delivery models that are not well understood. While the extent to which this is even possible is debatable (Moses et al (2005)), it is quite clear that efforts to make this work require thoughtful data analysis and rigorous approaches to operations management (Sainfort et al (2005)).

The primary objective of this chapter is to lay out a strategy toward gaining an understanding of these complex systems, identifying means to improve their performance and predicting how proposed changes will effect system behavior. We present this in the form of a 6-step process and provide some details regarding each step. We then close with a discussion of several projects in which our process has been applied. Along the way, we present representative data so that the interested reader can explore the approach in more detail.

6.2 A Representative Clinic: Part I

To make the remainder of our discussion more concrete let us re-introduce an outpatient clinic in Eastern Hospital to serve as a representative unit of analysis. For reasons related to privacy and data security, the data presented for this clinic presents a composite of clinics that we have studied but is not meant to be a complete representation of any particular unit. Envision a walk-in clinic within an AMC. We can consider the simple case of a patient visit for some new ailment and we will label this patient type as NEW. By NEW we mean to suggest that this the first visit of this patient to this particular clinic for this particular condition. This must be differentiated from a "RETURN" visit which would occur later. We will assume for now that this patient needs to be treated by the Attending. This distinction is relevant because some visits only involve a Nurse, a Nurse-Practitioner, a Physician's Assistant or some other provider.

Our analysis will focus on the management of Processes that deliver care. A Process is designated by a <u>Route</u> along which <u>Resources</u> perform <u>Activities</u> designed to alter the state of <u>Flow Unit</u>.[2] This clinic visit can be defined as a 4-step process as outlined in Figure 1.

In Activity 1 the patient interacts with staff at the front desk. We will label this step **Check-In** with the understanding that it may include data collection, and perhaps some patient education. In Activity 2 a Nurse leads the patient into an Room, collects data on vital signs, and asks a few questions about the patient's condition. We will label this step **Vitals**. In Activity 3 the Attending enters the Room and interacts with the patient. We will refer to this step using the label **Exam**. Finally the patient returns to the front desk for **Check-Out**. This Activity may include time spent to make one or more appointments for a future visit as a "RETURN" patient. For ease of exposition, we will frequently refer to this as Process A, and note that this structure is quite common in private practices without a teaching mission.

For the sake of illustration, let us also consider a parallel operation that includes a medical trainee (Resident). We will frequently refer to this arrangement as Process B, and note that this structure is quite common in AMCs. In this process after

---

[2] A route is simply a sequence of steps or Activities and need not be taken to be a physical path.

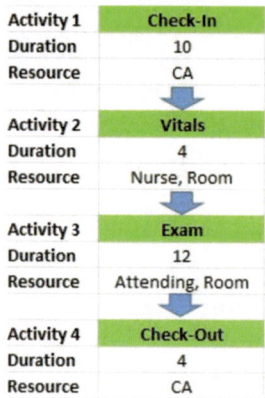

Activity 1	Check-In
Duration	10
Resource	CA

Activity 2	Vitals
Duration	4
Resource	Nurse, Room

Activity 3	Exam
Duration	12
Resource	Attending, Room

Activity 4	Check-Out
Duration	4
Resource	CA

Fig. 6.1 Four Step Clinic Process

the patient is led to the Room, the Resident reviews the patient record before entering the Room with the patient. Consequently, we can say that the step labeled
RESIDENT actually consists of 2 parts; reviewing the patient record followed by
interaction with the patient. Once this step is completed the Resident presents information about the case to the Attending. We will label this step **TEACHING**. After
this conversation, both doctors enter the room and interact with the patient. This
modified process flow is presented in Figure 2.

Managers of these processes need a working understanding of process standing
and performance. It is quite natural to ask questions such as:

1. What is the capacity of this process, or how many patients per hour can be seen?

2. How long does a typical patient stay in this process?

3. What is the average waiting time in this clinic?

4. How long will it take to serve all of the patients on the clinic schedule?

For our purposes we can think of Capacity as the maximum rate at which patients
may exit this system after being seen. This is the maximum rate of Throughput for
this clinic. The average time in the process will be referred to as Cycle Time, and the
span of time from the start of the first case to the completion of the last case on the
schedule is known as Makespan. We may also have more subtle questions including,
"How does the added education mission affect these metrics?" and "What is the best
appointment schedule for this clinic?"

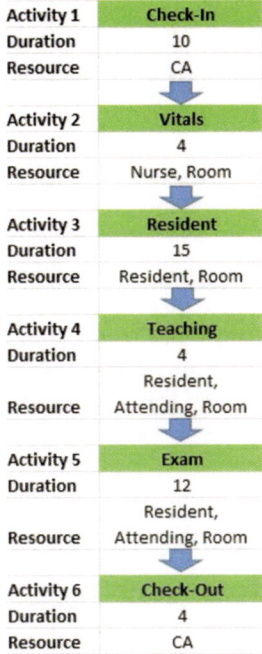

Fig. 6.2 Four Step Clinic Process

6.3 How to Fix Health Care Processes

Much of the development of research oriented universities in the US was driven by the needs for research related to health care (Chesney (1943)). Consequently, when working with physicians and other health care professionals a convenient starting point for the discussion is already in place. Much medical research addresses questions using randomized trials or pilot implementations. These typically center on formal experiments which are carefully designed and conducted in clinical or laboratory settings. This has proven to be highly effective and is assumed by many to be the best way to produce evidence based results on medical questions relating to things like the efficacy of a new drug or the efficiency of a new process. One way to get buy-in from practitioners in this industry is to take a very similar approach to issues related to process improvement.

At the same time, Operations Research has a long history of creating and applying tools to improve service delivery processes. Operations Research employs a predictive modeling investigative paradigm that uses mathematical equations, computer logic, and related tools to forecast the consequences of particular decision choices (Sainfort et al (2005)). Typically, this is done in abstraction without a formal experiment. This approach permits the consideration of alternative choices to be evaluated and compared to see which are most likely to produce preferred outcomes. Many traditional areas of Operations Research are prevalent in clinic management including appointment scheduling (Cayirli et al (2006)), nurse rostering problems (Burke et al (2004)), resource allocation problems (Chao et al (2003)), capacity planning (Bowers and Mould (2005)), and routing problems (Mandelbaum et al (2012)).

Given this confluence of approaches and needs, it seems natural for those working to improve health care delivery processes to employ Operations Research techniques to conduct controlled, actual or virtual experiments as part of the improvement process. However, when one looks more closely one finds that the history of implementations of results based on these findings is actually quite poor. For example, when looking at the current research on health care process improvement the tool most frequently cited as an aid for improvement projects is a technique known as Discrete Event Simulation (*DES*). This is the approach of creating a mathematical model of the flows and activities present in a system and using this model to perform virtual experiments seeking to find performance improvements. However, a review of over 200 papers that use DES in health care settings identified only 4 that even claim that physician behavior was changed as a result. (Wilson (1981)) A more recent review found only one instance of a publication which included a documented change in clinic performance resulting from a simulation-motivated intervention (van Lent et al (2012)).

This raises a major question since there is clearly an active interest in using Operations Research techniques to improve patient flow and there is ample talent working to make it happen, "What can we do to make use of this technique in a way that results in real change in unit performance?" Virtually any Operations Management textbook will provide a list of factors needed to succeed in process improvement projects such as getting all stakeholders involved early, identifying a project champion, setting clear goals, dedicating necessary resources, etc. However, we want to focus on two additional elements that are a bit more subtle and, in our experience, often spell the difference between success and failure when working in hospital units.

First finding an important problem is not sufficient to achieve good results. It is critically important to think in terms of finding the right question, which also addresses the underlying problem. This may be counter-intuitive, but when seeking buy-in from physicians in the AMC we can leverage the fact that they are also dedicated researchers. As outside agents or consultants, we are not in a position to pay faculty and staff extra money to get improvements done. We need a different form of payment to motivate their participation. One great advantage in the AMC model is that we can use the promise of publications in lieu of a cash payment to induce participation.

Second, we need to find the right technique. Modeling by itself does not improve the system, and mathematical presentations that feel completely abstracted do not resonate with practitioners. One meaningful advantage of DES modeling is that it helps clinicians project themselves into the model in a way that is more salient then the underlying equations could ever be. The key idea is that value exists in finding a way to merge the research paradigm of Operations Research such as model building and simulation with those more common in medical research such as controlled experiments. In this chapter we lay out a process whereby research can be conducted that has a high likelihood of generating interesting findings that will actually be implemented to improve clinic flow.

6.4 The Process Improvement Process

Given this background, we need a systematic approach to describing, analyzing, and predicting improvements in performance based on changes that can be made to these systems. In order to do this we need to accomplish at least six things, and this list forms the statement of our method.

Step 1:   Describe the process in a relevant way.

Step 2:   Collect data on activity times and work flows.

Step 3:   Create a DES of the system under study.

Step 4:   Develop performance metrics of interest.

Step 5:   Propose changes to processes.

Step 6:   Predict changes in metrics stemming from process changes.

We now turn to providing a bit more detail about each of these steps.

6.4.1 Step 1: Process Description

Much has been written concerning process mapping in health care settings. The common themes of these approaches are that we: define discrete steps in the process, determine any setup times and run times associated with each step, describe any buffers between steps, specify resources involved, and describe any exceptions to the usual process flow. In many instances the activity of process mapping itself suggests multiple changes that may improve process performance.

Perhaps the most obvious way to begin this step is to ask the agents in the system what the work flow is. We have found that this is absolutely necessary but have also found that it is never sufficient. Agents in the system often provide misleading descriptions of process flow. In many cases physicians are not fully aware of what support staff do to make the process work, and Residents are fairly new to what is going on and are going to be very careful not to appear to contradict more senior physicians. To get high quality process descriptions we need insights from multiple perspectives and levels of the organization. Ideally, this will include support staff, nursing, Residents, and Attendings. In some cases other administrators are valuable as well, especially if there is a department manager or some other person who routinely collects and reports performance data. It is ideal to have all of these agents working on the development of a process map as a group. However, if this cannot be done it is even more vital to carefully gather information to describe process flows from as many different angles as possible.

Second, we have found that no matter how much information about the process has been gathered, direct observation is ALWAYS required. We have yet to find a process description created by internal agents that completely agreed with our observations. Health care professionals put patient care above all other considerations. Consequently, they make exceptions to normal process flows routinely and do not give them a second thought. As a result, their daily behavior will almost always include several subtleties that they do not recall when asked about process flow.

6.4.2 Step 2: Data Collection

In our experience, this is the most time consuming aspect of the improvement process. Given a process map, it will be populated with some number of Activities undertaken by various Resources. The main question that has to be asked at this stage is, "How long does each Resource spend to complete each Activity?" Gathering this data is critical for several reasons. First, the dominant patient complaint in outpatient settings is waiting times. Thus, time is a crucial metric from the patient's perspective. Second, many costing systems have been developed in which total cost is based on hourly or minute by minute costs of various Resources. Consequently, time is most often the crucial metric from the process manager's perspective as well. Therefore, how long each Activity takes becomes the central question of interest.

We have utilized several approaches to uncover this information. Agents within the system can be asked how long an Activity takes. This is useful as a starting point and can be sufficient for some Activities that are highly standardized. On the other hand, quizzing agents about activity times when more variability is present is problematic because most people think in terms of averages and find it difficult to articulate variances. This can only be done after a sufficient number of observations are in hand.

We have also used approaches in which the care givers record times during the patient visit. For example, in one clinic we attached a blue form to each patient record. When the patient arrived, staff at the front desk created the form and recorded the arrival time for the patient along with the appointment time. When the patient was led to the Room, the times at which the Nurse entered and left the room were added. The Attending then recorded times upon entry and exit as well. Front staff then recorded when the patient was last seen at the desk along with patient departure time. This approach can be automated in a number of ways through the use of aids such as phone or Ipad apps where applicable.

While this approach can provide excellent data, it introduces several issues as well. Recording data interrupts normal flow and it is not possible to convince the participants that data recording compares in importance to patient care. As a consequence, we repeatedly see instances where providers don't get to record the data in real time and then try to fill it in later in the day when things are less hectic. This produces data sets where mean times may be reasonable estimates but the estimates of variance are simply not reliable.

A common approach to data collection used in AMCs is to use paid observers. This approach can generate highly reliable information as long as the process is not too complex and the observer can be physically positioned to have lines of sight that facilitate accurate observations and do not interfere with the work flow. This approach is commonly used in AMCs because they are almost always connected to a larger university and relatively high quality, low cost labor is available in the form of students or volunteers. While we have used this technique successfully on multiple occasions, it is not without its issues. First, the observers need to be unobtrusive. This is best done by having them assigned to specific spaces. If personnel travel widely, this becomes problematic. For example, a Radiation Oncology clinic that we studied had rooms and equipment on multiple floors so, tracking becomes quite complex (See Elnahal et al (2015a), Elnahal et al (2015c), and Conley et al (2016)). Second, the parties serving patients know they are being observed. Many researchers have reported significant improvements to process flow using this approach, only to find that after the observers left, the system drifted back to its previous way of functioning and the documented improvement was lost.

Given this backdrop it is useful for the reader to learn about a fourth approach to data collection. Many hospitals and clinics have been equipped with Real-Time Location Systems (RTLS). Large AMCs are often designed to include this capability because tracking devices and equipment across hundreds of thousands of square feet of floor space is simply not practical without some technological assistance. For example, we have studied the movements of Heart Rate Monitors that are needed when a patient is moved form an OR to an ICU or to another ward. Each of these pieces of equipment was issued a tag that could be tracked by censors in the ceilings or floors throughout the hospital.

These sensors can also pick up signals from transmitters that can be embedded within tags (or badges) worn by personnel or patients. Each sensor records when a tag comes within range and again when it leaves that area. When unique tag numbers are given to each care giver, detailed reports can be generated at the end of each day showing when a person or piece of equipment moved from one location to another.

This approach offers several dramatic advantages. It does not interfere with the care delivery process. Once the system is in place, the marginal cost of using it is virtually 0. Since these systems are always running, the observation period can be managed easily. Data can be analyzed from any span of time, before, during, and/or after an intervention. Consequently, the agents are not constantly reminded that observations are being made, and changes in behavior can be tracked over much longer periods of time to verify the evolution of a process.

6.4.3 Step 3: Create a DES of the System

Consider a simple two-step process. We label Activity A **Registration** and Activity B **Attending**. Activity A takes 4 minutes and Activity B takes 5 minutes. Activity A involves one resource which we will refer to as STAFF and Activity B involves one resource which we will refer to as ATTENDING. Let us assume that patients arrive to this process once every 10 minutes, and that all times given so far are deterministic, meaning there is no variability in their realizations. We can deduce several facts immediately. First, the Cycle Time for this process is $4 + 5 = 9$ minutes. The utilization level for the two resources 40% and 50% respectively. The Attending is the bottleneck resource, and the patient experiences no waiting. Up to this point, we have employed only the most basic tools of process mapping and process analysis.[3] Clearly this analysis is not sufficient for our purposes because it ignores variability which is a fact of life in the settings of interest to us.

One straightforward way to include variability is to assume that these times are drawn from some well understood distribution such as an exponential distribution. If this is the case, then simple results from queueing theory can be applied. Queueing theory is a branch of OR in which the interactions of arrivals and servers is modeled using mathematical formulas. To get closed form solutions for these models, several strong assumptions have to be made. Unfortunately, the most common assumptions that these models make are routinely violated in clinic settings. For example, some processing times are not exponentially distributed, processing times are often not from the same type of distribution, and if arrivals are based on appointments, inter-

---

[3] The term Bottleneck refers to the Resource that limits the Throughput of the process.

arrival times are not exponentially distributed.

However, we argue that none of these issues pose the largest challenge to applying queuing models in outpatient clinics. Consider three additional issues. First, the basic results of queueing models are only averages which appear in steady state. Steady state means that the inflows and outflows balance over the relevant period of time, such as a clinic session. However, a clinic does not start the day in steady state - it begins in an empty state. It takes some time to reach steady state. This probably sounds like a small issue. However, if one plots average waiting times for a simple, single server queue over time with a utilization above 80%, one quickly sees that it may take dozens or even hundreds of cases for the system to reach steady state. Clearly a clinic with one physician is not going to schedule hundreds of patients for that resource in a single session. Thus, this kind of system never reaches steady state, and predictions based on the assumption that it does are not entirely valid.

Second, in practice processing times often change depending on the status of the system. We have found that staff and physicians unconsciously alter their processing times depending on the state of the system, in the sense that when they get behind schedule, they try to speed up (Chambers et al (2016)). We have also observed that care providers are frequently interrupted to deal with issues involving other cases.

Third, none of this discussion so far has accounted for the extra steps added by the teaching mission present in the AMC. Different clinics make use of Residents in different ways, and how the Resident is used can also depend on the state of the system. Consequently, there is no single, tractable queueing model that could possibly capture all of these possibilities.

Clearly, what is needed is a tool that can account for all of these factors simultaneously, make predictions about what happens when some element of the system changes, and can give us information about the broader distribution of outcomes - not just means for systems in steady state. DES is a tool with the needed capabilities.

To create the DES we begin with a process map like the one developed in Step 1. From there we add information about distributions of the activity times collected in Step 2. We can select an activity time at random from our collection of observations. Alternatively, we can fit a distribution to the collected activity time data. We have found both approaches to work satisfactorily.

Once a DES model is created it is easy to simulate a clinic session and collect data on metrics such as waiting times, cycle times, utilization levels, and session completion times. With a little more effort a simulation model can be set up to collect data on more complex measurements such as the use of overtime or waiting times within Rooms. Finally, DES models can be set up to have patients take different paths or have activity times drawn from different distributions depending on system status. Finally, we have found it useful to have DES models collect data on subgroups of patients based on system status because many changes to system parameters affect different groups differently.

6.4.4 Step 4: Metrics of Interest

As one famous adage asserts, "If you can't measure it you can't manage it." The idea being that focusing on measurable quantities makes many approaches to improvement feasible and tractable. Using measurements removes ambiguity and limits misunderstandings. If all parties agree on a metric, then it is easier for them to share ideas about how to improve it. However, this begs an important question - what metrics do we want to focus on?

Both patients and providers are concerned with system performance, but their differing perspectives create complex trade-offs. For example, researchers have often found that increases in face time with providers serves to enhance the patient experience (Thomas et al (1997); Seals et al (2005); Lin et al (2001)). When patients arrive at a clinic, their immediate objective is to receive treatment from the provider. Health care is unusual as a service in that the consumer views the provider as an expert and consequently may have some trouble evaluating the quality of what the provider does. However, one clear indicator of service quality that the consumer always understands is how much time is spent with the provider. This creates an unambiguous metric and almost all consumers will agree that more is preferable to less. On the other hand, there is also almost universal agreement that increases in waiting times degrades the patient experience (Meza (1998); McCarthy et al (2000); Lee et al (2005)). Again, the patient may not fully understand what the provider is doing but they can always understand that waiting for it is not productive.

The fact that patients care about both face time and waiting time creates a complex trade off. Given a fixed level of resources, increases in face time result in higher provider utilization, and higher utilization increases patient waiting times. Consequently, the patient's desire for increased face time and reduced waiting time creates a natural tension. Fortunately, in many systems there is much room for improvement. Considering several clinics that we have studied, waiting times are routinely 2-5 times the levels of face time. However, such results can be misleading. Most systems measure waiting time as the time between patient arrival and the time the patient is lead to an Room. This masks two key issues. Putting a patient in an Room does not mean that waiting has ceased. We have frequently measured wait times in the Room that exceed waits in the waiting room. Since most systems only measure waits outside the Room, one easy way to eliminate reported waits is to add another room. However, moving the problem from one large room to several small ones does not necessarily improve things.

Consider a patient that we observed recently. This patient arrived 30 minutes early for an appointment, and waited 20 minutes before being lead to the Room. After being lead to the room the patient waited for 5 minutes before being seen by a Nurse for 5 minutes. The patient then waited 15 minutes before being seen by the Resident. The Resident spoke with the patient for 20 minutes before leaving the room to discuss the case with the Attending. The patient waited 15 minutes before being seen by the Resident and the Attending working together. The Attending spoke with the patient for 5 minutes before being called away to deal with an issue for a different patient. This took 10 minutes. The Attending then returned to the Room and spoke with the patient for another 5 minutes. After that, the patient left. By summing these durations we see that the patient was in the clinic for roughly 100 minutes. The patient waited for 20 minutes in the waiting room. However, the patient also spent 45 minutes in the Room waiting for service. Time in the Room was roughly 80 minutes of which 35 minutes was spent in the presence of a service provider. Thus, we may say that Face time was 35 minutes. However, of this time only 10 minutes was with the attending physician.

Within this scenario a wide variety of different metrics could be considered, depending on what aspect of the service we are working to improve. Possible metrics include:

1. Patient Punctuality

2. Time spent in the waiting room before the appointment time

3. Time spent in the waiting room after the appointment time

4. Total waiting time in the Examination Room

5. Cycle Time

6. Proportion of Cycle Time spent with a care provider

7. Proportion of Cycle Time spent with the Attending

8. Time from start of clinic session to completion of clinic schedule

The key message here is that the metrics of interest will be specific to the problem that one seeks to address and the nuances of the process in place to deliver the services involved.

6.4.5 Step 5: Propose Process Changes

Many types of process changes are possible. Changes can be made to affect patient arrival patterns. This includes changes to an appointment template as well as penalties based on arrival behavior. Changes can be made regarding the role of the Resident. These can include pre-processing meaning that the Resident can discuss the case with the attending prior to patient arrival. Other options include omitting the Resident from the process for some cases because they offer limited opportunities to learn or because the system is falling behind schedule. At the other end of the spectrum we may be able to almost eliminate the Attending from the process for routine matters where risk is very low.

We wish to emphasize two critical issues at this stage, confounding variables, and unintended consequences. Confounding variables refers to system or behavioral attributes that are not completely controlled when conducting an experiment. For example, consider looking at a system before an intervention, collecting data on its performance, changing something about the system, and then collecting data on the performance of the modified system. This is our desired approach, but implicitly assumes that nothing changed in the system other than what you intended to change. If the appointment schedule changed due to increased demand, or some other procedure changed due to administrative necessity, these changes could be part of the explanation of why system performance changed. It is critically important to eliminate as many of the possible explanations as possible before concluding that your proposed change fully explains any improvements in the selected performance metrics.

It is also critical to account for unintended consequences. For example, adding examination rooms is often touted as a way to cut waiting times. However, this also makes the relevant space larger, increasing travel times as well as the complexity of resource flows. This must be accounted for before declaring that the added room improved performance. It may improve performance along one dimension while degrading it in another.

6.4.6 Step 6: Predict Impact of Process Changes

We have found that it is extremely difficult to predict how changes will affect system performance simply by looking at a process map. More formal explorations have proven invaluable to include controlled experiments and numerical simulations. Controlled experiments are widely understood in the context of AMCs for the simple reason that the physicians, nurses, and some administrators are also instructors and researchers. Consequently, the AMC presents a unique environment in which management by fact is valued and application of well defined protocols is accepted practice. One can leverage these characteristics when working to improve system performance. The basic steps will be understood by all parties other than the patients.

Measurements are made of the system performance in its current state. An improvement is suggested and trial improvements can be implemented. Measurements of the same metrics can be gathered by observing the modified system. By comparing metrics before and after the intervention, statistical tools can be used to talk about whether a statistically significant change has taken place. Using this data, managers are positioned to make decisions about whether the change should be made permanent or extended to other units.

On the other hand there are a few drawbacks to this approach. Data collection can be costly or time consuming. It may be hard to get staff and care providers to buy in to a change with no prior proof that it is effective or beneficial. Finally, it will be virtually impossible to get care providers to try doing things a new way if they feel there is some chance that patient care or safety could be adversely affected. Given these issues, it is often better to experiment with process changes in a virtual way. This is where the use of DES models becomes particularly valuable. We can make a model of the system which is a numerical abstraction. Changes in process flow, schedules, or work assignments can be done in this simulated world, and evidence can be gathered which suggests whether a change will have the desired outcome in practice. Using this approach we have been able to show care providers the impacts of proposed changes to help get the buy-in needed to facilitate a more formal experiment or to motivate an implementation.

6.5 Experiments, Simulations, and Results

Our work has included a collection of experiments that have led to system improvements for various settings. We turn to a discussion of these efforts to provide examples of the kinds of measures that can be taken. In these examples we focus on a single clinic visit. Each visit consists of an arrival process under an appointment system. In this prototypical arrangement **Check-In** is followed by interaction between the physician and the patient. In the AMC this is made more complex by the addition of a Resident. One measure to counter this added processing time is to have some visits handled by a PA or NP. Finally, the system hopes to account for all of these things when searching for an optimized schedule. We discuss several of the issues that naturally arise in turn.

6.5.1 Arrival Process

Historically, almost all research on health care systems assumes that when patients come to a clinic for an appointment, they arrive on time - but is this true? One obvious complication is that some patients are no-shows, meaning that they do not show up for the appointment at all. No-show rates as high as 40% have been cited in prior works (McCarthy et al (2000); Huang (1994)). However, there is also the more subtle issue of patients arriving very early or very late and this is much harder to account for. Early work in this space referred to this as patient unpunctuality. (See Bandura (1969); Blanco White and Pike (1964); Alexopoulos et al (2008); Fetter and Thompson (1966); Tai and Williams (2012); Perros and Frier (1996).) Our approach has been used to address two interrelated questions. Does patient unpunctuality affect clinic performance, and can we affect patient unpunctuality?

To address these questions we conducted a simple experiment. Patient unpunctuality was mapped over a 6 month period. We found that most patients do arrive early, but the range of unpunctuality (defined as arrival time minus appointment time) ranged from -80 to +20. In other words some patients arrived as much as 80 minutes early while others arrived 20 minutes late. An intervention was performed that consisted of three elements. In reminders sent to each patient before their visit, it was stated that late patients would be asked to reschedule. All patients were called in the days before the visit and the same reminder was repeated. Finally, a sign explaining the new policy was posted near the registration desk. Unpunctuality was then tracked one month, 6 months, and 12 months later. Additional metrics of interest were waiting times, use of overtime, and the proportion of patients that were forced to wait to be seen.

This lengthy follow up was deemed necessary because some patients only visit the clinic every month or every quarter, thus the intervention would take time to have an effect. However, this introduces a new problem. To ensure that changes in clinic performance were related only to changes in unpunctuality we needed a way to control for other confounding variables such as changes in the appointment schedule or changes in the number of patients served. It is impossible to hold so many variables constant over an 18 month period. This is a major problem when performing research on environments that change rapidly and include activity times with high levels of variability. Our response to this problem was to create a DES of the clinic, use actual activity times as proxies for activities in our simulation, and consider old versus new distributions of patient unpunctuality. This allows us to isolate the impact of our intervention and later to devise new performance metrics not envisioned initially.

Before the intervention 7.7% of patients were tardy and average tardiness of those patients was 16.8 minutes. After 12 months, these figures dropped to 1.5% and 2 minutes respectively. The percentage of patients who arrived before their appointment time rose from 90.4% to 95.4%. The proportion who arrived at least one minute tardy dropped from 7.7% to 1.5%. The range of unpunctuality defined as the maximum minus the minimum decreased from 100 minutes to 58 minutes. We also found that the average time to complete the session dropped from 250.6 minutes to 244.5 minutes. In other words about 6 minutes of overtime operations was eliminated. This is important when remembering that this improvement is realized over 2 sessions per day for the entire year. The likelihood of completing the session on time rose from 21.8% to 31.8%.

Our use of simulation also allowed us to create metrics of performance that had not been explored earlier. For example, we noticed that benefits from the change were not the same for all patients. Patients that arrived late saw their average wait drop from 10.7 minutes to 0.9 minutes. Those that arrived before their appointment time but did not get into the Room until after the appointment time saw their average waiting time increase by 0.8 minutes. Some patients arrived earlier and got into the Room before their appointment time. For this group their average waiting time increased by about 0.9 minutes. Finally, for those who arrived very early, their waiting time was unaffected. In short, we found that patient unpunctuality can be affected, but this has both intended and unintended consequences. The clinic session is more likely to finish on time and overtime costs are reduced. However, much of the benefit in terms of waiting times is actually realized by patients that still insist on arriving late.

6.5.2 Physician Processing Times

Historically, almost all research on process improvement in appointment based clinics assumed that the processing times for the physicians was not related to the schedule or whether the clinic was running on time. Many works did assume that different patient types would have different processing times. This is probably obvious. However, our basic tools of process analysis and queueing models break down if the activity times depend upon the status of the system. Is this indeed the case? To address this question we analyzed data from three clinic settings. One was a low volume clinic that housed a single physician, one was a medium volume clinic in an AMC that had one Attending working on each shift along with 2 or 3 Residents. The last was a high volume service that had multiple Attendings working simultaneously.

We categorized patients into three collectively exhaustive and mutually exclusive groups: Group A patients were those who arrived and were placed in the Room before their scheduled appointment time; Group B patients were those who arrived before their appointment times, but were placed in the Room after their appointment time, indicating that the clinic was congested; and, Group C patients were those who were tardy, meaning that they arrived after their appointment time. The primary question was whether the physicians spent as much time with patients in each group. This is basically the differences in average processing times for patients in Group A compared to those in Group B. We also had questions about how this affected clinic performance in terms of waiting times, and session completion times.

In the low volume clinic with a single physician, looking at average processing times and standard errors showed that these values are 38.3 (3.2) for Group A and 26.2 (2.2) for Group B. In other words, the physician moves faster when the clinic is behind schedule. Similar results had been found in other industries, but this was the first time (to the best of our knowledge) that this had been demonstrated for these clinics. This finding is important, because it implies that prior work done assuming that this did not take place needs to be reconsidered in light of this new evidence.

In the medium volume clinic the relevant values were 65.6 (2.2) and 53.5 (2.0). Again, the system works faster for Group B then it does for Group A. However, we note two key additional points here. First, the drop in average times is about 12 minutes in both settings. This suggests that the finding is robust, meaning that is seems to occur in different systems to a very similar extent. Second, we note that this setting is different because it also included Residents in the process flow. This suggests that the means that this system uses to achieve this increase in speed may be different. In fact, our data show that the average amount of time the Attending spends with the patient was no more than 12 minutes to begin with. This tells us that it is not just the behavior of the Attending that makes this happen. The AMC must be using the Residents differently when things fall behind schedule. (We will return to this issue shortly.)

In the high volume clinic, the parallel values were 47.2 (0.8) and 17.6 (0.2). We note that the standard errors are much lower here because we have many more data points due to the high volume nature of this clinic. Here we see that the drop in processing times is much more dramatic than we saw before. Again, the message is that processing times do change when the system is under stress. In hindsight, this seems totally reasonable, but the extent of the difference is still quite startling.

As we saw in the previous section, there is an unintended consequence of this system behavior as it related to patient groups. Patients who show up early help the clinic stay on schedule and receive longer processing times. Thus, their cycle times are longer. Patients wo arrive late, have shorter waiting times and also have shorter processing times. Thus their cycle times are shorter. If shorter cycle times are perceived as a benefit, this seems like an unfair reward for patient tardiness and may explain why it will never completely disappear.

6.5.3 Private Practice versus the AMC

The result from the previous section suggests that the way that the Resident is used and managed within the clinic makes a difference when considering clinic performance. To explore this point further we wanted to compare a clinic without Residents with a similar clinic that included them. This is difficult to do as an experiment, but it turned out that we were lucky when looking at this question. An Attending with a stable private practice was hired as the director of a clinic in the AMC. Thus, we could consider the same Attending, seeing the same patients in the two different settings. By analyzing data from both settings, we could compare the performance of the two processes and see what the additional mission of the AMC does to clinic performance. However, there are a number of factors that make this comparison surprisingly complicated. When comparing a low volume clinic to a medium volume clinic, how do we know that the differences in performance are not caused by the different appointment schedules? This is impossible to do by looking only at the metrics of immediate interest from each setting.

Here, the tool of DES proves invaluable. We collected data on activity times in both settings with the same Attending handling the same patients. Given these times, we could seed simulation models of both clinics and compare results. Since these were mathematical models we could look at both settings as though they had the same appointment schedule. This is invaluable because it allows us to conduct a virtual experiment controlling for many confounding variables that cannot be ruled out in practice without inconveniencing patients.

If we consider the two settings using the schedule in place for the AMC we see that the average Cycle Time in the AMC was 76.2 minutes and this included an average waiting time of 30.0 minutes. The average time needed to complete a full schedule was 291.9 minutes. If the same schedule had been used in the private practice model with the activity times realized in that setting, the average cycle time would be 129.1 minutes and the average waiting time would be 83.9 minutes. We note that these times were not realized in the private practice model because that clinic would never schedule as many patients as the AMC. The point being that the capacity of the AMC is clearly greater than it is in the private practice model. This is interesting because the flow times in the private practice setting using the schedule that was optimized for that setting were much lower. It turns out that the total processing time for each patient is greater in the AMC but the capacity is higher. This is explained by the use of parallel processing. In the AMC the Attending spends time with one patient while Residents work with other patients at the same time. The impact of this hybrid approach is very difficult to quantify without using a model for experimentation.

The use of DES also highlighted a less obvious result. It turns out that the waiting time in the AMC is particularly sensitive to the time that the Resident spends interacting with the Attending. To understand this, consider what happens when the

Resident and the Attending are discussing the case while the patient waits in the Room. In this scenario the three busiest resources in the system are the Resident, the Attending, and the Room. When the Attending is teaching the Resident while the patient waits in the room, all of these resources are occupied at the same time. Thus, it is not surprising that waiting times are so sensitive to the duration of this activity. In fact, we found that increasing the average duration of this activity by one minute increased average waiting time by roughly 3 minutes per patient. The clinic normally scheduled 17 patients per session, so this adds up to over 50 minutes of waiting time per session due to a one minute change in the duration of one activity.

6.5.4 Pre-processing

The finding that waiting times are so sensitive to teaching times in the clinic yields new understanding about system behavior. Recall the result that the system moves faster when it falls behind schedule. One obvious way to have this happen is to adjust teaching time. This suggests that one way to improve patient flow is to make this time shorter or have less variability. One idea with potential to do this is known as pre-processing. This is an old idea from Operations Management where part of the setup time for a task is moved off-line, meaning it is done before the job is submitted to the system. Anyone who has ever worked in a restaurant is familiar with this idea, but there it is simply called Prep-time. Items that will be served later are staged, set in place, and partially prepared before the customer arrives to cut processing time after the order is placed. We can use that same idea in the clinic. Our experiment was to alter the process flow a bit. Instead of having the Resident review the case after the patient is placed in the Room and then having the first conversation about the case with the Attending after the Resident leaves the Room, we can tell the Resident in advance which patient he/she will see. That way the Resident can review the file and discuss the case with the Attending before the session starts. This should not eliminate the teaching time while the patient waits, but it is likely to shorten it.

The structure of the study is straight forward. We record activity times using the original system. We then introduce the new approach and run it for 30 days. During this time we continue collecting data on all Activity times. Again a confounding variable is introduced if the appointment schedule is not exactly the same before and after the intervention. We work around this by using the DES to consider the impact of having different sets of activity times under the two practice patterns with identical appointment schedules. Before the intervention was made the average Teach time was 12.9 minutes for NEW patients and 8.8 minutes for RETURN patients. The new approach reduced these times by 3.9 minutes for NEW patients and 2.9 minutes for RETURN patients. These results suggest that slightly changing the approach to teaching could have meaningful effects on waiting times and cycle times.

However, in this instance, it was the unintended consequences that proved to be more important. When the residents had a more clearly defined plan about how to handle each case, their interactions with the patients became more efficient. The residents reported that they felt more confident when treating the patients than they had before. While it is difficult to measure this effect in terms of times, both the residents and the Attending felt that the patients received better care under the new protocol.

6.5.5 Cyclic Scheduling

Considering the works mentioned above, one finding that occurred repeatedly was that the way the Resident was involved in the process had a large impact on system performance, and how that was done was often state dependent. Recall that we found that the system finds ways to move faster when the clinic is behind schedule. When a physician is working alone, this can be done simply by providing less face time to patients. When the system includes a Resident, an additional response is available in that either the Attending or the Resident can be dropped from the process for one or more patients. Our experience is that doctors strongly believe that the first approach produces a huge savings and they strongly oppose doing the second.

Our direct observation of multiple clinics produced some insights related to these issues. First, omitting the Attending does not save as much time as most Attendings think. The Resident is slower than the Attending. In addition, the Attending gets involved in more of these cases than they seem to realize. Many Attendings feel compelled to "at least say hi" to the patient even when the patient is not really on their schedule, and these visits often turn out to be longer than expected. Regarding the second approach, we have noticed a huge variance in terms of how willing the Attending is to omit the Resident from a case. Some almost never do it while others do it quite often. In one clinic we studied, we found that the Resident was omitted from roughly 30% of the cases on the clinic schedule. If this is done, it might explain why a medium volume or high volume clinic within the AMC could reduce cycle times after falling behind schedule to a greater extent than the low volume clinic can achieve. This can be done by instructing the Resident to handle one case while the Attending handles another and having the Attending exclude the Resident from one or more cases in an effort to catch up to the clinic schedule.

Accounting for these issues when creating an appointment schedule led us to the notion of Cyclic Scheduling. The idea is that the appointment schedule can be split into multiple subsets which repeat. We label these subsets Cycles. In each cycle we include one NEW patient and one RETURN patient scheduled to arrive at the same time. A third patient (RETURN) is scheduled to arrive at about the middle of the cycle. If both patients arrive at the start of the cycle we let the Resident start work on the NEW patient and the Attending handles the RETURN patient without the

Resident being involved. This was deemed acceptable because it was argued that most of the learning comes from the visits of NEW patients. If only one of the two patients arrives the standard process is used.

Process analysis tools produce some results about average cycle times in this setting, but predictions about waiting times are much more complex. This is true because these measurements are sure to be serially correlated. This means that if the waiting time for one patient rises, it is much more likely that the waiting time for the next patient also rises. The fact that waiting times are not independent events makes it tricky to identify statistical significance in changes to the average value. However, the more important issue is that it also conflates the identification of "managerial significance." Consider a clinic with two patients on a schedule. Using one process both patients experience 10 minute waits. Using a different process the first patient has no wait and the second patient has a 20 minute wait. Both processes produce the same average waiting time, but complaints are likely to be rare using the first process and much more likely using the second. This result is important to the clinic manager even though the average waiting times are not different in a statistical sense.

Due to the nuances of process behavior sometimes we want a much clearer depiction of how each patient's waiting time compares to that for the following patients. Considering this question using a queuing model is extremely difficult because the relevant distribution of activity times is state dependent, and the number of cycles is small. Consequently, steady state results are misleading. Studying this approach within a DES revealed that average Makespan, waiting time, and cycle times are significantly reduced using our Cyclic approach and the Resident is involved in a greater proportion of the cases scheduled.

6.6 Key Take-Aways

It may be useful to rephrase many of the findings mentioned in earlier sections to highlight lessons or key points. With this in mind we leave you with 7 key take-aways.

1. Process mapping using a fresh set of eyes is a pre-requisite for process improvement. Experience provides a wealth of insight but also brings a set of pre-conceived notions about what is possible. If you wish to help you have to observe the system yourself.

2. Don't skimp on data collection. Hospitals have a plethora of information systems and it is easy to assume that this data is both sufficient and accurate. Our experience has repeatedly taught us that this assumption is a leap that is not justified.

3. Model building has immense value, but complexity is rarely our friend. A deep understanding of some central trade-off is preferred over an elaborate statement of how impossible the task can be.

4. Metrics have power. Meaningful goals can only be set when performance can be defined in simple terms that everyone understands. This may mean thinking outside of standard terms such as waiting time or utilization. More nuanced metrics may be needed.

5. Look for simple changes rather than grand schemes. A series of small victories is needed before the organization will provide the buy-in required for larger plans to work. If we cannot get compliance for small changes, we will never succeed with larger ones.

6. Simulation provides many unanticipated benefits. The process mapping, data collection, model building, and virtual experimentation that it facilitates are all enlightening. Sometimes the unintended discoveries will be more useful than the original objective.

7. Incentives have power. When selling ideas about process changes, it is key to find a reward that resonates with the agents involved. Typically, we are not in a position to provide monetary incentives. In these settings we need to focus on some alternate outcome such as getting home earlier, or having time to go to lunch or attend a seminar. It is surprising how powerful these rewards can be.

In closing, while a great deal of time, effort, and money have been spent to improve health care processes, the problems involved have proven to be very difficult to solve. In this chapter we focused on a small but important sector of the problem space - that of appointment based clinics in Academic Medical Centers. One source of difficulty is that the medical field favors an experimental design based approach while many Operations Research tools are more mathematical and abstract. Consequently, one of our core messages is that those working to improve these systems need to find ways to bridge this gap by combining techniques. When this is done progress can be made and the insights generated can be spread more broadly. Our use of DES builds on tools of process mapping that most managers are familiar with and facilitates virtual experiments that are easier to control and use to generate quantitative metrics amenable to the kinds of statistical tests that research physicians routinely apply.

Finally, we would be remiss if we closed without emphasizing the fact that analysis of data is never sufficient to bring about the desired change. Hospitals in AMCs are often highly politicized environments with a hierarchical culture. This fact can generate multiple roadblocks that no amount of number crunching will ever overcome. One, not so subtle aspect of our method is that it typically involves embedding ourselves in the process over some periods of time and interacting repeatedly with the parties involved. We have initiated many projects not mentioned above because they did not result in real action. Each and every project that has been successful involved many hours of working with faculty, physicians, staff, and technicians of various types to collect information and get new perspectives. We have seen dozens of researchers perform much more impressive data analysis on huge data sets using tools that were much more powerful than those employed in these examples, only to end up with a wonderful analysis not linked to any implementation. When dealing with health care professionals we are often reminded of the old adage, "No one cares how much you know. They want to know how much you care." While we believe that the methodology outlined in this chapter is useful, our experience strongly suggests that the secret ingredient to making these projects work is the attention paid to the physicians, faculty, and especially staff involved who ultimately make the system run.

6.7 Review Material

To ensure that the material covered here can be applicable to your settings develop your responses to the scenarios laid out below.

6.7.1 Searching for a Better Appointment Schedule

Recall the appointment template for the specialty outpatient clinic described in the Prologue. Given the process improvement process laid out in Section 6.4 consider what would happen if the schedule shown in the prologue were replaced with a simple schedule of 9 appointments spaced 30 minutes apart.

1. What would you anticipate as the change in waiting times?

2. What would you anticipate as the change to the likelihood of finishing the schedule on time?

3. What would you anticipate as the change to the level of utilization of the key resources including the Nurse, the Attending, and the Exam Rooms?

6.7.2 Searching for a Better Appointment Schedule

Recall the appointment template for the specialty outpatient clinic described in the Prologue. Given the process improvement process laid out in Section 6.4 briefly discuss the questions listed below.

1. If the clinic is considering adding one NEW and one RETURN patient to the schedule, what metrics would you suggest they focus on to think about the repercussions of this change?

2. What data do you want to collect to help inform this decision?

3. Describe an experiment in the clinic to test the feasibility of this idea if you do not yet have all of the data that you want.

4. Explain how you would approach the problem of creating a new scheduling template for this modified setting.

5. Describe three process changes you would suggest they consider as part of this effort.

Chapter 7
Discrete Event Simulations: Concepts, Metrics, and Canonical Models

Abstract Our approach to improving health care delivery processes involves mapping of process flows, collection of detailed data on activity times, and discrete event simulation (DES). When information collected from an actual care delivery system is input into a DES, a virtual model of the system is created. Although process mapping is a pre-requisite for this step, many key elements of health care delivery systems make it insufficient for the analysis needed. These elements include high levels of variability, parallel processing, shared resources, state dependent behavior of patients and providers, mixing of different types of jobs, and emergency cases. In addition, though managers are often concerned with waiting times and overrunning scheduled end times, analysis of these systems is made much more complex by the fact that processing and patient waits take place in multiple stages that are often uncoordinated. In this chapter we introduce the reader to a collection of small models to convey the logic of the DES approach and present lessons on process management. None of these models will be sufficient to represent an entire clinic or hospital. However, out goal is to focus on pieces of the system in a way that highlights key issues and conveys enough information to explain why these models are needed, and how they can be profitably used.

7.1 Introduction

Organizations that deliver health care services can be incredibly complex. Consider a rather typical larger hospital. This hospital will include emergency departments (EDs), outpatient clinics, operating suites (ORs), several intensive care units (ICUs), inpatient beds in a variety of wards, and a host of additional departments/groups providing a plethora of supporting services. These units will be staffed by a mixture of salaried personnel, hourly workers, and contract labor. Patients will range in age from those not yet born, to those over 100 years old. Some patients will be in the system seeking advice from one provider while others will involve dozens or even hundreds of doctors, nurses, technicians, orderlies, social service workers, students, and other staff playing many roles. Consequently, a single model of this entire system is impossible to follow and impossible to construct without making a wide range of simplifying assumptions.

With all of this in mind we introduce representations of proto-typical units, each based on a small portion of the system in digestible bites. In particular we focus on a collection of stylized models of ED's, OR's, ICU's, and outpatient clinics. The purposes of these presentations are three-fold. First, we want to convey basic characteristics of each of these settings in a way that allows a user or visitor to quickly recognize fundamental trade-offs taking place. Second, we wish to highlight basic principles that are useful to understand any system that involves variability along multiple dimensions, and third, we seek to prepare you to take subsequent steps in efforts to improve the functioning of these system pieces.

We previously presented material focused on a proto-typical outpatient clinic that managed a collection of appointments. At that stage we included simple process maps that led to the construction of discrete event simulation (DES) models. We then used those models to facilitate quantitative discussions of a variety of issues related to Cycle Times (CTs), Throughput, waiting times, and Makespan. (Recall that Cycle Time refers to the duration from the start of a job to its completion. Throughput, is the rate at which jobs exit the system. Makespan is the duration between the start of the first job on a schedule and the completion of the last job.) The question arose as to why such model construction is needed when simple tools (also discussed in prior chapters) are available such as process mapping, Gantt Charts, or queuing models. The short answer to this question is that those tools provide valuable insights but are often insufficient to guide an improvement process, because the trade-offs that must be made take place along multiple dimensions and human decision makers have great difficulty handling all of these issues simultaneously.

Here we discuss a collection of issues and complications that are rather difficult to fully convey using simpler tools. Along the way we will present an argument that the use of DES models are invaluable to process improvement efforts. In addition we develop and highlight a number of generalizable insights that are broadly applicable to many health care settings. Although this note is not meant to be a primer on any particular simulation software, we aim to provide enough detail to give you a feel for how these approaches work and why further study of them is valuable.

As a word of caution, we reiterate that health care settings are so varied, so complex, and so important that no single model or chapter (or book) could ever hope to address all of the relevant issues. Rather than waving the white flag and saying that the system is too hard to understand, we choose to focus on stylized models of key parts. In some instances a small model of one part is enough to make headway on an important problem. In other settings a broader perspective is needed. (For a more detailed review of existing literature in the field see Zhang (2018), van Lent et al (2012), and Günal and Pidd (2010).) For those settings these smaller models can serve as building blocks for instances where a more comprehensive representation is required. Along the way we will interact with a number of small DES models. Copies of these models are available through the web page created to accompany the text. Instructions are also provided there on how to gain some access to the software involved. To organize our presentation, we mention a collection of issues that we have found DES particularly well suited to describe. In particular, our work has led us to a sort of top ten list of reasons that DES is so often critical to the process improvement process. In no particular order we provide that list below.

1. It's the variability stupid! We all have tremendous difficulty conceptualizing the significance of variability. Variability is the key driver of congestion and waiting times in almost all of the systems that we discuss here. If this significance cannot be conveyed to system managers, efforts to improve performance cannot work.

2. Patients and providers do not arrive on schedule. This statement is not meant to imply that the appointment schedule doesn't matter. For example, double and triple booking will obviously force someone to wait. However, the relationship between the schedule and arrival times is more nuanced than is commonly assumed. In addition, we repeatedly find that late arrival of providers is an important problem and more common than many would like to admit.

3. Specialization leads to waiting. Specialization is at odds with resource pooling. Division of labor leads to resources being dedicated to specific types of tasks but also increases waiting times. Sharing resources decreases waiting times, but the shared resources become stressed in subtle ways.

4. Mixing types of jobs increases waiting times. For example, it is quite common for NEW patients to take much longer than RETURN patients in a clinic setting, and blending them on the schedule can have counter-intuitive effects.[1]

5. Providers behave differently when they fall behind schedule. This simple fact has been observed in many other systems, and we have documented such behavior in multiple clinics. However, quantifying the linkages between this behavior and performance metrics is very difficult with most common process analysis tools.

6. Some jobs must take priority over others. Emergencies and unexpected complications will always arise, and the system must adjust to accommodate these events. If adjustments are made, then average times or the average level of a chosen metric may not be fully informative about process performance.

7. Waiting is not confined to waiting areas. Contrary to popular belief, moving a patient from a waiting area to an examination room (Room) has very little to

---

[1] We use the labels NEW and RETURN throughout this text to name specific types of patients and/or jobs.

do with waiting times. Is it proper to report that waiting times declined when an additional Room is added if it means that patients simply wait in an examination Room instead of a waiting area?

8. Metrics can drive performance. If clinic managers are assessed based only on a single metric such as waiting times in designated areas, we create a system that is easy to game and will produce multiple unintended results. Alternate measurements may be more illuminating and do a better job of driving desired behavior.

9. Some resources float from job to job. Having nursing staff or Residents pre-process or pre-position patients can greatly increase the productivity of more expensive providers. However, these actions make the environment much more difficult to visualize and monitor, because steps are being added to a process and perfect coordination of additional resources is tricky.

10. Waiting is BAD - but is certainly not the worst thing in the world. It is quite common to witness providers work long stretches without breaks in efforts to cut patient waiting time, but trade offs are being made. For example, it is easy to cut waiting times by increasing the gaps between appointments. However, the resulting increase in Makespan may be very expensive. In addition, processing rates and error rates will change over time when any resource is over-loaded for more than a few minutes.

In the remainder of this chapter we expound upon many of these observations as we discuss small DES models of key portions of a medical center. None of these models is complete. Each is designed to isolate the significance of key points, and we hope that their consideration leads to some general rules that may prove useful in more complete settings. We also note that we restrict our discussion to DES models focused on system performance. DES models that focus on disease progression, screening, of health behavior (Zhang (2018)) are outside the scope of this work. System dynamics and agent-based models are also used in the study of healthcare but are different in focus and nature (Günal and Pidd (2010)).

7.2 Outpatient Clinics

As a convenient starting point, we focus on the modeling of a simplified outpatient clinic with 12 patients arriving according to a simple schedule of one visit every 20 minutes. Thus, we plan to see three patients per hour for 4 hours. The process is defined by four steps or activities which we will label **Check-In**, **Vitals**, **Exam**, and **Check-Out**.

Upon arrival each patient goes through a process at a reception desk labeled **Check-In**. This step involves the front desk staff and has a minimum activity time

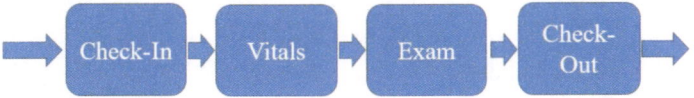

Fig. 7.1 A simplified process for a walk-in clinic

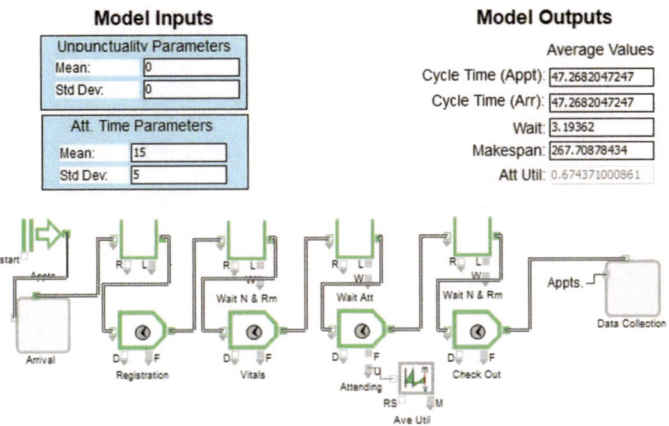

Fig. 7.2 Schematic of discrete event simulation for a walk-in clinic

of 5 minutes along with an additional duration (above this level) drawn from a log-normal distribution with a mean of 10 minutes and a standard deviation of 5 minutes.

After **Check-In** is completed, the patient resides in a waiting area until called upon by the nurse for the **Vitals** step. This involves the CA who leads the patient into an examination Room. The nurse also collects vital information and, upon leaving, flags the Room so that the attending physician (Attending) knows that a patient is waiting in the Room. The **Vitals** step involves both the nurse and a Room. The duration for this step has a minimum of 2 minutes plus the value of a log-normal variable with a mean of 5 minutes and a standard deviation of 2 minutes.

After some delay, the **Vitals** step is followed with the **Exam**, which involves the Attending along with the Room. This is the actual face-time between the Attending and the patient. The duration of this activity is drawn from a log-normal distribution with a mean of 15 minutes and a standard deviation of 5 minutes. Upon completion of this step the patient heads back to the front desk for **Check-Out**. This activity has a duration of 2 minutes plus the value of a log-normal variables with an average of 5 minutes and a standard deviation of 3 minutes. A simple map for this process is shown in Figure 7.1. A schematic of the DES model for the same setting is shown in Figure 7.2.[2]

---

[2] ExtendSim blocks copyright © 1987-2022 Imagine That Inc. All rights reserved.

Note that Figure 7.2 shows space for "Model Inputs" and "Model Outputs." When we discuss output from this DES model we will present average values collected over 1000 simulated 4-hour sessions. Modeling in this way allows us to experiment with this virtual system and isolate the impact of changes on behavior or structure.

The model inputs shown include information about the <u>unpunctuality</u> of the patients. Unpunctuality is the patient's actual arrival time minus the appointment time. Those who arrive early, as most patients do, will have a negative value for Unpunctuality. We treat this difference as a normally distributed random variable. In the simplest case, we will assume that all patients arrive on time. To simulate this scenario, we can set the mean and standard deviation of Unpunctuality to 0.

Since arrivals are 20 minutes apart and service times average 15 minutes (for the Attending) intuition suggests that the utilization for the Attending will be roughly 75% and waiting times will be minimal. After simulating 1000 sessions we present results in Table 1. All values of average times are reported in minutes, and all utilization levels are written as percentages. In addition, all utilization levels are calculated as busy time for that resource divided by the Makespan of the entire schedule. This definition ensures that calculated utilization will never exceed 100%. Alternative definitions may allow utilization to be greater than 100%. For example, if we define utilization as busy time divided by the target session length, we may get higher utilization values. The key point is that we keep in mind how our metrics are defined to avoid confusion and faulty conclusions.

TABLE 7.1: AVERAGE VALUES FOR BASE CASE

Metric	Average Value
Cycle Time (Appt)	47.28
Cycle Time (Arr)	47.28
Average Wait	3.19
Average Makespan	267.76
Attending Util.	67.44

Table 7.1 shows average CTs calculated in two ways. Each patient has an appointment time and an arrival time. As long as Unpunctuality is set to 0, these times are identical. CT is the exit time minus some start value. We show results when this start value is either the appointment time (Appt) or the Arrival time (Arr). These values are identical for the moment, but that assumption will be relaxed later. The table also shows average waiting times of 3.19 minutes. For now, this is only the time spent in the waiting room before the **Vitals** step. As expected, this setting produces minimal, but positive waits. We see that the average Makespan is roughly 268 minutes. Recall that the clinic was assumed to run for 4-hours or 240 minutes. Hence, on average the clinic is running 27 minutes beyond this point in each session. Fi-

nally, the table shows an average utilization level for the Attending of roughly 67%. This is below the expected value of 75% because Makespan routinely exceeds the 240 minute target. Since average Makespan is higher, the calculated utilization level drops below the expected value.

Several additional observations are of note at this stage. First, in this basic model we assumed that all patients arrive exactly on time. This is a common assumption in most of the formal research in this field, although it is surely not accurate. The assumption is often made to keep the focus on the impact of changes within the clinic. Second, we note that the overtime operations of this clinic must incur some cost, even though the Attending is busy roughly 2/3 of the time. This is a fundamental problem. Most hospitals cannot stay solvent if they pay the most expensive personnel to be idle one third of the time, especially if they must also pay (in some form) for 1/2 hour of overtime operation for a typical clinic session.

One of the main advantages of using DES as a portion of the process improvement process is that it allows us to eliminate some confounding variables from a model and introduce them in a controlled way. By adding a variable into a model or altering a variable in otherwise identical models, we can showcase the impact of a single change as the selected variable interacts with the rest of the system. One example of this idea is the inclusion of Unpunctuality. The obvious fact is that people do not arrive exactly at the appointed time, and the variance may alter system performance. This patient behavior is easily added to our model by adjusting the parameters of the distribution from which Unpunctuality is drawn. In the schematic of the DES model shown in Figure 7.2 one block is labeled "Arrival." In this block we add a log-normally distributed variable to the appointment time to get the actual arrival time. Since most patients arrive before their appointment time, the mean of this variable is negative. Making the mean and variance of this value -15, and 5 minutes respectively, we can re-run the model and see new results. We label this setting Case A and display results from the Base Case along with Case A in Table 7.2.

TABLE 2: AVERAGE VALUES WITH PATIENT UNPUNCTUALITY VS BASE CASE

Metric	Base Case	Case A
Cycle Time (Appt)	47.27	37.20
Cycle Time (Arr)	47.27	50.92
Average Wait	3.19	6.81
Average Makespan	267.76	254.26
Attending Util.	67.44	70.88

We immediately note that average waiting times are still quite attractive at roughly 7 minutes per patient. This is a wonderful result if our only concern is waiting times and lends support to the idea that the appointment schedule and Unpunctuality are not factors that should be of great concern. We also note that Makespan has declined significantly, largely because most patients arrive before the appointment time. Early arrivals frequently allow the last patient to leave the system near the targeted ending time of 240 minutes. In addition, the average CT has dropped from 47.04 to 37.20 minutes when it is calculated based on appointment times, it increases slightly when it is calculated based on arrival time. Since patients typically arrive early, they may be seen prior to their appointment time. Accounting for this behavior results in a significant decrease in the value of exit time minus appointment time.

These data highlight the fact that the selection of a metric is deceptively important when studying these systems and that this selection is not to be taken lightly. One can make a system look much better or worse simply by selecting different metrics at different stages of the analysis. It is critical to be consistent across problem settings in the display of metrics to avoid misleading the reader or manager.

A study of these results also reveals an additional point. When Unpunctuality is accounted for, average CT calculated with appointment times falls but average CT calculated with arrival times rises. Using metrics and insights drawn from research that ignores the difference between appointment times and arrival times can induce perverse incentives. Urging patients to show up earlier while using CT metrics based on appointment times may lead one to conclude that system performance is excellent from an administrator's perspective even though it is getting worse from the patient's perspective. Models that ignore Unpunctuality may lead someone to conclude that a system change improves performance when in fact it does not.

Table 7.3 shows results from the same setting summarized in Table 2 with one additional adjustment. We modify Case A by delaying the start time for the first patient by an exponentially distributed amount with an average of one minute. It is not unusual to have some delay in rooming the first patient on the schedule for a variety of reasons including tardiness of staff or the Attending, a morning meeting where the Attending interacts with staff or Residents, or traffic delays for the first patient on the schedule. Including this small change (Case B) leads to the results shown below.

TABLE 3: AVERAGE VALUES FOR BASE CASE, CASE A, AND CASEB

Metric	Base Case	Case A	Case B
Cycle Time (Appt)	47.27	37.20	40.44
Cycle Time (Arr)	47.27	50.92	52.74
Average Wait	3.19	6.81	8.82
Average Makespan	267.76	254.26	254.71
Attending Util.	67.44	70.88	70.48

Note that while an event such as provider tardiness is likely to directly affect only the first patient on the schedule, the total increase in waiting time can ripple through the rest of the day. The increase in waiting time of roughly 2 minutes is spread among all patients. In other words this increase of 2 minutes per patient is actually an increase of 24 minutes of waiting time for the population. Each minute of tardiness for the provider produces 2 minutes of increased waiting for the patient group. In this sense, the system is much more sensitive to provider tardiness than to patient tardiness.

7.2.1 Variability and System Performance

Unfortunately, these results are not at all what we typically see in practice. The fiscal reality of most health care settings is that having a clinic in which the most expensive resources are utilized roughly 2/3 of the time is not a viable option. It is most likely that a private practice with this level of utilization would find it difficult to stay in business, and no upper level administrator in an academic medical center (AMC) could afford to let this stand. To make our model more realistic, let us adjust the Attending's average visit time to be 18 minutes, instead of 15. This change should increase utilization to around 90%. Since 18 is still significantly less than the 20 minutes between arrivals, the schedule remains feasible. Making this adjustment yields average waiting times of 11.5 minutes and an average Makespan of 264 minutes. Thus, a more realistic assumption about a target utilization level significantly increases waiting times and the need to run beyond the scheduled completion time for the clinic.

Of course, there is one critical element that we have deliberately understated to this point. Let us make our model more realistic again by increasing the variance of the service time as well. Standard queueing models assume that service times are exponentially distributed. If this is the case then we will have the standard deviation of service time equal to the mean. Making this change (Case C) implies that the mean and standard deviation of the Attending's time should both be 18. Table 7.4 displays results for these 4 scenarios.

TABLE 7.4: AVERAGE VALUES FOR BASE CASE, CASE A, AND CASEB

Metric	Base Case	Case A	Case B	Case C
Cycle Time (Appt)	47.27	37.20	40.44	56.99
Cycle Time (Arr)	47.27	50.92	52.74	70.71
Average Wait	3.19	6.81	8.82	23.99
Average Makespan	267.76	254.26	254.71	283.46
Attending Util.	67.44	70.88	70.48	74.35

These changes result in average waiting times and Makespan values of roughly 24 minutes and 283 minutes respectively. These values are much closer to what we expect to see in practice. If we make a parallel increase to the variance of Unpunctuality we get values of 27 and 289 minutes respectively. These results lend support to two key observations. First, variability is the key driver of waiting times and the need for overtime. Second, the variability within the clinic walls is much more important than the variability outside of it, in the sense that the variance of the Attending's processing time has a much greater effect on waiting times than the variability of Unpunctuality.

Finally, note that standard queueing models are not capable of capturing all of the nuances of patient and provider behavior that we have included here, even in these very simple models. The vast majority of queueing models assume that processing times are exponentially distributed. This assumption also implies that the point in time with the highest probability of job completion is in the first minute. In several steps included in our models we impose a minimum duration, because each provider is obligated to collect basic information. Thus, a lower bound of 2-5 minutes is reasonable for many process steps. In addition, our usage of log-normally distributed variables allows us to separate the impact of changes to the means as opposed to changes in the variance. This ability to isolate an effect is a key benefit of using DES models.

7.2.2 Pooling Resources

Each issue raised on our list of concerns presents characteristics that are difficult to convey in a simple diagram and/or produce counter-intuitive results that demand elucidation. One classic trade-off in health care settings is the value of specialization when balanced against its impact on congestion. To be clear, we are only referring to assignment of resources to specific job types where there is no medical imperative to do so. Clearly a podiatrist and a psychiatrist cannot be interchanged in a care protocol. However, for some resources such as Rooms and staff there are many instances in which assigning a resource to a specific provider is not medically critical and has unintended negative consequences.

Consider a modification of our Base Case to focus upon a setting without appointments. In this example, let us assume that there is no appointment schedule, but instead patients arrive on average every 10 minutes (instead of 20) and that the time between arrivals follows an exponential distribution. (We also double the capacity at the front desk for sake of consistency.) To eliminate the number of arrivals as a confounding variable, let us assume that the clinic closes each day after serving 50 patients. Let us also assume that we have two Attending physicians in this clinic and two Rooms. We have two obvious choices here. We can assign one Room to each of the two Attendings. Alternatively, we can simply let each arriving patient go to the first available Room. For now let us assume that patients are assigned to a physician randomly. When patients go to the first available Room, we say that the Rooms are pooled. Given two Rooms and two Attendings we label this scenario Base Case 2. (Table 7.5)

TABLE 7.5: AVERAGE VALUES WHEN ROOMS ARE POOLED

Metric	Average Value
Cycle Time (Arr)	80.52
Average Wait	25.12
Average Makespan	591.89
Attending Util.	76.49

Figure 7.3 shows the DES model for a slightly different arrangement in which each of the two Rooms is assigned to one provider [3]. The main change is that after patients move through **Check-In** they are split randomly to represent assignment to one of the two Attendings (Case 2B). After that happens the patient experiences the same process flow as in Base Case 2. After patients leave the Room these two flows merge into one before moving on to **Check-Out**. Table 7.6 shows the performance metrics including this modified case.

TABLE 7.6: AVERAGE VALUES WHEN ROOMS ARE PARALLEL

Metric	Base Case 2	Case 2B
Cycle Time (Arr)	80.52	100.40
Average Wait	25.12	97.76
Average Makespan	591.89	639.82
Attending Util.	76.49	70.53

Running two parallel systems increases the average waiting time by roughly 70 minutes. Since the same amount of work is being done in both settings, we would hope that the utilization would be roughly the same. However, this is clearly not the case. Makespan for the parallel setting is almost 48 minutes longer, even though the busy time for the Attendings should be the same. Consequently, Attending utilization has decreased.

When the system is run in parallel, patients experience longer waits because they may need to wait for a provider even when a Room is available, if that Room is assigned to the other provider. Consequently, waiting times and Makespan both increase. As a secondary problem, we will also miss opportunities in which one Attending could have patients in both Rooms simultaneously if the other Attending is

---

[3] ExtendSim blocks copyright © 1987-2022 Imagine That Inc. All rights reserved.

not needed at that time. Allowing two patients to be roomed for the same provider provides a small time savings because **Vitals** can be carried out in one Room while the Attending examines a different patient in the other. The absence of pooling hurts in both respects.

It can be difficult to accept how large this difference in CT is for these two cases. Let us consider another context. In a supermarket we typically see multiple cashiers with a line of customers waiting at each one. Imagine that you are in a line and a customer in front of you attempts to buy an item that requires a price check. This process may involve another store employee literally running back to some shelf space to find a price. Now imagine if this happens multiple times for the same basket of goods for some customer. The processing time for that job may become 10 times longer than the average. In the supermarket setting those waiting behind this customer can simply change lines. If you could not change lines, then your waiting time could be 10 times longer than the average. Having pooled Rooms is akin to being able to change lines when some job takes much longer than expected. Having dedicated Rooms eliminates this option, and average waiting times can explode.

Before leaving this topic, we note that these models assume that the clinic closes after treating 50 patients. We made this assumption to make each scenario comparable to the others in this section. Thus, a 97 minute average waiting time applies to each of the 50 patients treated. When comparing these two settings the total waiting time has increased by 50 * (97 - 25) = 3600 minutes. For the sake of argument let

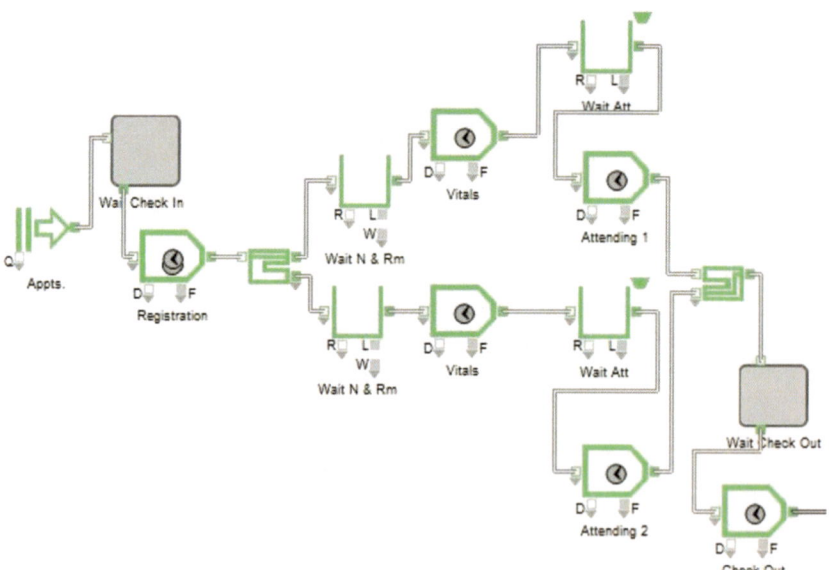

Fig. 7.3 A walk-in clinic with parallel processing

us place a value on this waiting time of $1 per minute. Using this scale, researchers typically assume that the cost of an additional minute of Makespan is 10 or 20 times the per minute cost of patient waiting. Assuming a value here of $15 per minute of added Makespan, we can say that the cost of running these two Rooms in parallel is roughly $3600 + 15 * (639.82 - 591.89) = $4318.95. When quantified in this way we can put a price on the behavior of assigning resources to specific providers. This type of information can help guide decisions about process design.

The trade-off is that, in all likelihood this assignment was made for some reason other than medical requirements. For example, assigning providers to Rooms may cut down on confusion or allow each Room to be set up in some way that is idiosyncratic to that provider. This benefit must be balanced against some coherent measure of cost to decide whether it makes sense. Similar arguments can be made about sharing any other resource such as desk staff, machinery, equipment, etc. The intuition that assigning assets exclusively to a more expensive resource will increase the productivity of that resource must be verified, and its benefits must be carefully weighed against the increase in congestion that such an assignment will create.

In practice we have seen this arrangement play out in a surprising proportion of clinics in which physicians or service lines share common resources. Rarely do we see any well thought out justification for such practices. More commonly, it simply evolves over time based on habit or preferences of the providers involved. No one intends to increase waiting times and overtime operations. It is often difficult to see these unintended consequences of simple efforts to allow care providers to be comfortable in the working space. We are not claiming that such accommodations are always unwarranted. However, we do see value in exploring the ramifications of such arrangements and DES is a useful tool for doing so.

7.2.3 Mixing Patient Types

It is common for health care providers to deal with cases that have widely varying characteristics. One simple example is an outpatient clinic that mixes NEW and RE-TURN patients. Virtually every clinic that we have studied uses this approach and has significant differences in processing times for these different populations. It is almost inevitable for the first visit of a NEW patient to be longer if it includes some data collection related to patient history. This data collection is likely to extend the activity times for the **Check-In**, **Exam**, and **Check-Out** activities. Let us return to the setting of Table 7.2 and make another small change. Instead of having all patients require an average of 18 minutes of Attending time, let us have half of these cases need an average of 9 minutes. These cases may be our proxy for RETURN patients. We allow the other half to need an average of 27 minutes. This is our proxy for NEW patients. (We ignore the increases in activity times for the other steps for the time being.) The average total activity time across all cases is the same as before, and remains 18 minutes for the **Exam** step. Table 7.7 shows average metrics across these two settings: all cases of one type that each average 18 minutes (Case A) vs cases of two distinct types that blend those that average 9 and 27 minutes respectively (Case NR, which blends NEW and RETURN cases).

TABLE 7.7: SINGLE CASE TYPE VS MIXED TYPES

Metric	Case A	Case NR
Cycle Time (Appt)	61.14	63.97
Cycle Time (Arr)	74.40	77.29
Average Wait	27.35	23.96
Average Makespan	289.85	296.30
Attending Util.	73.80	70.76

We note that CT and Makespan have each increased, but average waiting times have actually fallen even though the total work to be done is the same (on average). These results highlight the fact that variability can take multiple forms and has varying effects. In this model we have a variance within each job type, and we are also adding variance across job types. Simple process analysis would not suggest that this would be an issue because, in expectation, the workload is the same. When dealing with variability along multiple dimensions simultaneously, it becomes very difficult to predict how a system change will play out. Thus, simulation models often provide important insights that were not expected and not easy to find using other means.

7.2.4 State Dependent Face Time

Virtually all of the published works in health care that focus on process improvement assume (either explicitly or implicitly) that processing rates do not change over the course of a day or a clinic session. This assumption facilitates simple approaches including the use of standard queuing models, which also typically assume exponential service times. In our experience the assumption of exponential service times is problematic because it overstates the probability of having extremely low processing times. The shape of the exponential distribution ensures that the minute with the greatest likelihood of completion for each job is the first. However, examination times very close to 0 are virtually impossible in practice because any patient will become irate if the Attending does not stay in the Room long enough to find out why the patient is there. This issue can be dealt with fairly easily within a DES model by simply adding some lower bound on the service time as we have done here. On the other hand, this type of adjustment is very difficult to account for in standard queueing models.

If face time actually changes depending on the state of the system, we have a much more difficult situation to analyze. Queuing models do exist in which the server speed is set as a function of queue length. These esoteric models are uncommon and not well understood by most readers. In addition, the assumption is not entirely consistent with our observations. Many attending physicians never set foot in the waiting area and don't know how long the queue actually is. Even if the Attending looks in the waiting area, it is not clear how many of the inhabitants are patients as opposed to friends and family. However, experienced care providers do develop a sort of sixth sense that tells them when they are falling behind schedule.

If I am scheduled to see a patient every 20 minutes and I have been in clinic for 2 hours and completed only 3 patients, I know I am behind schedule; it is quite natural to assume that I will respond in some way. As mentioned elsewhere, we have observed this behavior in a variety of clinics including private practices with one Attending, medium volume clinics with one Attending on duty working with Residents, and larger volume clinics with multiple Attendings and Residents on service (Chambers et al (2016)). In each of these cases we verified that when the clinic gets behind schedule the system simply runs faster. There are also nuances to how this gets done.

In the single-physician setting we have documented that the Attending simply spends less face time with each patient. In teaching hospitals the interaction is more complex. In some instances the Attending and a Resident can use parallel processing in which the Attending deals with one patient while the Resident deals with another. In other cases the Attending has the option to simply omit the Resident from the process for selected cases. These measures can dramatically increase processing rates because the Attending is typically much faster than the Resident when dealing with the same information.

Modeling this reality in a simple way is tricky for several reasons. First, the acceleration is state dependent, meaning we cannot simply assume it is in place from start to finish. Second, this change in behavior works in response to congestion. Since the server speeds up when behind schedule, the system has the capability to get back on schedule. Thus, to an outside observer considering an entire clinic session, the system may look fairly stable even though variability has actually increased. Finally, since it is not the queue length that triggers the change, but the time itself relative to prior throughput, this element is very difficult to build into a queuing model. Standard queuing models are designed to provide steady state results. This term means that the mathematical formulas provide long term averages assuming that no behavior changes. When the system behavior changes from one minute to the next, the system never reaches a steady state - thus steady state results are not very informative.

Fortunately, DES models can be built that capture this feature without too much added complexity. We can accomplish this feat by adding a collection of blocks that check the time at which a patient reaches the **Exam** step. This time is compared to the appointment time to determine whether the system is running on time or behind schedule. If the system is behind schedule, the predicted face time with the Attending is scaled back by some proposed amount in our virtual clinic. We can make the magnitude of this acceleration whatever value we like. Table 8 shows metrics of system performance under the same schedule used to develop the data shown in Table 7.2 with an important additional element labeled <u>Factor</u>. A value of 0.8 for this factor means that the face time with the Attending for a patient when the system is behind schedule is set to 80% of its original value for that patient. In other words, we include an acceleration for the Attending when the system is running behind schedule.

TABLE 7.8: AVERAGE VALUES WITH STATE DEPENDENT PROCESSING RATES

Factor	1.0	0.9	0.8	0.7
Cycle Time (Appt)	58.36	52.45	46.71	42.98
Cycle Time (Arr)	72.07	66.14	60.46	56.66
Average Wait	75.03	71.55	67.50	64.14
Average Makespan	285.47	279.67	269.14	265.47
Attending Util.	75.03	71.55	67.50	64.14

As expected, system performance improves noticeably when the acceleration effect is accounted for. Several observations are warranted here. First, we did not claim that the Attending accelerates for all patients. If that had been the case, the improvements would have been much greater. Second, we are implicitly working with the assumption that this behavioral adaptation is free. Workers of many types can simply "run faster" for a time, and this behavior is quite natural. However, it will have its limits. The more face time is cut, the greater the risk of errors and decreased patient satisfaction. Finally, the magnitude of this effect suggests that it must be accounted for when considering data before and after any intervention. Ignoring this fact makes it impossible to be completely sure that a singular system change is the only explanation for changes in process performance. Having agents accelerate in an effort to show results can confound the results seen in many improvement efforts.

It is worthwhile to pause for a moment and think through some aspects of what this means. We have seen instances where a change has been made to a delivery system and an improvement was recorded over a short period of time. One possible explanation for the improvement is that the change had a permanent effect. However, another explanation is that some element of the system "runs faster" while the system is being watched. Once the novelty of the change wears off, the system may drift back to older patterns and performance levels. On the other hand, some changes can be made to a system that actually make matters worse, but some agent in the system may be able to compensate by operating under greater stress for a while. The result can be that you have done damage to the system, and staff have simply accommodated to prevent the change from harming patients. The nobility of health care providers can make research on process improvements deceptively difficult. These sorts of adjustments can make your decent ideas seem better than they are (for a time) or make your bad ideas seem less damaging. Consequently, deep familiarity with the system and its participants is necessary to do effective work in this space. You should always be wary of numerical analysis based only on data draws from various information systems if those doing the analysis do not spend extended periods of time observing the process in action.

7.3 Emergency Departments

For most episodes of care, the outpatient clinic is the entry point into the health care system. However, an alternate entry point of note is the ED. These facilities are unique in that they are almost exclusively set up to handle random arrivals, including many cases that are "true emergencies." By this term we mean people with life-threatening conditions that must be attended to in very short order (bleeding, difficulty breathing, loss of consciousness, severe chest pains, signs of a stroke, etc.). However, the economic reality of the health care marketplace in the US has created incentives for many people without a regular primary care provider to use the ED as a makeshift walk-in clinic. Consequently, these facilities routinely handle a mixture of critical cases and other visits with a much lower level of urgency. In Figure 7.4 we depict a very simple simulation model of a generic ED.[4] Salient features of this model include:

1. The time between arrivals follows an exponential distribution and we set the mean at 20 minutes.

2. 20% of arrivals are emergency cases and are assigned a higher priority than the other cases.

3. 20% of ED arrivals result in an admission to the hospital.

4. Admitted patients can leave the ED once a room is available in the hospital, and these resources become available randomly.

One odd feature of ED waiting times in the US is that for many years hospitals were allowed to define the term as they saw fit and to advertise these values even when neighboring hospitals defined the term differently. To cut down on these discrepancies, the Centers for Medicare & Medicaid Services (CMS) established a standard definition for ED waiting time as the interval between the time a patient walks in the door and the time that the patients is evaluated by a licensed provider

---

[4] ExtendSim blocks copyright © 1987-2022 Imagine That Inc. All rights reserved.

(a doctor, physician's assistant or nurse practitioner). For patients who are admitted to hospitals after passing through the ED, the hospitals also report the waiting time between when this decision is made and when the patient is placed in a room. Unfortunately, these values are often entered by hand, which raises some concerns about their accuracy. In addition, we know that some patients leave the ED before being seen. Estimates of this proportion range from one to 9% (Peterson et al (2019), Vieth and Rhodes (2006)).

Just as we did in the outpatient setting, we assume in this model that the average time for the Attending is 18 minutes. Simulating this system for 50 cases yields an average cycle time of 104 minutes and an average wait of 61 minutes. These averages mask great differences in the experiences of different types of patients. In our basic model we simply assumed that patients are treated using a first-come-first-served protocol. If we change the function of the queue before the step of putting a patient in an Room such that higher priority patients move to the front of the line, we can look at the waiting times for these two populations. We see that waiting times for high and low priority patients are 22 and 70 minutes respectively. Thus, a priority system that naturally occurs in these settings creates vastly different experiences for the system users. These differences may be entirely necessary. A patient who enters the ED and is bleeding may die if nothing is done immediately whereas the medical condition of many other patients may not change over several hours. One

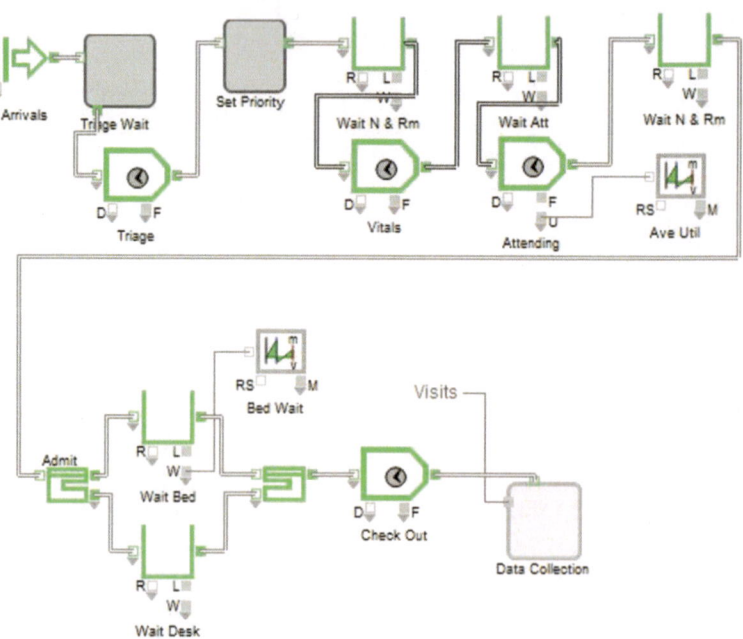

Fig. 7.4 An ED with random arrivals

clear down side of this reality is that 80% of these patients are likely to be highly upset after waiting roughly 100 minutes to be seen for a condition that was not life threatening to begin with.

7.3.1 Downstream Resources and Blocking

Though a significant percentage of patients processed through the ED will need to be admitted to the hospital, these admits do not necessarily flow immediately upon discharge from the ED to a bed on one of the floors (Kolker (2013)). One way to explore the nature of this delay is to assume that these beds become available after random intervals. In other words, we can model this as an "arrival" of an available bed with inter-arrival times defined by an exponential variable. Note that, even if beds become available at the same rate (on average) as requests for a transfer from the ED to the floor, we will still have instances in which patients have to wait to be moved from one space to the next. Adding this complication allows us to focus on an additional metric for waiting time, which is the wait between the decision to admit and movement into a room in one of the hospital wards. To simulate this aspect of the process we added a **Bedding** Activity to simulate the "arrival" of an available bed. By selecting different parameters for the average time between arrivals of bed availability we can simulate systems with different lags related to patient transfers. Average **Bedding** values and the resulting waiting times are shown in Table 7.9.

TABLE 7.9: AVERAGE VALUES OF SYSTEM METRICS WITH VARYING AVERAGE TIMES
TO THE NEXT AVAILABLE BED

Mean Bed Arrival Time	10 Min	20 Min	30 Min	40 Min
Cycle Time (Arr)	101.93	109.41	170.52	340.77
Total Wait	60.05	62.67	104.61	252.25
Wait for Bed	1.16	3.52	85.62	406.17

Again, we recognize that these values may seem shocking to those who have never experienced such a wait. However, several researchers report average transfer times in excess of 6 hours (Singer et al (2011)). One report involving California hospitals found an average value of roughly 336 minutes. In our model this wait time would be achieved with an average **Bedding** time of roughly 27 minutes. These results highlight several key points. First, blocking is quite common in these systems. Blocking refers to the phenomenon in which part of the system has performed the needed tasks but patient flow is blocked because a needed downstream resource is unavailable. Second, system performance can be very sensitive to the rate as which a downstream resource becomes available. Finally, we note that we have simplified the model in that we are implicitly assuming that ample examination Rooms are always available. If they are not, then the blocking experienced by patients who need to be admitted will eventually cause a deterioration in the performance of the ED itself. We have witnessed ED's work around this problem by staging patients in hallways as holding areas until beds become available. This fix presents a stressful and unpleasant experience for all involved.

Note that this simple ED model also implicitly assumes that all of the steps needed for patient evaluation and treatment in the ED are carried out by the attending physician. This is obviously a very strong assumption. For example, virtually all patients admitted to the ED will require some lab work as part of their work-up. Hence, a request must be made for some outside resource. That work will be done once the resource is available and information must be returned to the ED staff before a patient can move on to a subsequent step. In other words, the delay that we model here related to movement to a bed actually had parallels earlier in the process. The ED may have been forced to wait for multiple external resources including a pathology lab, an imaging center, and one or more specialists from another department. If we have similar delays regarding the availability of these resources, it becomes easy to understand why 6 to 12 hour ED visit times are actually quite common.

7.3.2 Length of Stay from ED to Discharge

The examples in the previous section were written as though all ED patients are either discharged or sent directly to a bed on one of the hospital floors. Clearly, the reality is much more complex. Let us add a bit more realism by considering a common sequence for trauma cases. We will have this subset of the patient population arrive in the ED at a rate of one every 2 hours. Service time in the ED will average 4 hours. For the sake of clarity we will assume that all inter-arrival and service times in this example are exponentially distributed. Let us then have these patients travel to the OR for some procedure and spend an average of 2 hours there. After leaving the OR these patients spend an average of 24 hours in an ICU followed by 48 hours in a regular bed. Finally, the patient is discharged through a process that takes 60 minutes. This step may include locating a rehabilitation facility, arranging transportation for the patient, providing prescriptions and instructions, updating of all records and billing information, and other assorted sign-offs and approvals. A simple schematic of this system is shown in Figure 7.5.[5]

If we seek to track flows through this network we have multiple capacity constraints to consider. To make the problem easier we assume that the capacity in the ED is effectively infinite. For ease of scaling, we consider 6 ORs, 24 ICU beds, and 48 beds on the floor. Since the ED never closes we will simulate these flows for 360

---

[5] ExtendSim blocks copyright © 1987-2022 Imagine That Inc. All rights reserved.

days. One complicating characteristic of this system is that if no unit of the downstream resource is available, the patient will be held in the current unit until he or she can be moved. In other words, if the OR is full, the patient will be stabilized in the ED. If no bed in the ICU is available, the patient will be boarded in the OR until space is cleared, and so on. In this setting, blocking of the flows is the critical issue. Again, blocking means that a job is ready to proceed to the next step but cannot do so because some resource is busy with another task. Table 7.10 shows the proportion of the time that each of the four key resources listed are full given different levels of the average discharge time.

TABLE 7.10: PERFORMANCE METRICS OF TRAUMA RELATED FLOWS

Mean Discharge Time	60 Min	90 Min	120 Min	150 Min
Discharge full (%)	49.29	75.49	97.67	96.67
Floor full (%)	0.00	0.00	67.62	97.50
ICU full (%)	0.00	0.00	58.84	97.11
OR full (%)	0.00	0.00	45.21	96.67

Consider the impact on this system when longer times to facilitate discharge are required. If the discharge process averages one hour, then the associated resources are occupied roughly half the time and no blocking occurs earlier in the system. However, if this process averages 2 hours (120 minutes) instead of one, the entire system backs up and most patients will experience at least one instance in which movement to the next step in the chain is blocked.

One may ask why those managing this system would allow the activity with the shortest processing time to cause congestion throughout so much of the hospital. While the reasons are myriad, some components are clear. First, reducing the speed of the discharge process leads to blocking that may be realized much earlier in the series of activities. Thus, it may not be at all obvious to the parties involved that discharge execution is ultimately the cause. Second, ED's, OR's and ICU's are incredibly expensive units to build, equip and staff. Consequently, maximizing their utilization is something of a priority, and everyone expects these units to be busy all the time. It does not set off an alarm to see them full as long as patients are cared for until they can be moved.

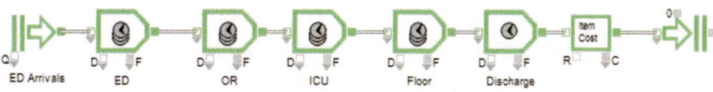

Fig. 7.5 Flows from emergency department (ED) through discharge. ICU, intensive care unit; OR, operating room.

In addition, as the patient becomes healthier, he or she is more able to tolerate waiting. Having to spend an extra few hours resting in bed before going home is likely to be the least of their worries and it is hard to intuit how reducing this time should ever be a priority. Finally, the discharge step involves coordination with some entities outside the control of the hospital. Either a step-down unit such as a rehabilitation center must be identified and managed, or more commonly family members must be willing and available to handle multiple elements of the process. As a consequence, needing a few hours to facilitate this activity is not surprising in the least. The fact that a process often viewed as an afterthought plays such a vital role in ensuring that patient flow proceeds according to plan is easy to overlook in the grand scheme of things. Using simple models such as those presented here is immensely valuable for gaining insights into this system behavior.

7.4 Key Take-Aways

Health care service delivery processes are infinitely varied in terms of resources used, volumes faced, activity time distributions involved, arrival methods, and real time adjustments needed to accommodate emergencies, resource shortages, blocking and interruptions. Consequently, it is literally impossible to argue that any single approach or tool tells the entire story for every setting. Process mapping conveys much information about process structure and resource placement. These maps are useful snapshots of reality but are often insufficient for detailed planning. Its like trying to run a corporation based simply on what is shown on a balance sheet. The information is quite valuable but clearly incomplete.

Other tools from Industrial Engineering such as Gantt charts provide a useful depiction of a finite number of cases as they flow through a system over time. These are great supplements to arocess analysis but say little about the effect of variability. The sophisticated models found in queuing theory embrace the significance of variability and provide some insights when the assumptions of the models are not too far afield from reality. The trade-off with these models is that they provide long term averages, and it is often dangerous to use these values as proxies for reality.

Our use of DES for the study of these systems was made necessary by the plethora of times in which we observed that the living, adapting system never perfectly fits a process flow diagram or the limiting assumptions of a queuing model. A variety of factors are difficult to build into a map or a simpler model. The output of DES includes a collection of user-defined metrics that can be created to fit the problem of interest and changed from one setting to the next as needed. This capability facilitates experimentation in a virtual world that can mimic what is found in practice. This quality makes these models invaluable in efforts to describe, predict, and prescribe remedies related to system performance. We close with a listing of several key messages from the models discussed above.

1. Accounting for tardiness and early arrivals is necessary to have a healthy under-standing of case flow.

2. High levels of variability are inherent in the nature of many health care processes and must be included in models of systems that deliver care if they are to be most useful.

3. The use of specialized resources is natural in complex settings but can dramat-ically alter system performance. Consequently, this practice should be thought through carefully if patient flow is valued.

4. Variability exists along multiple dimensions including inter-arrival times, service times, mixture of job types, evolving processing rates, and flows along multiple paths simultaneously. It is often very difficult (if not impossible) to predict how all of these dimensions of variability will interact without some formal modeling to capture them.

5. When viewing a resource in isolation, it is impossible to account for block-ing caused by the occupation of downstream resources or for resources that are starved of work owing to the variable loads on upstream resources. Consequently, the study of a resource network requires analysis that extends beyond the walls of a single clinic or unit.

6. We must fight against thought patterns that lead us to focus only on the most ex-pensive resources, or assumptions that steps at the end of the chain are of lessor importance. It often takes a formal model to make this clear.

One of our primary aims in this work is to illustrate these points and to provide tools that support these findings and help manage settings in which the complexity discussed here must be dealt with on a daily basis.

7.5 Review Material & Prior Works

Although this is not a manual on the creation of DES, we do wish to help develop an understanding of the types of settings and questions that are best addressed with them. With this in mind we provide a collection of small DES models that the reader can interact with to deepen the understanding of the material presented and to ex-plore the tool for application to other settings.

These models are each built using ExtendSim and related software is available from ExtendSim.com. The trial version or student version of the software is sufficient to rum the models referenced here. Whenever one of these models is opened, an area of the model is labeled "Input Parameters." Users can make adjustments to the relevant activity time and arrival time distributions in this area of the model to address questions posed below. Detailed explanations and tutorials on the use of this software package to model healthcare settings is available in Karuppan et al (2021), Strickland (2010), and Laguna and Marklund (2005). Several similar models using an alternate software platform are discussed in Kolker (2010a), Kolker (2010b), Kolker (2011), and Kolker and Story (2012).

While none of these models are complete depictions of settings that we have studied, they are each distilled from settings that we have simulated in greater detail using the same software platform referred to above. Details about our use of DES in system analysis and improvement projects are available in Chambers et al (2016), Chambers and Williams (2017b), Chambers and Williams (2017a), Chambers et al (2018), Conley et al (2016), Elnahal et al (2015a), Williams et al (2012), Williams et al (2014), and Williams et al (2015).

7.5.1 Patient Unpunctuality

Many clinics use an appointment system to manage the arrival of patients. However, the assumption that the appointment schedule will be strictly followed is rarely justified. Model 1 presents a simplified process flow for an outpatient clinic with no teaching mission. The schedule sets times for 12 patients and each patient is allocated a 20 minute block. The model facilitates changes to a random variable that defines patient Unpunctuality. In short, patients arrive at some time offset from the appointment time. In this example we model arrival times as the appointment time plus a log-normally distributed variable with a mean μ and a standard deviation of σ minutes. In this construction, negative values mean that the patient arrives before the appointment time, which is the norm. The base case sets $\mu = -15$ and $\sigma = 10$. By adjusting these parameters one can depict changes in arrival behavior. One can alter this model to address the following questions.

1. Describe clinic performance if all patients arrive on time.

2. Explain how this performance changes when Unpunctuality is included. Consider changes to the mean and/or variance.

3. Explain how you would create an experiment (in an actual clinic) to uncover how a change in policy might create a change in this behavior and how such a change affects clinic performance.

4. Create a flow chart that lays out how you might alter Model 1 to report results for groups of patients such as: those with negative Unpunctuality, those with positive Unpunctuality, and those with appointment times near the end of the session.

5. The DES assumes that if multiple patients are in the queue, the patient with the earlier appointment time is always seen first, even if they arrived late. Create a flow chart that lays out how you would modify the model to reflect a setting in which the Attending waits for late patients but only up to some limit of "w" minutes rather than seeing the next patient as soon as the server is free.

7.5.2 An Academic Model with Distributions of Teaching Time

The process flow within the academic medical center differs from Model 1 in that it includes additional steps and resources made necessary by the hospital's teaching mission. One key aspect of this mission is to have a consultation between the Attending and the Resident after the Resident interacts with the patient but before the Attending and Resident return to the patient together to complete the visit. Model 2 reflects this setting and labels the meeting between the Attending and the Resident as Teach Time. It also provides as way to alter parameters of the distribution of this activity time. Intuition suggests that clinic performance will change if these parameters change. Use the attached model of the academic medical center (Model 2) to address the following questions.

1. How do the average values of Cycle Time, Waiting Time, and Makespan respond to changes in the parameters that define Teach Time?

2. Describe the linkage between Resident utilization in this system and the amount of time they spend with patients. How much of their busy time is not explained by patient-facing tasks?

3. Describe the linkage between the number of Residents and the utilization of other key resources in the system.

4. Explain how you would create an experiment (in an actual clinic) to uncover how changing the educational process is linked to Resident productivity and clinic performance.

5. Create a flow chart that lays out how you could alter Model 2 to reflect a new approach to Resident education aimed at increasing the share of their time that adds value to the patient?

7.5.3 State Dependent Activity Times

Common sense suggests that service providers may speed up when they sense that they are falling behind schedule. This adjustment is very difficult to depict with simple models like Gantt charts or queueing models. However, it seems obvious that this behavior must alter clinic performance. With this in mind Model 3 includes a reduction to processing times for the Attending when the system is busy. The model inputs include an entry labeled <u>Factor</u>. This value is multiplied by the Attending activity time to reflect the phenomenon of speeding up. In this model the behavior is triggered by having a patient reach the Attending after the appointment time. For example, if this factor is set to 0.75, and the system is behind schedule, then the applied activity time is the normally predicted value multiplied by this factor. Consider this model to address the following questions.

1. How do average values of Cycle Time, Waiting Time, and Makespan change when the Attending gets faster in a busy system?

2. Note that when <u>Factor</u> is below one, we are reducing face time to help the system get back on schedule. As an alternative, consider leaving Factor at one and adding examination Rooms to the system instead. Is there any evidence produced by the DES to suggest that one approach is better than the other?

3. Describe the comparison between decreasing processing times when the system is busy to changing processing times for all settings.

4. Explain how you would create an experiment (in an actual clinic) to explore how this behavior affects patient flow and service quality. What extra factors do you need to control for?

5. Create a flow chart that lays out how you would alter Model 3 to separate the effects of patient behavior (including Unpunctuality) from the effect of physician behavior (including tardiness and changing processing times)?

Chapter 8
Case Study: Miller Pain Treatment Center

Abstract Introductory courses in Operations Management typically introduce students to process analysis and queuing theory. We apply these tools to consider patient flows in an outpatient clinic where processes are made more complex by inclusion of the teaching mission of an Academic Medical Center. The case narrative deals with a physician who moved his practice from a setting with no teaching mission to the academic setting. This created a natural experiment because he began treating the same patients using a different process flow. Students are asked to use data collected at both settings to compare and contrast these flows. The protagonist weighs options designed to improve an appointment schedule, change patient punctuality, and introduce a type of pre-processing of patients. Evaluation of these proposals calls for a different style of analysis. Students are introduced to the use of discrete event simulation to address such questions. Simulation models are provided corresponding to the two clinic settings. This allows students to conduct and learn from virtual experiments using calibrated models. The case fills a need for material that covers issues in healthcare delivery, which the basic tools of process analysis and queuing theory are insufficient to fully address.

8.1 Introduction

On a cool Saturday morning Dr. Keith Weems walked briskly down the hallway toward the main entrance to Eastern Hospital (EH). He was on his way to visit in-patients in several wards as part of his duties as the pain specialist on call for that weekend. However, his mind kept drifting to issues he was facing as the new manager of the Miller Pain Treatment Center in the neighboring Eastern Hospital Outpatient Center (E-HOC). Dr. Weems had been working as part of the Eastern system for several years. However, he recently merged his successful private practice into the Miller Pain Treatment Center and was appointed as its director. In so doing he moved from a setting where he was the clear boss to one in which he was dealing with a collection of more established doctors already set in their ways. He also had to figure out how to improve the care delivery process in this environment, which considered itself to be part of the premier teaching hospital in the world. After reviewing the operations and meeting the staff he was coming to grips with the fact that this new setting was much more complex than his old practice in a myriad of ways. Additionally, between treating outpatients and in-patients, managing the clinic, teaching medical students, and conducting research, it was clear that the complexity of the job mirrored the complexity of the operating environment. However, he was confident that he could find ways to get this larger clinic to surpass the success of his old, simpler practice.

8.2 Eastern Hospital and E-HOC

Eastern Hospital (Eastern) is a 918 bed general medical and surgical facility founded in the 19th century. The hospital currently handles roughly 47,000 admissions per year and 400,000 outpatient visits. This includes over 22,000 inpatient surgeries and 86,000 emergency room visits annually. Eastern is considered by many to be the preeminent medical facility in the world and was ranked #1 by US News and World Report for over 20 years. However, such rankings do not paint the total picture for all areas, especially when considering outpatient care. As the journal states, "our intent when we published the first Best Hospitals annual ranking in 1990 was to help people who find themselves in need of unusually skilled inpatient care."

Over its long history Eastern Hospital has evolved to include a large outpatient service. Much of this service is housed in the neighboring E-HOC, but this is supplemented by a number of outpatient clinics in surrounding communities. Many metrics of quality related to outpatient care, differ from those most often discussed when considering inpatient services. For outpatient care, key metrics typically revolve around 1) access to care, 2) preventive measures, and 3) treatment outcomes including the reduction in complication rates. In some areas these are relatively easy to identify. For example, for clinics that focus on chronic conditions such as diabetes or cardiovascular disease, we can look at outcomes such as modification of risk factors, the number of patients with cardiovascular diseases who remain stable, or the number of diabetics who remain stable. Complications in these areas include limb amputations brought on by diabetes or strokes and heart attacks in patients with cardiovascular disease. By comparison, many outcome measures in chronic pain clinics are more subjective because patients and health care providers focus on altering the impact of pain on functioning and quality of life. However, other metrics such as access to care are more readily measurable.

8.3 Private Practice

Before assuming the role as the lead administrator for the Miller Pain Treatment Clinic, Dr. Weems had been employed as the sole pain specialist at a private practice satellite clinic within the Eastern system. This practice was housed in a newer facility in a suburban location with ample parking and lush grounds. In this practice, he was the sole attending physician (Attending) and worked in conjunction with a Physician's Assistant (PA) and nursing and administration staff to deliver outpatient care to patients with chronic pain.

His clinic dealt with three types of patient visits. "New" patients were those coming to the clinic for the first time. These patients were instructed to arrive 30 minutes before the appointment time to fill out forms and provide insurance information. (Other patients are asked to arrive 15 minutes early.) New patients represent about 30% of all cases. For these visits special care was needed to gather data on the patient's medical history and other conditions. "Return" patients (roughly 40%) were those that needed additional care from the Attending. The practice also included a number of "Follow-up" patients (roughly 30%) who simply needed a prescription refill or to provide feedback on how they were progressing. As both a new doctor in the Eastern system, and the only doctor at this location, Dr. Weems felt that it was his responsibility to manage patient satisfaction in his clinic, as this would ultimately affect the clinic's profitability and reputation.

The process flow of the private practice was fairly straight-forward and is depicted in Figure 1. A sample of activity times is presented in Table 1. Virtually all patient visits are by appointment. The first patient is scheduled for 8 AM. For New and Return visits, the patient signs in upon entry to the clinic. Front desk staff retrieves the patient's records and completes any needed administrative activities. We label this step - Check-In . After an examination room becomes available, a clinical assistant leads the patient to one of 4 examination rooms and records vital signs. We label this step – Vitals . The patient's file is then left in a slot outside the door indicating that a patient is inside. The Attending reviews the file and enters the examination room to interact with the patient. We label this step – Attending. After completing the visit with the Attending, the patient proceeds to the front desk before exiting the system. We label this step Check-Out.

For Follow-up visits the PA replaces the Attending in the process flow, but does need to consult with the Attending in about ½ of such cases. Due to the nature of the medications involved, prescription refills are typically not authorized over the phone. For tightly controlled substances such as OxyContin or Percodan, the Attending must authorize each refill request by signature. However, most of these visits are routine, and the bulk of the review process is handled by a PA who is assigned one of the 4 examination rooms for the day. In these cases the PA sees the patient and prepares the prescription for the Attending's signature, which takes virtually no time. However, for about half of the follow-up cases, the PA needs to consult with the Attending before preparing the prescription. When this happens, the PA typically needs to have a conversation with the Attending. The average duration of this activity is 3 minutes.

8.4 Efficiency of Clinic Operations

Working in a small satellite clinic afforded Dr. Weems some control and flexibility. This was valuable to him because he had to juggle clinic sessions, time spent doing procedures that were not billed the same as clinic visits, and time in the hospital helping manage pain for inpatients. This type of autonomy had its appeal to many

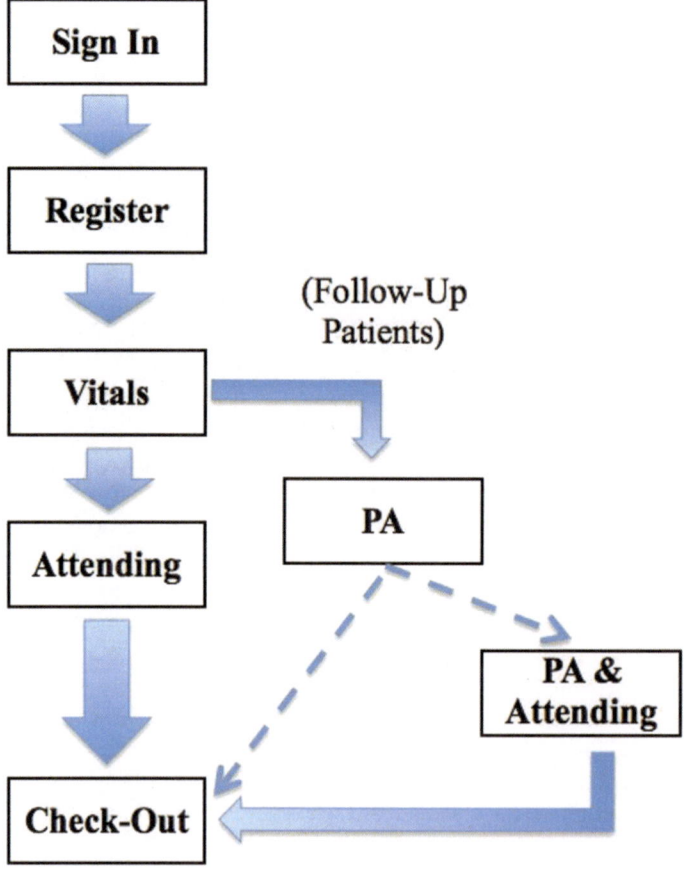

Fig. 8.1 Process Flow in Private Practice

TABLE 8.1: ATTENDING TIMES IN PRIVATE PRACTICE CLINIC

Record	Attending Time New Patients	Attending Time Return Patients
1	12	15
2	27	14
3	16	15
4	15	30
5	18	16
6	29	30
7	29	24
8	20	14
9	33	14
10	30	14
11	29	4
12	35	14
13	15	11
14	33	17
15	39	26
16	23	22
17	10	15
18	35	10
19	30	30
20	20	31
21	30	20
22	20	11
23	55	12
24	34	15
25	28	23
Average	30.97	16.94
Standard Deviation	12.41	

entrepreneurial practitioners. On the other hand, these small clinics were serving the same general population as E-HOC, and the barriers to entry for a doctor with a successful practice were fairly low. Consequently, these small practices were in competition with each other as well as larger elements of the Eastern system. This motivated many of the smaller clinics to develop and leverage a reputation for superior service.

For example, if Dr. Weems was available, he would often go into the waiting room and retrieve the next patient on the appointment schedule himself. If he was falling behind schedule, he would occasionally step into the waiting room to explain to patients why they were being asked to wait. Dr. Weems was also known to accommodate a patient who needed to reschedule an appointment, even if this meant starting before 8 AM or staying after 5 PM. At times Dr. Weems spent extra time with a patient that was having a particularly hard time managing their chronic pain. This time might include advising, counseling, or even praying with patients that were having an emotionally difficult time dealing with their circumstances.

In addition to these informal efforts to improve the patient experience, Dr. Weems quickly recognized that even though most patients didn't fully understand the complexities of medical care, they certainly understood that waiting for service was an unpleasant part of a stressful experience. Consequently, the doctor trained in medicine has to double as an operations manager. As Dr. Weems explains, "Given the realization that the era of multitasking physicians who double as clinic managers was at hand, the only way to survive was to roll up your sleeves and get on with the job."

As part of his efforts to develop and maintain a good reputation for service quality, Dr. Weems decided that he needed accurate data about how patients flow through the clinic. To collect this he had the front desk staff create a simple paper form when the appointment was made. This form would be attached to the patient's file when they checked in. Staff at the front desk would record the appointment time, the time when the patient signed in, the time when the patient got back to the desk to check out, and the time that the patient completed the exit procedure. The clinical assistant (CA) would record when the patient was led to the examination room and when she left the room after collecting vital data. Dr. Weems recorded when he entered the examination room, and when he finished. This data was collected over the course of several years. Table 2 shows samples of selected activity times recorded in the clinic for the steps that did not involve the Attending.

8.5 Patient Tardiness and Waiting Times

Dr. Weems hoped to use the data that he had collected about clinic operations to help improve some aspects of service quality. Past research had repeatedly demonstrated that patient satisfaction with an outpatient service was significantly related to waiting time, and Dr. Weems hoped that waiting times were an area where improvements could be made. When he looked at the data that had been collected Dr. Weems noticed that some patients arrived late to an appointment.[1] He suspected that this would set the clinic behind schedule. If that happens it might increase waiting times for patients scheduled to arrive later in the clinic session. Dr. Weems decided to attack this problem directly.

It was standard practice to send patients a letter about a week before their visit that contained a reminder of the time and date of their appointment. The standard

---

[1] While it is common to refer to this behavior as lateness, or tardiness, much of the published literature on the subject uses the term patient unpunctuality and is defined as Arrival Time minus Appointment Time. Thus, unpunctuality is negative for patients who arrive early and positive for those who arrive late.

TABLE 8.2: ACTIVITY TIMES IN PRIVATE PRACTICE CLINIC

Record	Registration	Vitals	Physicians Assistant	Check-Out
1	9	3	15	1
2	4	2	26	5
3	9	3	47	4
4	8	3	24	10
5	4	4	56	9
6	3	1	21	7
7	2	3	12	3
8	1	3	19	4
9	6	3	9	5
10	8	3	21	1
11	4	3	14	1
12	4	3	13	6
13	4	2	21	3
14	11	2	26	2
15	2	3	32	4
16	3	3	25	8
17	7	5	23	2
18	3	4	18	2
19	3	1	42	6
20	3	2	16	3
21	2	5	22	2
22	4	5	19	4
23	1	4	25	3
24	1	2	14	5
25	5	2	17	3
Average	4.33	3.53	22.62	4.72
Standard Deviation	2.68	1.75	13.7	3.26

letter included a sentence explaining that if the patient arrived late their appointment may need to be rescheduled. However, in practice, late patients were virtually always accommodated. Dr. Weems decided to be more proactive about enforcing this policy. The letters confirming each appointment were continued and the information about rescheduling late arrivals was highlighted. To make the policy more salient, a new activity was added to the clinic staff's job. Patients were called 24-48 hours prior to the appointment by clinic staff to remind them of their appointment time. During the call, patients were verbally reminded about the lateness policy. In addition, a sign stating that late patients would be asked to reschedule was displayed prominently on the front counter where patients checked in.

Since other clinics seemed to ignore the rescheduling policy it was not clear that patients would be convinced that the policy would be enforced in this clinic. Dr. Weems realized that in order to change behavior, he and the team would have to maintain consistency in the way in which the policy was carried out. After discussions with the staff, Dr. Weems settled on an approach that would involve letting the patients who arrived "late" know that if they were to be seen at that point, it would be taking time away from other patients who arrived on time. For dissenting patients, Dr. Weems employed the strategy of telling them that if the late patient was willing to face the next patient on the schedule who arrived on time and tell that patient that he/she would have less time with the physician because of the late arrival, then the patient who was "late" would be seen if the next patient on the schedule agreed. No late patient ever took up the "offer" to face another patient depriving them of their due time with the physician.

Dr. Weems was quite pleased with the results of this effort. The portion of patients who arrived late was cut in half, and over 12 months the need to reschedule patients due to their late arrival disappeared. Dr. Weems kept a continual record of patient sign-in times and appointment times. Table 3 shows patient appointment and arrival times before the policy was implemented, and 12 months later. This experience convinced Dr. Weems that simple changes in policies or procedures could have an impact on clinic performance.

8.6 Merging Clinics

After four years of operation, Dr. Weems received a call from the chief of his division, Dr. Ravinasa to inform him that the departmental chair, Dr. Qutowski decided that it would be best for the department if the satellite clinics were closed and the services they offered were moved into E-HOC. The reasons for this decision were two fold. First, after reviewing the Profit and Loss (P&L) figures for the department it seemed clear that collectively, the clinics were not operating at full capacity and this move would reduce fixed costs. Having staff at multiple locations duplicated several roles. In addition, real estate costs at the attractive suburban locations was rapidly rising. Second, the department found it difficult to attract new faculty to the satellite facilities given the allure of the teaching and research missions of the main hospital.

Dr. Weems would continue to see "his" patients, have the same number of clinic sessions per week, and work with the same PA. The clinic space in E-HOC was similar to his clinic in that it also offered four examination rooms for patient assessment, including one that could be assigned to the PA. As part of the consolidation effort, Dr. Weems would be appointed as the director of operations for the larger clinic with responsibilities to help improve the Profit and Loss performance of the Center.

TABLE 8.3: PATIENT UNPUNCTUALITY BEFORE AND 12 MONTHS AFTER POLICY
CHANGE

Record	Appointment Time Minus Arrival Time Before Policy Change	Appointment Time Minus Arrival Time After Policy Change
1	0	-21
2	-13	-23
3	-40	-15
4	-20	-38
5	-10	-23
6	-5	-5
7	-10	-2
8	-30	-15
9	-18	-36
10	-1	-20
11	-34	-30
12	-2	-36
13	-10	-10
14	-10	-49
15	-31	-37
16	-16	-53
17	-60	-52
18	-30	-45
19	-15	-24
20	-29	-34
21	4	-18
22	-36	-29
23	-35	2
24	-26	-29
25	-35	-17
Average	-24.09	-25.55
Standard Deviation	24.77	16.14

8.7 Miller Pain Treatment Clinic

The Miller Pain Treatment Center located in E-HOC offers a comprehensive range of services for patients suffering from acute or chronic pain. It also functions as an Academic Medical Center (AMC) which means that it doubles as a training ground for Residents and Fellows. These doctors have completed 4 years of medical school but are working toward a specialization as Anesthesiologists. In addition to the 4 examination rooms, the facility also includes a suite of rooms where a variety of more invasive procedures occur. For example, Dr. Weems uses this space to install Spinal Cord Stimulators in some patients. These stimulators are electronic devices that deliver electrical impulses directly to the spine as part of a larger pain management strategy.

The center staff includes 5 attending physicians along with a full time PA. However, for each 4-hour clinic session only one Attending will be present. A typical schedule for an Attending includes two, 4-hour sessions involving the examination rooms, and another two, 4 hour sessions using the procedure rooms. In addition, each physician typically visits in-patients 5 days per week and is on 24-hour call for 5 weekdays and one weekend, every five weeks. Beyond this load, Eastern physicians manage an ongoing research agenda that includes a mixture of funded and unfunded projects.

While many doctors enjoy the autonomy of private practice, operating under the umbrella of the AMC offers many advantages. Close proximity to colleagues facilitates research and makes it easier to form a network of collaborators. Famous institutions such as Eastern also attract the most challenging cases. As Dr. Qutowski explained, "we will always be the hospital of last resort. When your physician can't figure out what to do next, they know they can always send you to us." Documenting care delivered in such cases often leads to research publications. However, even for doctors not highly concerned about publication rates, the intellectual atmosphere of being at the leading research hospital in the world is a compelling attraction to many physicians who want to be at the top of their respective fields.

In addition to patient care, clinic administration, and research, Attendings working in the Miller Pain Treatment Center are actively involved in training the next generation of physicians. As the letter sent to all new patients states:

> Please be aware that your care at the Miller Pain Treatment Center will involve interaction with board certified physicians at various levels of medical training under the close supervision of your attending physician. While this may slightly extend the total time necessary for your visit, this academic approach provides a higher quality of care for our patients through more thorough discussion and review of patient problems and needs.

This added role of the clinic as an educational facility results in a more complex patient flow, as shown in Figure 2. After the Check-In step at the front desk and the Vitals step with the CA, the activities of the student are typically inserted into the patient flow. After the CA leaves the patient in one of the examination rooms, a resident is informed of the patient's presence. The resident then retrieves the patient file and reviews the case before entering the examination room (Resident Review). The resident then interacts with the patient (Resident) with no direct intervention of the attending physician, who may be visiting with another patient. After visiting with the patient, the resident then "presents" the case to the Attending. The Attending uses this interaction to get information about the patient and the issues at hand. However, the Attending also uses this time as a teaching step (Teach) to instruct the resident about what should be done next. This interaction can take several different forms.

The Attending uses this time to impart factual information, clinical insights, and lessons from experience about how to proceed. Factual knowledge might include a discussion of what different conditions can be causing the patient's symptoms. Clinical knowledge includes things like lessons on how to differentiate between conditions based on subtle findings from the physical examination of the patient or from information gained via specific tests such as X-rays or Magnetic Resonance Imaging. This is the "apprenticeship" part of the training where the resident learns by induction. Dr. Weems feels that it is important for each resident to spend some time with patients on each day. The Miller Clinic typically uses 3 residents at a time, and they take turns dealing with patients. Under this arrangement, each resident would typically see 2 cases during each 4-hour clinic session.

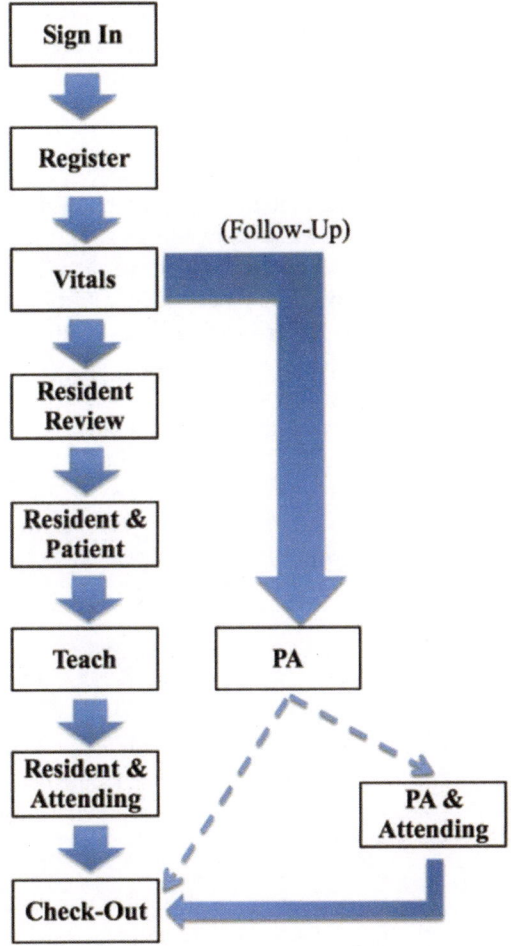

Fig. 8.2 Process Flow in Academic Medical Center

After this interaction, the Attending and resident re-enter the examination room, and the Attending speaks with the patient directly. Since the resident has done some preliminary work, the Attending's face time with the patient is typically shorter than it would be in private practice. After this, the patient is ready to head to Check-Out .

8.8 Issues in the AMC

The AMC model reflects a much more complex environment when compared to private practice, largely because the educational activities add steps to the process flow. This must have some effect on cycle times and throughput. However, Dr. Weems still wants the flow in the AMC to be as smooth as possible and is searching for ways to achieve improvement. As he had done in the private practice, he starts by collecting data on activity times in the AMC. Sample times involving new and returning patients are shown in Tables 4 and 5 respectively.

Dr. Weems has a few ideas on how to improve clinic flow. First, he suspects that the way patients are scheduled might be affecting the efficiency of the clinic. (A copy of the current scheduling template is shown in Table 6.) In the current schedule appointments are set at 15 minute intervals. However, the time required to treat a new patient is highly variable and can run much longer. If this happens, the clinic might fall behind schedule. On the other hand, if a new patient doesn't show up, this might have a big impact on performance. History shows that roughly 10% of scheduled appointments were canceled for a variety of reasons. The clinic typically finds out about these cancellations when the staff calls patients to remind them of an upcoming appointment. This means that the clinic staff finds out about an opening too late to fill it with another patient. Dr. Weems believes that if the scheduling of patient appointments is optimized, these variations in consultation length, and the impact of "no-shows," might be reduced. Unfortunately, he believes that trying a collection of new schedules to figure this out will be much too disruptive.

Another factor to consider is that while some patients arrive late, most actually arrive early. If the first patient of the day arrives prior to 8 AM, they have to wait until the front desk processes them before they can be seen. In his private practice the staff often started work a little early, so that the first patient could be seen by 8 AM. He believes that this is key to keeping the clinic on schedule but is not quite sure. He wonders if the policy regarding late arrivals that worked in his private practice would make a difference in the AMC.

Another issue nags at Dr. Weems. While the clinic typically schedules 3 residents to be in clinic, there is some variability regarding their availability. Residents are students with multiple duties within the hospital. Occasionally, 1 or even 2 residents miss a clinic session because they are away, performing other tasks. Some of these events are predictable because they are related to seminars that the residents

TABLE 8.4: ACTIVITY TIMES FOR NEW PATIENTS

Record	Resident Review	Resident & Patient	Teach	Resident & Attending
1	1	27	15	1
2	5	17	26	5
3	7	9	47	4
4	0	17	24	10
5	6	27	56	9
6	2	13	21	7
7	4	32	12	3
8	4	15	19	4
9	9	17	9	5
10	3	10	21	1
11	23	33	14	1
12	34	20	13	6
13	2	13	21	3
14	3	11	26	2
15	18	6	32	4
16	5	14	25	8
17	10	17	23	2
18	22	6	18	2
19	23	30	42	6
20	10	48	16	3
21	4	7	22	2
22	3	30	19	4
23	15	11	25	3
24	4	17	14	5
25	5	21	17	3
26	10	22	6	9
Average	10.44	20.16	7.85	12.45
Standard Deviation	9.38	10.82	5.62	7.44

are required to attend. He is not sure how this affects flow times for patients on the schedule for that day.

The data collected in the AMC shows that the time Attendings spend teaching residents during the clinic visit varies considerably from one doctor to the next. Since teaching is a critical activity for the AMC, he needs to know how the duration of this activity relates to clinic performance. He suspects that this time has a big impact on waiting times. After thinking about this issue for a while Dr. Weems came up with an idea that he called pre-processing. In this approach each patient would be assigned to a resident in advance. This would allow the resident to review the case the night before the patient's scheduled visit. It would also allow the Attending to do some of the case-specific teaching offline after the resident's review. This might improve flow through the clinic on the following day by reducing the resident's review time, and the teaching time that routinely occurs while the patient waits in the examination room. If pre-processing is used it might be possible to cut the average

TABLE 8.5: ACTIVITY TIMES FOR RETURN PATIENTS

Record	Resident Review	Resident & Patient	Teach	Resident & Attending
1	1	27	15	1
2	11	17	26	5
3	17	9	47	4
4	9	17	24	10
5	4	27	56	9
6	4	13	21	7
7	9	32	12	3
8	1	15	19	4
9	9	17	9	5
10	2	10	21	1
11	1	33	14	1
12	1	20	13	6
13	4	13	21	3
14	20	11	26	2
15	4	6	32	4
16	2	14	25	8
17	12	17	23	2
18	4	6	18	2
19	32	30	42	6
20	4	48	16	3
21	32	7	22	2
22	1	30	19	4
23	15	11	25	3
24	9	17	14	5
25	2	21	17	3
Average	9.30	12.99	5.17	9.24
Standard Deviation	10.60	7.96	4.07	8.71

TABLE 8.6: APPOINTMENT SCHEDULE IN AMC

Appointment Time	Patient Type
0800	New
0800	Follow-Up
0815	Return
0830	New
0845	Return
0900	New
0930	Follow-Up
1000	New
1015	Follow-Up
1030	Return
1045	Return
1100	Follow-Up
1115	Return

times for these activities in half.

Each of these ideas is fraught with risks. Getting staff to come in early might increase costs and has to be approved by the AMC. However there is a possibility that the hospital administration could be convinced to stagger the starting time for one of the patient service coordinators (PSC). This would involve having one PSC at the front desk by 7:30 AM. This would guarantee that a PSC is available for the patients who come in early for an 8:00 AM appointment. Changing the schedule would mean changing the work environment for Dr. Weems and the rest of the attending physicians as well. Convincing other attending physicians to try any of these ideas might be a tough sell.

How can he convince these experienced doctors, some of whom were more senior in academic rank, that the clinic should try some of these policy changes? Many of these ideas might seem rather radical for any hospital. However, this might be especially true for a hospital that has done things its own way for over 100 years and considers itself to be the best in the world. How could he argue that it was time to change anything now?

8.9 Review Material

Consider the tables of output data that were generated by simulating various scenarios for the pain clinic. This information is provided as MillerData.xlsx. Use this data to supplement the information written in the case the consider the following issues.

1. Describe the linkage between patient punctuality and clinic performance. Is patient punctuality a serious problem for the clinic? Why or why not?

2. Describe the linkage between teaching time and clinic performance. Is this a serious problem in this clinic? Why or why not?

3. Does the teaching mission of the clinic make the patient experience better or worse?

4. Using the data and results provided, make your best argument that pre-processing is best for 1) Patients, and/or 2) Attendings, and/or 3) Residents.

5. How would you go about getting other Attendings to implement a preprocessing protocol? Create 3 slides that you would use in a short presentation to get other Attendings to adopt the preprocessing policy.

Chapter 9
Case Study: Collecting Activity Times Using a Real Time Location System

Abstract In an effort to improve system performance in health care settings, one must first collect accurate information about patient flow and asset utilization. Much of this information can be deduced from start and end times for key activities. Use of a Real-Time Location System can be an excellent way to gather the needed data. This case looks at the collection of such data in the context of a complex outpatient setting, and the work needed to translate this raw data into useful information.

9.1 Collecting Activity Time Data in Eastern Hospital

The confluence of health care insurance coverage expansion and an aging population has created a need to expand access to medical care. Financial pressures and reimbursement systems favor the use of outpatient clinics to deliver a growing share of the related services. Increasing the workload in outpatient clinics adds to congestion which almost always increases waiting times. Increased waiting times inevitably lead to reduced patient and provider satisfaction. The dual need to focus on both access to care and waiting times means that evaluations of proposals to expand capacity require a detailed analysis of clinic operations. Cycle times (time from patient arrival to patient exit), throughput levels (patients per hour moving through the system), and makespans (duration between arrival of first patient on the schedule to the exit of the last patient) can be evaluated only with accurate representations of activity times related to patient visits.

When evaluating process improvement projects data accuracy is key, but such data can be deceptively difficult to come by. In addition, efforts to ensure data integrity must be managed in a way that does not interfere with patient care. Hence, we need thoughtful approaches to data collection efforts.

Let us peer into the workings of a Department of Radiation Oncology and Molecular Radiation Sciences at Eastern University Hospital to determine how to manage activity time data collection in a large clinic.

Radiation Oncology clinics are spaces used by patients who receive radiation treatments for conditions that include many types of cancer. These clinics can be rather large and have a waiting room adjacent to areas where radiation is administered on one floor. Another waiting area and clinic space with multiple examination rooms are typically close by, but on a separate floor. The clinic space will have multiple attending physicians (attendings) on site at the same time. Typically, each attending focuses on cases involving specific regions of the body. For example, some will focus on head and neck cancers, whereas others focus on gastrointestinal cases, lung cancer cases, and so on. In teaching hospitals, these clinics will also involve a collection of residents and students in various stages of the extended educational process.

Staff, attendings, and residents often are called upon to move between the clinic space and the radiation treatment areas on another floor. Patients will visit the clinic for a round of treatment that can run from 3 to 30 consecutive days. Because of the operation's scale, the mix of cancer types treated, patients involved, attendings on site, and nurses, residents, and technicians moving into and out of this space, the patient flows are extremely complex. The more complex the setting, the more data are needed to describe it, and the more important it is for the collected data to be accurate. As our observations begin we listen in on a meeting among key players as they work to initiate efforts to collect the needed information.

9.1.1 Kick-Off Meeting

Dr. Mary Hartman: I have asked you all here today to help get our heads around a very important issue. As you know, I became the department head here at Eastern a couple of months ago. I am still getting used to the way things are done around here, so I am going to need some help with this. The hospital is under increasing pressure to improve the financial state of each department. To help improve revenue projections, the administration wants us to increase capacity so that we can handle 20% more visits.

Now, I'm certainly in favor of providing access to more people, but I want to find a way to do this that will not increase waiting times. The monthly reports that I get show that we do a really good job of keeping times spent in the waiting rooms low and I want to keep it that way. After thinking this through I believe the only way to accomplish both of these objectives is to get us more examination rooms. I have asked you folks to join me on this task force so that I can build the case for that extra space. The problem is that the bean counters think space is like gold, and if we want more of it we need to make a better case for it than other clinics will.

OK, so that's the back-story. Let me get to exactly why I have asked each of you to help with this project. The way our space is accounted for, we effectively pay rent to the hospital for each exam room. I always assumed that rooms pay for themselves as long as we keep them full so there isn't too much to worry about there, but if we want to handle more visits we have got to get more space.

I have asked Dr. Bill Conrad to be here because he is the lead of our GI (gastrointestinal) team, and I believe that we can use his group as a sort of model case to show how this will work. Dr. Francis Knight is the resident right now on the GI team and she has agreed to do a lot of the leg work on this. I asked Nurse Elliott Weiss to be here because the nurses input a lot of the data that we are going to need. Tommy Tesch is here because he has some ideas on how to collect data very quickly. Finally, Professor Maxwell is here from the business school. He has had students help us collect data in other clinics and has some ideas about how to pull all of this together.

Now, my understanding is that our Appointment Management System (AMS) stores data on appointment times and patient arrival times. The nurses input times that patients enter (IN) and exit (OUT) the exam rooms. I think if we just pull the arrival times along with these IN and OUT times for each visit, we should have all that we need.

Nurse Weiss: Well that's a pretty simple problem. When patients are placed in the room we make an entry into the AMS, and we make another entry when they leave. I sent out copies of this data from last week to show what I mean. If that's all we need, we can pull this data whenever we like. The arrival times shown in the AMS are collected from the kiosks patients use when they first sign in upon entering the waiting area, so we can find waiting times using those figures.

Dr Conway: That's a relief. I thought you guys were going to ask me to track room times on some sort of form. That's not a good idea because I run from room to room, and sometimes I have to run down to the treatment room to sign off on a plan or report. The exam rooms are always full because we are a teaching hospital. The patient waits for the resident. The resident then sees each patient. After that, the resident and I meet about the case before we both go in as a team to do the final consult. That's why the rooms are always full and we need another one.

However, I really want to be clear that we are not going to sacrifice care for any efficiency measurements. Some of these visits are emotional events for patients, so face-time is a big deal, and I'm not going to cut into that just to increase volume. But it sounds like we are about done here. Nurse Weiss can give the data to Dr. Knight and she can compile what you need for your figures or whatever, right team?

9.1.2 Additional Issues

Prof. Maxwell: It sounds like you guys have a good plan, but if you don't mind, I do have a couple of small questions. (After a few bemused nods from the department head, the professor goes on.) The patient sees the nurse first, and then the resident, and finally the attending and resident together. It sounds like someone is in the room with the patient for the entire time between the patient's entry and exit. Is this correct?

Nurse Weiss: Not exactly. I leave the patient in the room and make the change in the AMS when I get back to the nurses' station. I make the next entry when the patient passes by on the way out, but I don't know all that happens in between. I have had a couple of patients complain on their way out about waiting in the room after I leave them, but I explain to them that the system is very busy and each doctor does the best they can.

Prof. Maxwell: Got it. So you create a time stamp the minute the patient enters the room. Now I was looking over the data from one day last week and I noticed that one entry time was missing and four patients left at midnight. Is this normal?

Nurse Weiss: Oh, you must mean last Wednesday. Well what happened there was that an in-patient was brought down from one of the wards and they don't use the kiosk because they just come off of the back elevator. In another case, after escorting a patient into the exam room, I was called away to one of the treatment rooms to deal with a patient having a bit of a panic when he was being placed in a machine. Some patients get claustrophobic in those things and freak out. I didn't get to make the entry until I got back, and I may have missed a couple of exits. If that happens, I make adjustments to the records at the end of the day.

Prof. Maxwell: I see, so when you are called away for another task, you might miss an exit, but you always record the room in time, and the waiting times that you track include the time spent waiting in the exam room. Is that right?

Dr. Hartman: Let me jump in here. Waiting time is time spent in the waiting room. If the nurse is busy, I might grab a patient from the waiting room, but that's pretty rare. Time spent in the exam room can't be that much, so I am not sure it's worth worrying about. But I'm sure the data will prove that. Do we have ideas on how to get the data we need to do this?

TommyTesch: You know we may have a simple way to deal with data collection. All of you folks have badges that trigger our Real-Time Location System (RTLS). You see, each room and hallway has a little sensor above the door that sees the badges and sends a signal to a server in the workroom. The server records the entries and exits from each space and creates a spreadsheet showing those time stamps at the end of the day. If you like, we can pull that data for a couple of weeks so you can see what I mean. Of course, this will tell us when the attending, the resident, or the nurse enters or exits a room, but it won't work for the patients because we don't have badges on them.

Dr. Conway: So now it sounds like we have an easy solution. If we pull the data from the AMS and the resident pulls data from this RTLS for the same spans of time, she can figure out the real entry and exit times. That should take care of it. Now that we have that figured out we can get back to real work.

Prof. Maxwell: Great ideas here. Let me add a few small points. I looked at a bit of RTLS data from a project in another clinic and I noticed a couple of small things to be aware of.

First, whenever data are entered by hand, there are bound to be occasional errors. These might include missing entries for times or room numbers, or just a typo on the times themselves. If we have a process to reconcile the AMS data with the RTLS data, we may be able to make the needed corrections.

Second, the RTLS data can tell us a lot about real face-time in the exam rooms. If we subtract face time from total time spent in the room, we will be able to verify that the waiting time in the room is not an issue. We really want to be sure that if we have to change the schedule to increase volume, patients can still get the face time that they need.

9.2 The GI Team

The care team in the GI service treats patients in a defined space that encompasses a patient waiting area, a nurse's station, a work-room for residents, and four examination rooms. Over an 8-hour day, the appointment schedule includes 15-20 patients. Appointment types include: 1) initial consultations (CON); 2) post-treatment follow-up visits (FU); 3) on-treatment visits (OTV) for weekly symptom evaluation during the course of radiation therapy; and 4) nursing visits (NUR), which address issues such as symptom management, review of information related to medications, and handling of consent forms. For Consults, Follow-Ups, and OTV's, a patient is typically seen by a nurse, then a resident before being seen by the attending. These visits to the clinic are differentiated from visits for radiation treatments, which involve machinery on another floor.

The AMS creates a new record when an appointment time is set at time A. Staff add to that record by recording any change in patient status. Status changes include: arrival (at time C), which is entered via the kiosk in the waiting area; entry to an examination room (IN) which is recorded at the nurse's station; and closing of the patient record when the patient leaves (OUT) also recorded at the nurse's station. The AMS generates a daily report of all recorded changes in patient status. Ideally, entry to the examination room occurs at time IN, and the record is closed at time OUT. Using these values total cycle time (CT) for the visit is $CT = OUT - C$, waiting time (W) is $W = IN - C$ and time in room (Room-time, RT) is $RT = OUT - IN$.

When data are entered manually there is a natural lag between when the patient enters the room and when that time is recorded. Similarly, there is also a lag between the time that the last provider leaves the room and this final status change is added to the system. These lags can be as short as one minute but can be considerably longer if staff are interrupted or called away.

9.2.1 Processing AMS and RTLS Data

In the days after the kick-off meeting, files of data are delivered to Dr. Fran Knight. She decides to look at a small data sample to figure out how to get the required information. After struggling with this a bit, she sends copies of the data to Prof. Maxwell and they agree to a short video conference to discuss the work.

Dr. Knight: Professor Maxwell, I really appreciate you meeting with me to help work through this. I sent you a copy of a small file that shows the AMS and the RTLS data related to a few patients. I noticed a few odd values that I need help figuring out.

Patient ID	Appointment	Check-In	Room-In	Room-Out	Room
1X327	4/12/2018 7:00	4/12/2018 6:30	--	4/12/2018 7:40	1
8QR79	4/12/2018 7:45	4/12/2018 7:00	4/12/2018 8:15	4/12/2018 9:20	1

Fig. 9.1 AMS Data Related to Exam Room 1 for First 2 Patients

Provider	Entry Number	Provider-In	Provider-Out	Room
Attending	1	4/12/2018 8:50	4/12/2018 9:15	1
Resident	2	4/12/2018 8:50	4/12/2018 8:55	1
Nurse	3	4/12/2018 8:42	4/12/2018 8:44	1
Attending	4	4/12/2018 7:25	4/12/2018 7:45	1
Resident	5	4/12/2018 7:15	4/12/2018 7:30	1
Nurse	6	4/12/2018 7:10	4/12/2018 7:14	1

Fig. 9.2 RTLS Data Related to Exam Room 1 for First 2 Patients

First, I noticed that the first patient has no value recorded for IN. Looking at data for other patients I found that sometimes we see one or more patients leaving at the same time. In one case I saw a value for OUT of 11:59 PM so we know this cannot be correct. I also noticed that we often show one patient leaving a room and another entering the room at the same time. I know that is not what is really happening, because it takes time to walk out and get the next patient, but that's what the data seems to show. I am really confused about why this data is so mixed up and what I can do about it.

Prof. Maxwell: I looked over the files that you sent and noticed the same problems. Fortunately, I was also able to sit in your clinic for a few hours to watch the flow. Whenever data are entered by hand, like some AMS entries, errors can happen. Fortunately, we can use data collected by the RTLS to correct many of these errors. It still won't be perfect because the RTLS data only looks at providers, but it will be an improvement.

Whenever we have data that we know are likely to have some of these kinds of issues we have to find a process to clean it up before we do anything else with it. I have been thinking about how I would scrub these data to make it useful, and I do have a couple of ideas.

When I see room-out times that are identical to room-in times for the next patient ($OUT_i = IN_{i+1}$ where i is an index for the Patients), I suspect that the nurse missed the actual exit time and just typed something in when he input the entry time for the next patient. If this happens, then the values for OUT_i are really upper bounds on the actual unobserved values. You can think of this as a Latest Finish time for Patient i (LF_i) because this is the latest point in time that the event could have actually happened. On the other hand, you can also think of it as the Earliest Start time for the next patient (ES_{i+1}).

Dr. Knight: I get that, but why do we have to worry about it?

Prof. Maxwell: Well it might be an issue or it might not. We can't really tell if it matters until we work through some of the calculations that we need. We always have to be careful when we pull data from an information system that wasn't set up specifically for what we are trying to do. Since the system designers can't anticipate all of the possible future uses for the data involved, they can't control for the infinite number of ways that people estimate things.

Fortunately, the fact that we have a clear sequence of patients creates a natural precedence time line for each room. In other words, we know that events in a room that involve the second patient must come after all events that involve the first. This is similar to what you see in a project management network. Knowing that Activity B cannot start until Activity A is completed creates a natural discipline that the real data must follow. Any data point that does not fit this logic needs to be looked into.

If we use our data to determine Earliest Start, Earliest Finish, Latest Start, and Latest Finish times for each patient, then the logic that we use to do that will also serve to correct a lot of the data entries that look fishy.

Dr. Knight: I think I get it, but I am not a project manager. Is there some way to give me a recipe to do this?

Prof. Maxwell: Since the patients use the kiosk to check in, I am going to assume that the arrival times recorded there are accurate. These arrival times are also the earliest times that work on a patient can start. Also, when we look at the RTLS data, it is safe to say that the last provider exit time was related to the last patient seen. So now we have an Earliest Start for the first patient and the Latest Finish for the last patient. To get a complete picture of the entire sequence of events in between, I will need similar values for all patients on the schedule. I also need to find a Latest Start (LS_i), and Earliest Finish (EF_i) for the same patients. I have written out an algorithm to get all of this done. (See Figure 9.3). So as you can see, this is a really easy problem.

Initialization	
Step 0:	Let $LF_0 = \max(7{:}00 \text{ AM}, CI_1)$
	$RI_{I+1} = \max(PO_{max}, CO_I)$
Main Loop	
For $i = 1,...., I$	
	$ES_i = max(LF_{i-1}, CI_i)$
	$EF_i = ES_i$
	$LF_i = min(RO_i, RI_{i+1})$
	$LS_i = LF_i$
	For j such that $ES_i \leq PI_j < LF_i$
	If $PO_j > LF_i$ then $LF_i = PI_j$; Next j
	Else
	$LS_i = min(LS_i, PI_j)$
	$EF_i = max(EF_i, PO_j)$; Next j
	Next i
End	

Fig. 9.3 Algorithm to Scrub AMS Data Using RTLS Information. CI, check-in; CO, check0out; RI, room in; RO, room out; PI, provider in; PO, provider out; ES, earliest start; EF, earliest finish; LS, latest start; LF, latest finish

Dr. Knight: Now, hold on there Professor. None of this looks simple to me. First, we can't move patients around like jobs in a project. Second, I really don't understand this code you have here at all. Can you walk me through it?

Prof. Maxwell: Well, you are certainly correct that we cannot go back in time and change where the patients were. We just want to use a consistent logic to scrub the data that we have. To explain how this works, let's apply the algorithm to the first 2 patients on the schedule.

We have two lines in the algorithm labeled Step 0. In this example, we are considering $I = 2$ patients but we pretend that we also have a Patient 0 and a Patient $I + 1 = 3$. The first line (Let LF_0 = max (7:00 AM, CI_1)) says that Patient 0 is finished when the clinic opens or when Check-In occurs for Patient 1 - whichever is greater. Since the Check-In time for Patient 1 is missing we get $LF_0 = max(7 : 00, --) = 7 : 00$. To get ES_3 we use the latest entry in the AMS data (9:20 in this example). Thus, $LF_2 = ES_3 = 9 : 20$. Since we have dealt with the missing arrival time for Patient 1 and we have a definite end point for Patient 2 we can calculate makespan. Once we find the busy time for each resource, we divide that by makespan to figure out utilization levels.

Dr. Knight: I think I understand what you want to accomplish, but what does all of this gibberish in your algorithm mean?

Prof. Maxwell: Since we are just looking at the first 2 patients on the schedule, $I = 2$ refers to the total number of patients being considered. Let J be the total number of sets of provider time stamps, where a set refers to a Provider-In time (PI_j) and a matching Provider-Out time (PO_j). We have six of these sets (6 lines in Figure 9.2) so $J = 6$. I write these 6 lines in reverse orders based on entry times so that it fits with the way my algorithm works. We keep track of the Patients using i and the provider time stamps using j. I have created a little table showing how I work through the steps for the first two patients. Let me show you that screen now. (See Figure 9.4.)

Line #		ES	EF	LS	LF
1	Patient 0				7:00
2	Patient 1	7:00	7:00	7:40	7:40
3	Patient 1	7:00	7:00	7:40	7:25
4	Patient 1	7:00	7:00	7:40	7:15
5	Patient 1	7:00	7:14	7:10	7:15
6	Patient 1				7:15
7	Patient 2	7:15	7:15	9:20	9:20
8	Patient 2	7:15	9:15	8:50	9:20
9	Patient 2	7:15	9:15	8:50	9:20
10	Patient 2	7:15	9:15	8:42	9:20

Fig. 9.4 Steps of Algorithm Applied to First 2 Patients. ES, earliest start; EF, earliest finish; LS, latest start; LF, latest finish

From Step 0 we input 7:00 AM as the Late Finish for Patient 0. That's all that we have for Line 1. We use the Main Loop to fill in Line 2. We are working on Patient 1 so $i = 1$. We get $ES_1 = max(LF_0, CI_1)$. This becomes $ES_1 = max(7 : 00, 6 : 30) = 7 : 00$. We then set $EF_1 = ES_1 = 7 : 00$. We know this value is wrong, but it will get updated later. Next we get $LF_1 = min(RO_1, RI_2)$. Since we haven't gotten to Patient 2 yet, we have no value to use for RI_2, so we just get $LF_1 = min(RO_1, --) = RO_1 = 7 : 40$. Finally, we get $LS_1 = LF_1 = 7 : 40$. That explains the entries on Line 2.

There is another loop within the main loop (*For j such that ...*). We see that Patient 1 has $ES_1 = 7 : 00$ and $LF_1 = 7 : 40$ so we have to look at all Provider-In times that fall within this span. As we read down Figure 9.2 we see three of them 7:25, 7:15, and 7:10 , which are entries 4, 5, and 6. Look at the provider entry at 7:25 (Entry Number 4). We see that this provider did not leave until 7:45. This value is after the time we had recorded for $LF_1 = 7 : 40$. Since $PO_4 > LF_1$ we have to reset $LF_1 = PI_4$. In other words, LF_1 becomes 7:25. The other entries for Line 3 are just copied from Line 2.

Dr. Knight: Why do we change the value in this way?

Prof. Maxwell: At this stage we have more confidence in the RTLS data than we do in the AMS data. It is customary for the provider to leave the room before the patient. So if we have a Provider-Out time that seems out of place, we guess that the Room-Out time that we had recorded earlier is most likely to be incorrect. Our initial data had suggested that this provider block of time involved Patient 1. We are now assigning that time to Patient 2. Thus, we conclude that Patient 1 left just before this provider entry. That's why we make this adjustment.

Getting back to the figure, for Line 4 we start by looking at $PI_5 = 7:15$. Since 7:15 is between 7:00 and 7:25 we have to check PO_5. This value is 7:30, which is greater than $LF_1 = 7 : 25$. Thus, we update LF_1 to equal $PI_5 = 7 : 15$. The rest of Line 4 was copied down from Line 3.

Finally, for Line 5 we start by looking at $PI_6 = 7:10$. The associated Provider-Out time is 7:14. This value is below 7:15 so we do not have to adjust LF_1. In this case we finish the algorithm by setting $LS_1 = min(LS_1, PI_6) = min(7 : 40, 7 : 10) = 7 : 10$. In addition, we get $EF_1 = max(EF_1, PO_6) = max(7 : 00, 7 : 14) = 7 : 14$. This completes the analysis for Patient 1. I then go through the same steps for Patient 2.

Dr. Knight: Why do we need so many steps?

Prof. Maxwell: The AMS data are enough to get us started, but not enough to come up with all of the needed values. To get the other values we need some additional information. That is where the RTLS data comes in. The main reason we have so many steps is that patients only enter and exit the room once, and a room only deals with one patient at a time. On the other hand, we have three different providers, and each one can enter and exit multiple times. We are really just looking at each block of time a provider is in the room and thinking about what patient had to be involved, and whether we need to update our information about that patient visit.

Dr. Knight: This is starting to make sense, but I still wonder whether this fixes all of the issues with the data.

Prof. Maxwell: Well, this works as long as we don't have too many missing data points. It is easy to come up with scenarios where this still won't work. For example, if we are missing the Check-In and Check-Out times for two patients in a row, we don't have enough to work with. Once we work through all of these steps for each patient we can use the resulting data for the rest of our analysis. It still won't be perfect since your data were not perfect, but it should be a lot better than what we had before.[1]

9.3 Review Material and Prior Works

The setting discussed above is based on multiple discussions and projects that involve a Radiation Oncology clinic within the Johns Hopkins Hospital. Names are changed as a courtesy to all parties involved. A bit of poetic license is involved in bringing all of the parties together in a single meeting. For more background on this work consult Conley et al (2016), Elnahal et al (2015a), Elnahal et al (2015b), and Chambers et al (2016).

With this background in place, review the data provided in the linked spreadsheet to address the following questions. The sheet labeled Vis1AMS.xlsx presents the IN and OUT times from the AMS for all patients who passed through Examination Room 1 over the span of one clinic session. The sheet labeled Vis1RTLS.xlxs shows the RTLS data for that same room over the same span of time, and indicates entry and exit times for the nurse, resident, and attending. Use these values to address the following questions.

1. Are the values of IN and OUT accurate for Patients 1 through 4? If cases exist for which the values are not accurate, correct them as best you can.

---

[1] The loop sequentially assigns providers to patients within the pre-computed ES and LF times. As providers are assigned to the room, LS is non-decreasing and EF is non-increasing. The IF statement identifies an exception; a consequence of RO being inaccurate is that a provider enters the exam room before RO but exits after that time. Since RO is an upper bound on the actual departure time, we lower LF to the entry time of the provider. This ends the iteration for that patient and also ensures that ES for the next patient is also set to this earlier time since the final $LS_{i+1} = LF_i < RO_{i+1}$. At this point all providers have been assigned uniquely to patients, and we can use ES as a surrogate for RI and LF as a surrogate for RO.

2. Calculate cycle time for the first four patients on the schedule; i.e. how long do each of the first four patients spend in the clinic?

3. Adjust IN and OUT values for all patients on the schedule, and find the resulting cycle times.

4. Given these values, calculate average time in the waiting room, average time in the exam room where no provider is present, and utilization rates for the examination rooms, attending, nurse, and resident.

5. Discuss what assumptions you made to address these questions and what additional data you would like to have to make the depiction of clinic operations better.

6. Discuss what policy you would like to see put in place to ensure that you get more reliable data in the future.

Chapter 10
Case Study: The RadOnc Clinic Expansion

10.1 Analyzing Flow Data

A large scale radiation oncology clinic collected data that focused on time stamps showing entry and exit times for patients, nurses, residents, and attending physicians to and from examination rooms. The datasets produced were analyzed with an eye toward justifying additional space to accommodate a projected 20% increase in patient volume. Data collection included downloads from an Appointment Management System (AMS). In this system the nursing staff types in IN and OUT times to indicate when a patient enters and exists an examination room. Since staff enter much of this data manually, issues often arise including data entry errors and omissions. To address resulting inaccuracies, the analysts retrieved supplemental data from a Real Time Location System (RTLS) that was installed in the clinic space. Hospital staff and physicians wear badges that the RTLS reads. Thus, the RTLS provides additional information on the movement of key resources. This combined data set was scrubbed (See Case Study: Collecting Activity Times Using a RTLS) and is now available to analysts working to understand the linkages between the number of examination rooms and clinic capacity.

In this short case we turn our attention to two analysts (Professor Maxwell and Mo Manzana) who are collaborating to establish ways to process the data and share results. In this sense the work is to transform raw data into useful information. This needs to be done in a fashion that helps management make critical decisions about renting additional examination rooms. Decision makers will need to combine this information with their understanding of the system to generate the knowledge necessary for process improvement. The clinic currently pays rent for four examination rooms, and clinic management anticipates a 20% increase in patient volume. Intuition suggests that if the clinic is expected to handle 20% more patients without an increase in waiting times, an additional examination room is required.

C. Chambers et al., *Improving Processes for Health Care Delivery*,
https://doi.org/10.1007/978-3-031-19043-8_10

With representative data in hand the remaining challenge is two-fold: 1) determine how much space is actually needed, and 2) establish a way to present information to the stakeholders involved in a fashion that is both clear and useful. As is often the case the analysts involved are trained as engineers and programmers, whereas the decision makers will be managers, nurses, and physicians.

10.2 Visualizing Key Data

We begin with a peek into a discussion between our two analysts.

Prof. Maxwell: Mo, did you finish the data visualization project that I asked you about on Friday? You've had the entire weekend to work on it.

Mo Manzana: Not quite. However, I was able to do a little with the sample that you gave me and I have come up with a couple of things that might help. Let me show you what we have so far.

I've printed out a few pages for you to look at. The nurses gave me IN and OUT times for a list of patients. The RTLS data adds the room entry and exit times for the resident, the nurse and the attending. It's a bit overwhelming when looking at tables of these raw values, so I am working on better ways to show what is happening. The first page (Figure 1) presents the raw data for a single room. The section at the top of the figure shows the IN and OUT time stamps for the patients along with entry and exit times for each resource depicted as the black blocks on a timeline. This is a lot like a Gantt chart in that there is one row of bars for each resource. This makes it a little easier to see what is happening.

In the next segment, I added a different color for each patient. In the third segment I assigned the resource time blocks to patients. The shaded areas in this part of the figure show when a resource is in the room with the patient. In most cases, it's pretty obvious which patient is being seen by which resource. However, I did notice that we still have some cases where things don't line up quite the way they should.

I had to make some decisions about a few time blocks that had to be assigned to patients. Once I did that I developed the depiction on the bottom part of the figure (Figure 1). I also did not have an exit time entered for Patient 7, so I used the last exit time for a provider as a replacement. This is why the bars on the bottom of the figure stop at 5 o'clock.

All of these busy times are now shaded areas in the figure. This shows face time. The times when the patient is in the room with no provider present are colored to match the patient. I also built a simple app that allows you to assign resource busy times to patients. I created a set of instructions that I have for that over here.

Prof. Maxwell: Got it. So I see that you have the data organized by room. That should help when we want to talk about room utilization, but we also need to think about the busy times for the doctors and face time. How do you suggest we look at that?

Mo Manzana: If you look at the next page (Figure 2) I organized the same data to show busy times for each resource by room. In this figure each of the four rooms is represented by four rows. The top row shows when each patient is in the room using the corrected times from the first page. The patients are in the room for the block of time that is a solid color. The next three rows show the spans of time when the resident, the nurse, or the attending are in the same room. I pushed those blocks up to the top row to show spans of time when the patient is in the room with at least one other person.

Prof. Maxwell: So why are there two colors on that top row?

Mo Manzana: For each room, the black bars in the top block show when the patient is in the room alone. The other colors show the presence of a service provider. When the room is empty, the space is blank. We can use this schematic to convey a few key points. The black blocks show that the room is almost always full, but most of the time, the patient is in the examination room alone. On the other hand, face time is any time that a resource is in the room with the patient. This can get a bit messy because more than one resource can be there at the same time, and a resource may leave the room and come back later. For example, in several instances, the attending enters and exits the room more than once to see the same patient.

The next page (Figure 3) shows the same data organized by resource. For example, the space at the top shows the busy times for a resource and includes a row for each room that the resource can visit. This is a different way to display the same information. The top figure shows this information for the nurse, followed by the attending, and then the resident. For each resource, I pushed the blocks up to the top row to represent utilization of that resource.

Prof. Maxwell: Well I suppose that's not bad for two day's work. Did you figure out how many extra rooms they need?

Mo Manzana: Maybe I misunderstood what you meant, but I looked at this in a different way. We can look at adding 20% more patients by adding a room. But why don't we just compress the current work into the rooms that they already have? If they can do that, then the fourth room that they pay for now is really the extra space that they can use to deal with the added load.

If you look at the next page (Figure 4) I collected the busy times for each patient in each room for one day. I used data from a different day to create this figure. In this analysis I treated the rooms as resources and looked at when they were occupied. The chart at the top shows busy times for the four rooms as things are now. I also add a bit more information here. After the patient is placed in the room there is a lag until the nurse or resident comes in. These blocks are assigned a lighter shade to point them out. In the second part of the page I show these same blocks after dropping this initial waiting time out of the equation. You can do this if you don't put a patient in the room until someone is ready to see them. Then, in the third section, I flatten these blocks to place them into three rooms.

Prof. Maxwell: It sounds like what you are saying is that to make waiting times look better, they put patients in rooms as quickly as possible, but this leads them to believe that they don't have enough rooms.

Mo Manzana: Well it's not quite that simple. After I looked at that room (Figure 4), I decided to push this a little further. I considered data from a different day, which is shown on the next page (Figure 5). For this dataset, it's not possible to compress the current work into 3 rooms without delaying some patients. If you look at time 1:45 PM in the second part of the chart, you see that we need all 4 rooms to serve the scheduled patients. The third part of the chart shows that we can fit all patients into three rooms, if we accept some delay. In other words, there is a trade-off between the number of rooms needed and the level of acceptable delays.

Prof. Maxwell: There may be a problem with delaying patients. It may cause some conflicts. Lets focus on the first case (Figure 4) when it was possible to fit all patients into three rooms without adding delays. If we wanted to move these patients to three rooms instead of four, we need a way to explain how to come up with a new schedule. I believe it is possible to mathematically formulate the assignment of patients to rooms in order to minimize the number of rooms used.

Mo Manzana: Well, I do have a couple of thoughts on that as well. We can solve this as a mathematical programming problem.[1] To do that we define a set of binary variables, X_{ir}. It's equal to 1 when patient i is assigned to room r and it's equal to 0 otherwise. Also, we need to define a binary variable for each room to determine if the room is occupied. So we define y_r to equal 1 if at least one patient is assigned to room r; otherwise it is 0. Do you have any thoughts on this plan?

Prof. Maxwell: We can write a constraint for each two patients with a time conflict that guarantees that they are not in the same room at the same time.

Mo Manzana: That's clever. I think I can formulate that in a spreadsheet.

---

[1] More specifically, this is a Integer Programming (IP) problem.

Prof. Maxwell: Let me share my screen as I write this out.

$$
\begin{aligned}
Z &= \min \sum_{j=1}^{J} Y_j \\
\sum_j X_{i,j} &= 1 \\
\sum_i X_{i,j} &\leq M * Y_j \\
X_{k,j} + X_{l,j} &\leq 1 \\
X_{i,j} &= 0 \text{ or } 1 \text{ for all Patients i, and Rooms j} \\
Y_j &= 0 \text{ or } 1 \text{ for all Rooms j}
\end{aligned}
$$

The only thing that is a bit clunky about this is that you have to create constraints that coincide with any conflicts. If patient k is in the clinic at the same time as patient l you create a constraint that they cannot both be assigned to the same room j. You can see by looking at the figure when two patients are there at the same time so this is not hard to do.

Mo Manzana: I understand that, but I am not sure that staff doing the scheduling or looking at this problem will be comfortable laying out the problem in this way. There may be a more intuitive way to look at it. We can think about this as a network flow problem. What I mean by that is that we create a network which represents each patient by a node. If two patients are in the clinic at the same time, we connect the associated two nodes with an arc. The neighbors of a node are defined as all nodes connected to it. In other words, nodes connected together overlap in time and all nodes that are not connected do not.

With this setup, each node can only be assigned to a room if that room is not taken by one of its neighbors. Here is the recipe to get this done. First, we create the network by connecting the nodes as we said before. We then create a list of candidate-rooms. In this case, this is just 1, 2, 3, and 4. We then start with Node 1 and assign it to the first room from a list of candidate-rooms. For Node 1 this will always be Room 1. We then remove Room 1 from the list of rooms available to all of the neighbors' candidate room lists. Then, we move to one of the neighbors of Node 1 and apply the same logic. We continue this process until all nodes are assigned to a room. (We attached a more detailed step-by-step description of this algorithm in an Appendix.)

Prof. Maxwell: That's a great idea! It gives us a way to lay out the solution without using any software or writing any code at all.

10.3 Review Material

The setting discussed above is based on multiple discussions and projects that involve a Radiation Oncology clinic within the Johns Hopkins Hospital. Names are changed as a courtesy to all parties involved. A bit of poetic license is involved in bringing all of the parties together in a single meeting. For more background on this work consult Conley et al (2016), Elnahal et al (2015a), Elnahal et al (2015b), and Chambers et al (2016).

Use the data and figures provided to consider the following questions.

1. Consider the information presented in Figure 4. Work through the network flow algorithm as described by Mo Manzana to demonstrate whether the cases can be processed in 3 examination rooms. Show your work as you move through the steps.

2. Consider the information presented in Figure 5. Work through the network flow algorithm as described by Mo Manzana to demonstrate whether the cases can be processed in 3 examination rooms within the allotted time. Show your work as you move through the steps.

3. Covert the problem formulation presented by Professor Maxwell into a spreadsheet model that you can solve there (using Solver in Excel or similar tools) and provide the solution showing the minimum number of examination rooms needed.

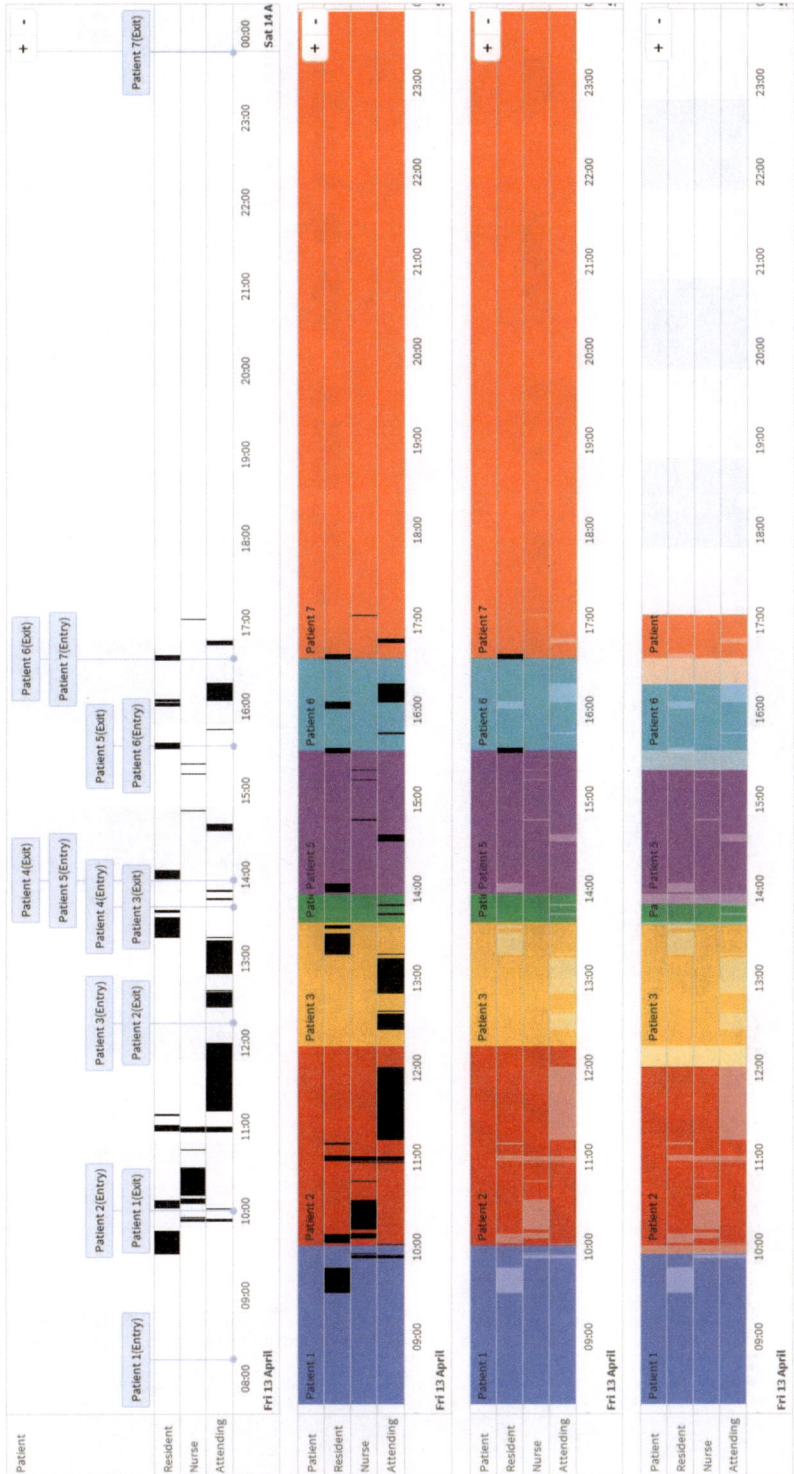

Fig. 10.1 Patient and Resource Times in Each Room

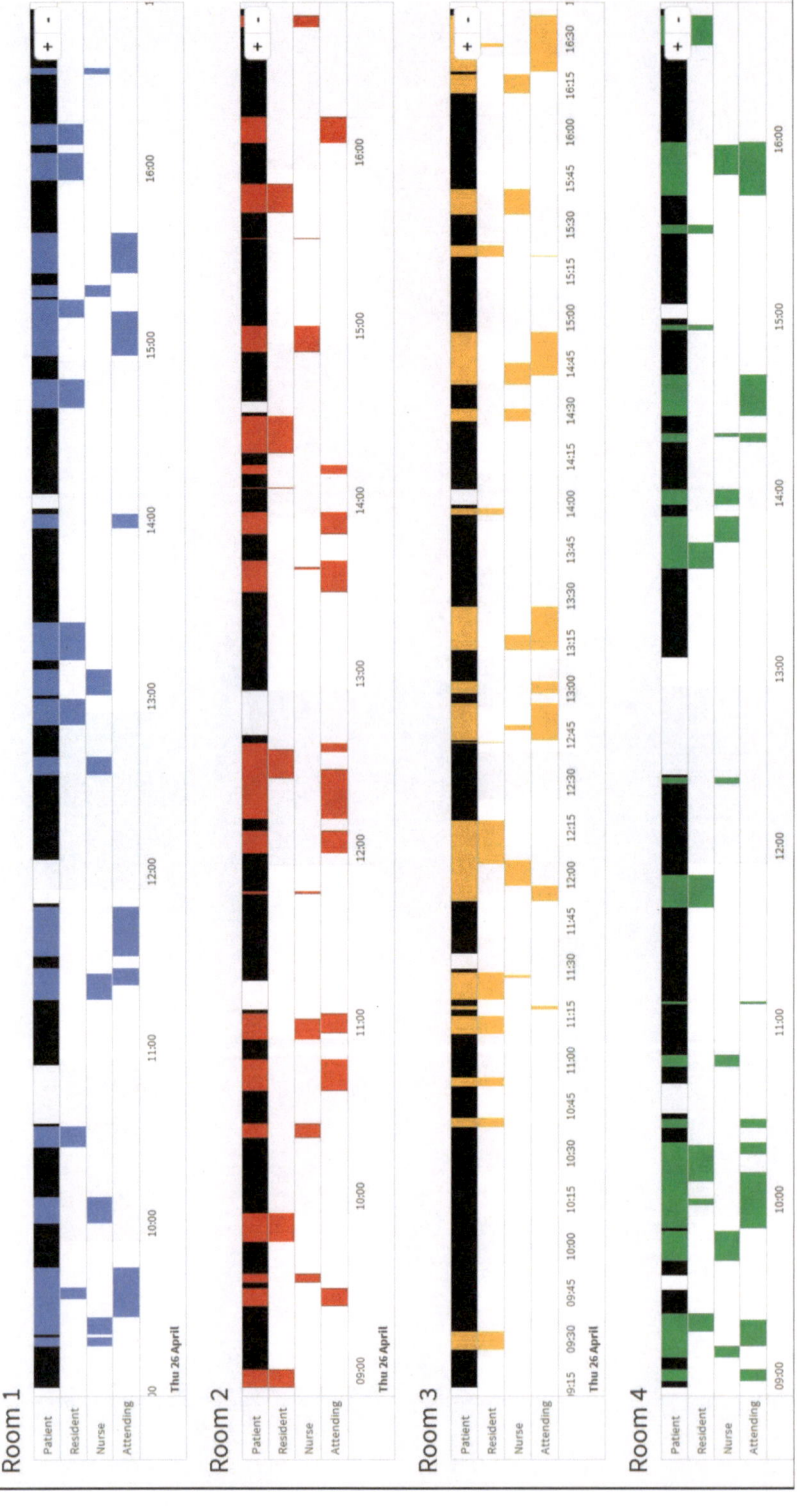

Fig. 10.2 Patient and Provider Times Organized by Room

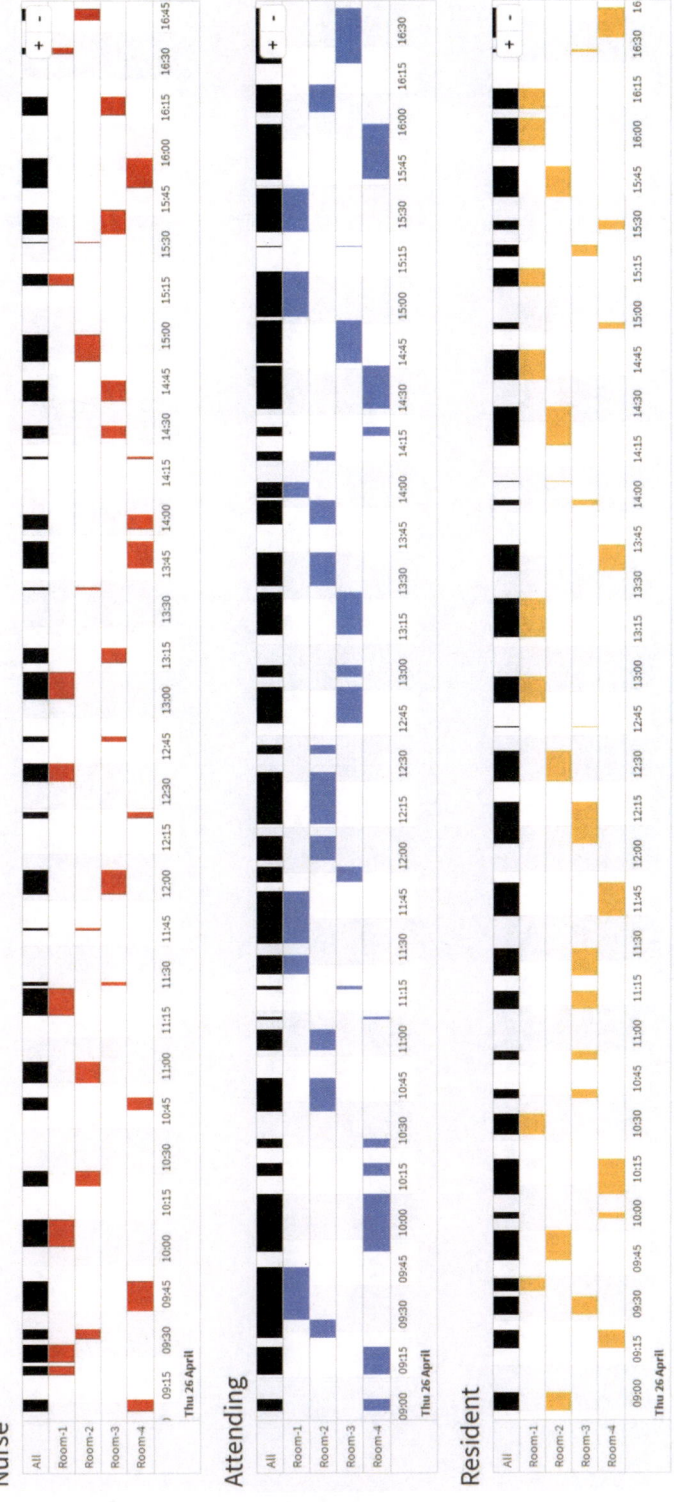

Fig. 10.3 Times Spent in Each Room Organized by Resource

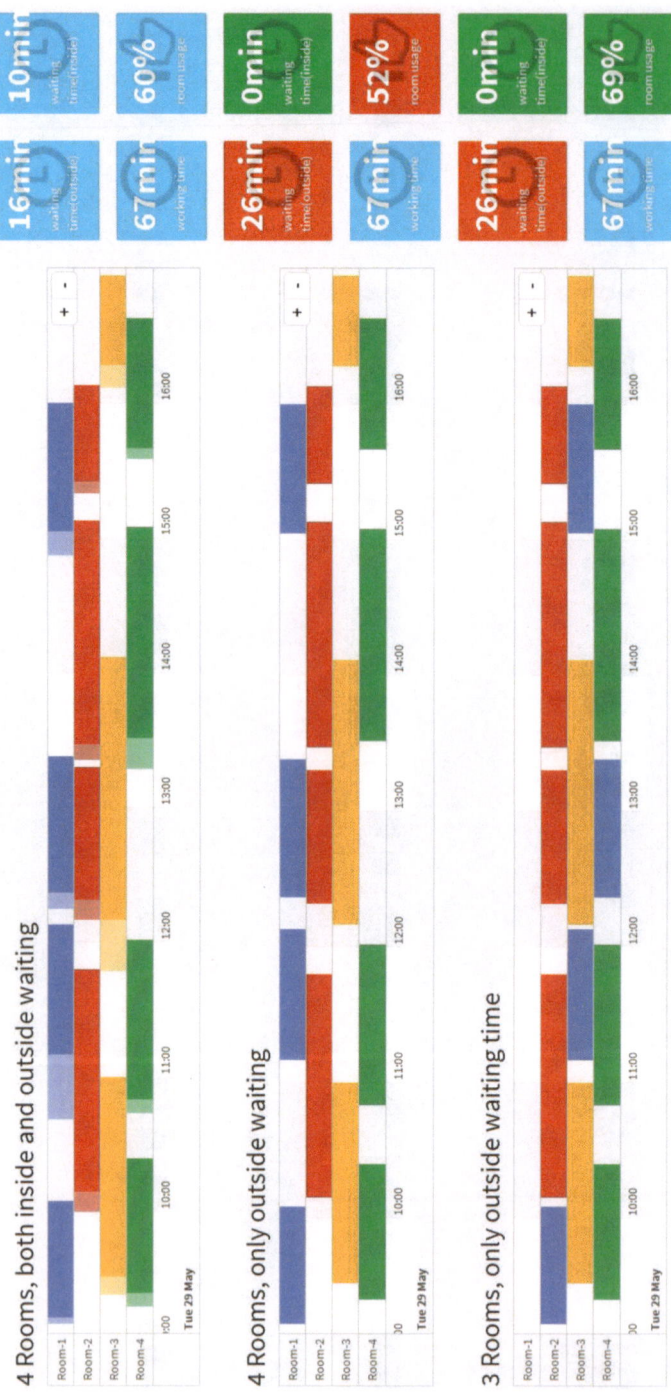

Fig. 10.4 Occupied Times Organized by Room and Patient

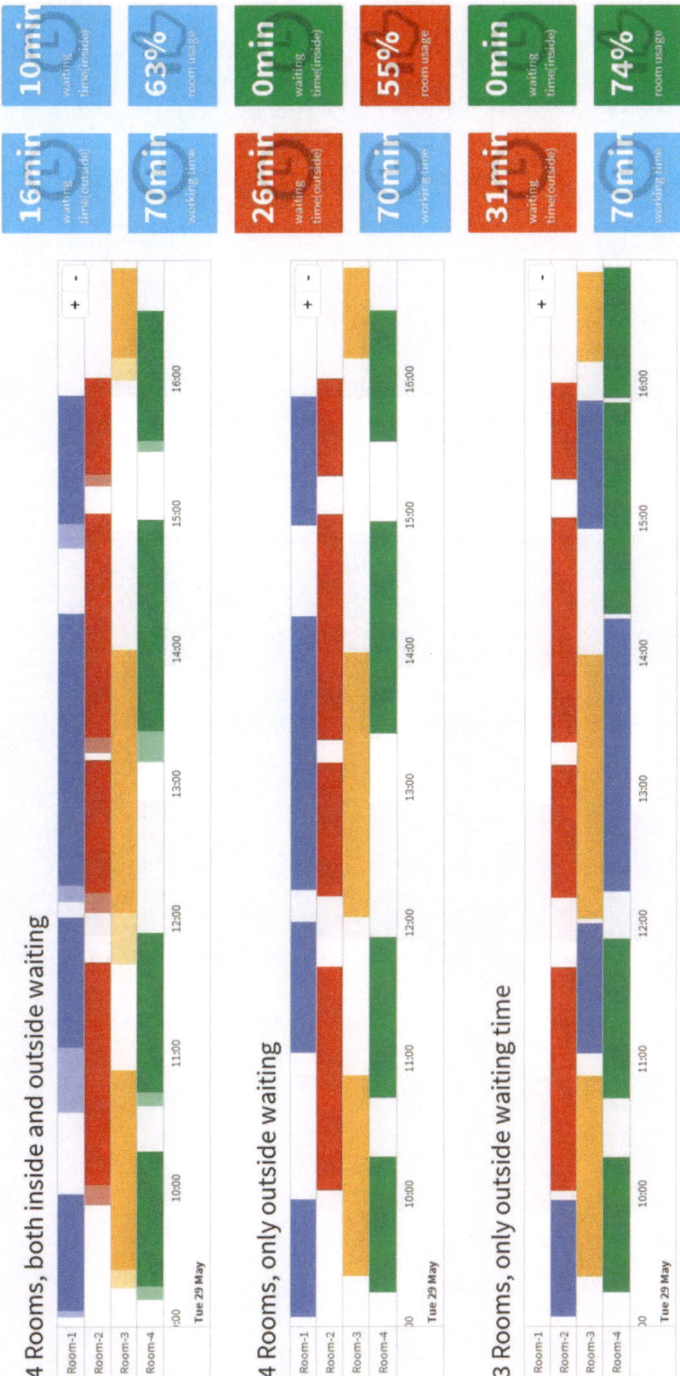

Fig. 10.5 Occupied Times Organized by Room and Patient

Chapter 11
Case Study: Safe Birth Clinic

Abstract Introductory courses in Operations Management typically introduce students to process analysis and queuing theory. We apply these tools to consider patient flows in an outpatient clinic where processes are made more complex by inclusion of the teaching mission of an Academic Medical Center. The case narrative deals with a physician who moved his practice from a setting with no teaching mission to the academic setting. This created a natural experiment because he began treating the same patients using a different process flow. Students are asked to use data collected at both settings to compare and contrast these flows. The protagonist weighs options designed to improve an appointment schedule, change patient punctuality, and introduce a type of pre-processing of patients. Evaluation of these proposals calls for a different style of analysis. Students are introduced to the use of discrete event simulation to address such questions. Simulation models are provided corresponding to the two clinic settings. This allows students to conduct and learn from virtual experiments using calibrated models. The case fills a need for material that covers issues in healthcare delivery, which the basic tools of process analysis and queuing theory are insufficient to fully address.

11.1 Introduction

The SafeBirth Clinic specializes in helping mothers manage a high-risk pregnancy.[1] The clinic uses advanced technology to help promote a safe, healthy delivery for mother and baby and provides diagnostic testing and specialized fetal care, including advanced fetal ultrasound, amniocentesis (amniotic fluid test), chorionic villus

---

[1] This case has reproduced with permission from Dawande, Milind, et al. "Case—The SafeBirth Clinic." INFORMS Transactions on Education 21.3 (2021): 148-151. The case is presented solely as a basis for engaging students in a classroom discussion on process capacity and its relationship with the capacity of a bottleneck resource. The setting depicted and the different processes described have been expressly designed for this purpose and do not necessarily reflect practice.

© The Author(s), under exclusive license to Springer Nature Switzerland AG 2022
C. Chambers et al., *Improving Processes for Health Care Delivery*,
https://doi.org/10.1007/978-3-031-19043-8_11

sampling (CVS), and fetal echocardiogram.

Currently, the following two physicians work at SafeBirth:

- Dr. Susan Wheeler, an obstetrician/gynecologist specializing in high-risk pregnancies

- Dr. Roger Sanders, a perinatologist

The clinic also staffs a sonographer for operating its state-of-the-art three-dimensional (3-D) ultrasound equipment, a nurse practitioner, and a receptionist.

Almost all the patients who come to SafeBirth are referred to the clinic by their regular obstetrician/gynecologist. In most cases, they need a perinatal procedure. These patients either seek prenatal diagnosis of genetic abnormalities and fetal infections or are women whose health puts them or their babies at risk for complications, such as heart disease, placental abnormalities, premature rupture of the membranes, diabetes, cystic fibrosis, multiple sclerosis, or cancer.

The two most common prenatal diagnostic tests for genetic defects are amniocentesis and CVS. Amniocentesis is a medical procedure wherein a needle is used to extract a small amount of amniotic fluid, which contains fetal tissues, from the amniotic sac surrounding the baby; the fetal DNA is then examined in a laboratory for genetic defects. In CVS, a sample of chorionic villi is removed from the placenta for testing. The sample can be taken through the cervix or the abdominal wall. CVS is usually done when the mother is between weeks 10 and 13 of pregnancy, whereas amniocentesis is usually done between weeks 14 and 17. For some patients, a fetal echocardiogram test is recommended to test the baby's heart for problems before birth. This test is done by a sonographer using an ultrasound machine and is typically conducted when the mother is about 18-24 weeks pregnant.

After arriving at the clinic, the patient follows a specific process. This process was updated in 2019, based on the feedback received from patients. Before discussing the current process adopted by the clinic, we discuss the earlier process that was followed until the end of 2018.

11.2 Process A: The Earlier Process (Followed by Patients Until December 2018

The earlier process consisted of the following five activities:

Activity 1: Check-In and Paperwork
The receptionist welcomes the patient, collects insurance information, and requires

her to fill out paperwork. Because the doctors make important medical assessments, it is critical that a complete medical history be obtained. For instance, if a patient has undergone a tonsillectomy, then this information may affect anesthesia decisions or a prior hernia surgery may influence surgical plans.

This activity takes about 10 minutes on average. The only resource used during the activity is the receptionist.

Activity 2: Nurse Check

Prior to the examination of the patient by the doctors, the nurse practitioner conducts a physical examination of the patient, updates the record of any medications that the patient is taking, and collects all documents relating to the patient's medical history.

The nurse check takes about 15 minutes on average. The only resource used during the activity is the nurse.

Activity 3: Examination and 3-D Ultrasound Examination by Dr. Wheeler

The doctor has a discussion with the patient about her previous medical history, family history, and past surgeries, and current lifestyle. The ultrasound pelvic exam examines the structures in the lower abdomen and pelvis. For most patients, this exam consists of physical checks and, given the high risk nature of the pregnancy, both transabdominal and transvaginal ultrasounds. The physical checks include an external genitalia exam, a speculum examination, and a bimanual exam. The transabdominal ultrasound examines fetal development, the position of the baby and the placenta, and the amount of amniotic fluid present around the baby. The purpose of the transvaginal ultrasound depends on the period of gestation: In early pregnancy, this procedure checks for any cysts, fibroid tumors, or other growths, whereas, in later pregnancies, it is done if preterm birth is a concern.

On average, the total time taken for this activity is about 50 minutes. This activity requires three resources, namely, Dr. Wheeler, the ultrasound equipment, and the sonographer, simultaneously.

Activity 4: Discussion and Perinatal Procedure by Dr. Sanders

The doctor first explains the risks involved in perinatal procedures to the patient and the interpretation of potential results. Depending on the period of gestation, either amniocentesis or CVS is conducted, guided by the ultrasound equipment. In some rare cases, a fetal echocardiogram is also done. Both amniocentesis and CVS require the administration of local anesthesia.

On average, the total time taken for the discussion and perinatal procedure is about 20 minutes. This activity requires three resources, namely, Dr. Sanders, the ultrasound equipment, and the sonographer, simultaneously.

Activity 5: Feedback on Service

The patient schedules a follow-up visit and is requested to fill a short feedback form for any suggestions she might have to improve service quality at the clinic.

On average, the total time taken for this activity is five minutes. The only resource used in this activity is the receptionist.

The process, as stated above is for the first visit of a patient to SafeBirth. This is referred to as a regular visit. The patients are also asked to schedule a followup visit to review the results of the procedure done during the first visit. A follow-up visit is relatively short. Each week, Friday is the day dedicated to follow-up visits. Thus, the process above is relevant for appointments on the first four days of each week.

In some cases, a repeat regular visit is necessitated if complications develop. For a repeat visit, the process above stays largely unchanged, except that the procedures done during the various activities may differ. For instance, in Activity 4, the perinatal procedures performed are different; instead of amniocentesis or CVS, a level 2 ultrasound for a comprehensive evaluation of fetal anatomy and development or some other perinatal procedure related to the specific complication is performed. Therefore, we will assume that, on average, the time taken for each activity above as well as the resources consumed remain the same during a repeat regular visit too.

The process is succinctly summarized in Figure 1.

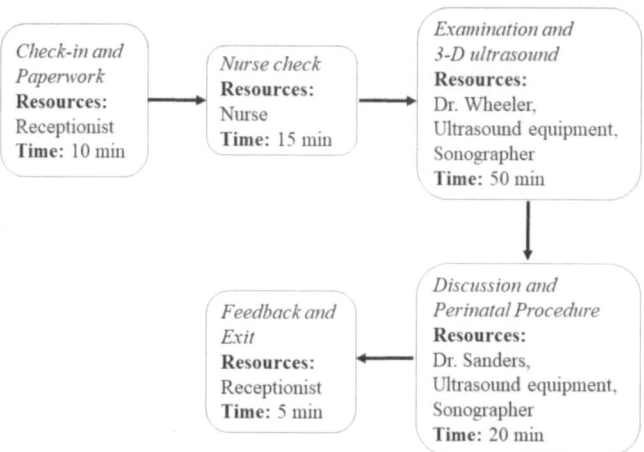

Fig. 11.1 The Process (Process A) Followed by Patients at SafeBirth Until the End of 2018

11.3 Process B: The Current Process (Being Followed by Patients Since January 2019)

In the process that was followed until the end of 2018, Drs. Wheeler and Sanders would meet the patient individually during their respective examinations in the course of Activities 3 and 4. Based on the feedback from the patients, it was discovered that they would be much more comfortable with a joint meeting with the doctors at the start. Often times, patients would question Dr. Wheeler about the impending perinatal procedure to be conducted by Dr. Sanders. Also, with most patients not being medically knowledgeable, there were instances where they either misunderstood or were not clear on the import of the discussion Dr. Wheeler had with them. This led to some confusion during their subsequent meeting with Dr. Sanders.

Based on this feedback, the doctors decided to update the process and introduce a joint meeting with the patient upfront to discuss the pros and cons of the procedures conducted during the visit.

The updated process is now the current process at SafeBirth and has six activities: Activities 1 and 2 of the earlier process remain the first two activities of the current process. The last activity (Activity 5) of the earlier process also remains the last activity (Activity 6) of the current process. The intermediate three activities of the current process are as follows:

Activity 3: Joint examination of the patient by Dr. Wheeler and Dr. Sanders
The two doctors first have a detailed discussion with the patient about her previous medical history, family history, past surgeries, and current lifestyle. This is followed by the pelvic exam, which consists of three physical checks: a physical and external genitalia exam, a speculum examination, and a bimanual exam. Dr. Sanders also explains the risks involved in perinatal procedures to the patient. Finally, the doctors briefly discuss any concerns they might have or issue some advice and instructions to the patient and ask the patient to proceed for ultrasound.

On average, the time taken for the joint examination is about 15 minutes. This activity uses two resources, namely, Dr. Wheeler and Dr. Sanders.

Activity 4: 3-D Ultrasound Examination by Dr. Wheeler
The transabdominal and transvaginal ultrasounds are conducted for most patients.

On average, the total time taken for the ultrasound exams is about 50 minutes. This activity uses three resources, namely, Dr. Wheeler, the ultrasound equipment, and the sonographer.

Activity 5: Perinatal Procedure by Dr. Sanders
With the help of the ultrasound equipment, either amniocentesis or CVS is conducted and, in rare cases, a fetal echocardiogram.

On average, the total time taken for the perinatal procedure is about 20 minutes. This activity uses three resources, namely, Dr. Sanders, the ultrasound equipment, and the sonographer.

Figure 2 illustrates the current process.

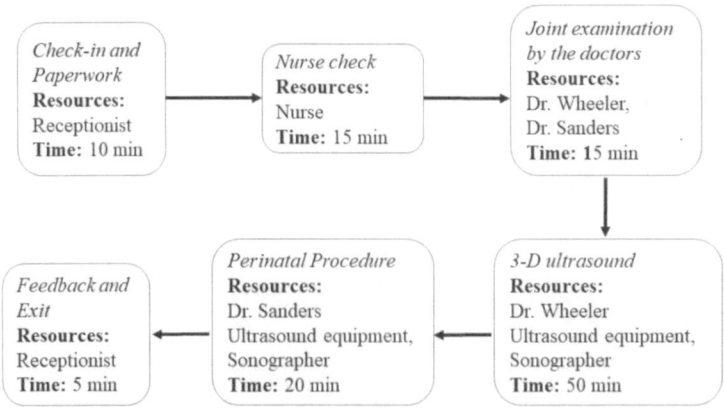

Fig. 11.2 The Process (Process B) Being Followed by Patients Since January 2019

11.4 A New Potential Addition: Genetic Counselling and Physical Therapy Session

A high-risk pregnancy can be extremely stressful. Most expectant mothers who come to SafeBirth face, to varying degrees, the risk of birth defects or genetic complications in their babies–some mothers have a family history of genetic disorders; some others are at risk because of advanced age, whereas some mothers have health issues of their own. To make matters worse, the plethora of information available on the internet about potential genetic disorders and fetal infections only serves to confuse and scare mothers. After carefully studying feedback from patients over the years, Drs. Sanders and Wheeler feel that mothers can significantly benefit from personalized counselling that would provide a meaningful interpretation of their individual data and circumstances and also much-needed emotional support.

Another area that the doctors feel would significantly help their patients is postoperative physical therapy. After having undergone a procedure such as amniocentesis or CVS, it is important to educate mothers on the physical activities to avoid at home and provide them with a specific set of maneuvers and exercises that would make them feel comfortable. Again, this advice would have to be personalized, taking into account the specific medical complications and the physical characteristics of a particular individual.

Keeping these needs in mind, the doctors are mulling over the possibility of offering a combined counselling and physical therapy information session for their patients. Over the past few weeks, they have also spoken to several patients; the feedback received was extremely positive, and they anticipate that almost all patients will sign up for such a session. The doctors expect such a counsellor to have a degree in genetic counselling and some prior experience in offering physical therapy. After a detailed discussion on the proposed agenda for the personalized counselling and therapy session, the doctors estimate the session to last about 80 minutes for each patient. The doctors have not yet decided how many such counsellors to hire.

If SafeBirth decides to offer the counselling session, then it would be offered after the perinatal procedure. Figure 3 illustrates the process after the (potential) introduction of this activity.

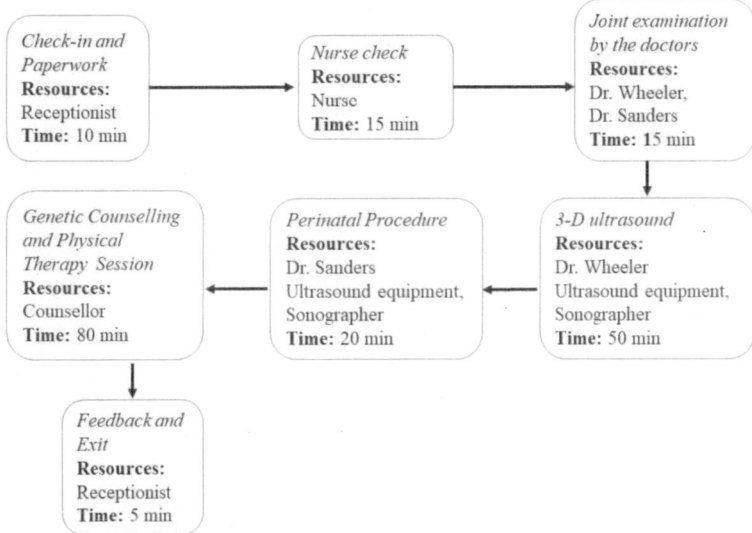

Fig. 11.3 The Process (Process C) to be Followed by Patients if the Counselling Session is Introduced

11.5 Process Redesign: Separate Upfront Examinations by the Doctor

In the current process (Process B) being followed by the patients at the clinic, the two doctors conduct a joint examination of each patient (Activity 3) prior to the medical procedure. After experiencing this process for more than a year now, the two doctors realize that the upfront examination has been extremely helpful to the patients. However, they believe that a joint examination is not necessary. Instead, they could examine each patient separately, first Dr. Wheeler and then Dr. Sanders, for 10 minutes each. If implemented, the new process (Process D) will be as shown in Figure 4.

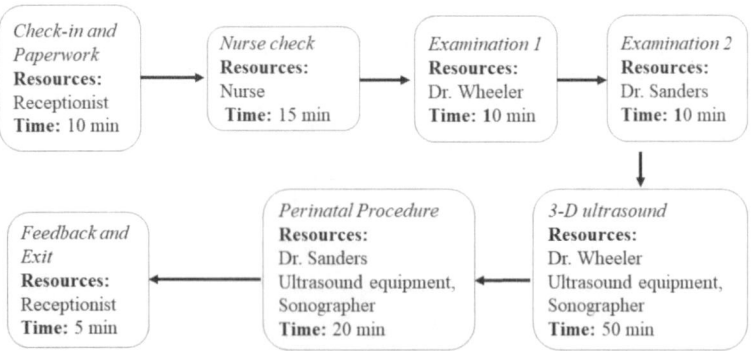

Fig. 11.4 The Process (Process D) to be Followed by Patients if the Upfront Examination by the Doctors is Replaced by Two Separate Individual Examinations

11.6 Discussion Questions

In order to make insights from the case more concrete, please work through the questions posed below. For each question, assume that each activity takes its average duration with no variability in service times.

1. For Process A: Identify the lowest-capacity resource(s) and determine process capacity. Draw a Gantt chart to illustrate the schedule that achieves the process capacity.

2. For Process B: Identify the lowest-capacity resource(s) and determine process capacity. Draw a Gantt chart to illustrate the schedule that achieves the process capacity. Is process capacity equal to the lowest capacity among all the resources?

3. For Process B: Consider Dr. Wheeler, Dr. Sanders, and the Ultrasound equipment. In the schedule you made, are all of these three resources in use at all times?

4. For Process C: Identify the lowest capacity resource(s) and determine process capacity.

5. For Process C: What will process capacity become if the clinic acquires an additional unit of the resource with the lowest capacity?

6. For Process C: Can capacity be increased without increasing the capacity of the lowest capacity resource?

7. For Process D: Assume the clinic has hired a single counsellor. Identify the lowest capacity resource(s). Suppose that SafeBirth acquires an additional unit of this resource. What is the capacity of this new process?

8. For Process D: Is it possible to increase the capacity of the process by increasing the capacity of some or all resources that are not the lowest-capacity resource while keeping the capacity of the lowest capacity resource the same?

9. Compare the capacity levels of the 4 processes and discuss the managerial implications of your observations thus far. What generalizable insights can you provide on the efficient investment in resources and productive use of available resources?

Chapter 12
Epilogue

12.1 Introduction

Frank Caldwell damaged his wrist in a recreational basketball game while he was a part time MBA student at Eastern University. He then worked through a collection of interactions with Eastern University Hospital's system including the Emergency Department, an Orthopedic clinic, Outpatient Surgery, and an overnight stay in the hospital.[1] Inspired by concerns raised during this series of events, Frank decided to concentrate his MBA studies in the area of Health Care Management. During this work, Frank completed one course in particular called "Immersion Projects in Health Care Process Improvement." As part of this course Frank was involved in process mapping, data collection on activity times and inventory levels, process modeling using Discrete Event Simulation (DES), idea generation, hypothesis testing, implementation, and a series of presentations to clinic and hospital managers aimed to help improve patient flow and waiting times in a Physical Medicine and Rehabilitation (PM&R) clinic. In fact, this work lead to a number of publications on the topic. (See Chambers and Dada (2014), Chambers et al (2018), and Dada and Chambers (2019).) The style of the course was heavily influenced by several prominent scholars doing similar work at other schools. (See Kolker (2010b), Kolker (2011), Laguna and Marklund (2005), and Ozcan (2009), and Ozcan (2017).)

After completing the MBA program Frank was offered a job in the Operations Integration Group within Eastern University Hospital. This unit serves as a sort of internal consulting group helping departments, clinics, and specialties work through process improvement projects. Many hospitals have developed similar units where a small staff, trained in project management, process modeling, and a variety of approaches to process improvement help teams of other health care professionals work

---

[1] Recall that Franks's journey was discussed in the Prologue. We exercise a bit of poetic license as Frank is a literary device. There was no single, former student that worked on all of these projects. However, the works mentioned throughout this text are a subset of projects that the authors worked on, and most of them involved various student teams over the last decade.

to improve quality, reduce utilization, or re-engineer processes to improve system performance. In this role, Frank worked on a number of projects. Given the connection to his old Business school, Frank often collaborated with faculty there to find, advise and make use of teams of students looking at various areas of the hospital. These teams were valuable to the hospital in part because they could be used to collect detailed data and analyze it in different ways. The projects were valuable to the students because they got an up-close view of how a hospital actually works.

Eventually Frank created a web page to highlight some of this work. After a few years, he was surprised to see that he had worked on projects spanning much of the system including a Neonatal ICU, a Medical ICU, Obstetrics, Pediatric Dermatology, the Pediatric ED, the Adult ED, Outpatient surgery, Radiation Oncology, a major pain clinic, Neurology, Orthopedics, Urology, and even Palliative care.

Frank was also asked repeatedly to provide input for other parts of the system including the Financial Analysis Unit (FAU). This group worked on projects including business plans for new units including new outpatient clinics, a peri-operative pain clinic, and a proposal for a Traumatic Brain Injury (TBI) institute. At other times Frank provided help with analysis at an insurance company that was part of the Eastern Hospital system. This included work that focused on alternate sites of care for Medicaid patients to improve access and to reduce costs.

Along the way, Frank was involved with a number of additional publications including Chambers et al (2021), that looked at creating a crowdsourcing approach to collecting and managing data about surgical protocols, Conley et al (2016), that focused on using a Real Time Location System (RTLS) to collect data that hoped to feed into an Activity Based Costing (ABC) system, and Elnahal et al (2015a), and Elnahal et al (2015b), that sought to develop a strategy to use an RTLS to collect data for simulations of a Radiation Oncology service to focus on costs and waiting times. Additional work looked at connections between congestion and patient safety (See Elnahal et al (2015c), and Elnahal et al (2016).)

Frank ended up performing a lot of work in a large pain clinic that led to more publications like Williams et al (2012), which compared capacity levels between services in a private practice to that in an Academic Medical Center (AMC), Williams et al (2014) that looked at how patient unpunctuality effects congestion, and waiting times in outpatient clinics, and Williams et al (2015) that looked at the use of pre-processing to alter patient flow in outpatient settings. Pre-processing refers to moving some of the educational activities in an AMC offline to reduce congestion during the normal clinic sessions. Chambers et al (2016) looked at how physicians adjust their service times in the face of clinic congestion in both private practice and the AMC. Chambers and Williams (2017b) became a case study that the instructors used in later sections of some courses in Frank's old MBA program. (See Chapter 8.)

Some of Frank's work took a very different perspective. This included Dada et al (2022), and Singh et al (2022), that looked at the financial and cost implications associated with moving the site of service from the AMC to other parts of the network, and Hanna et al (2019), that looked into creating a system-level response to the ongoing opioid crisis.

12.2 Complications in Projects to Improve Health Care Processes

Along the way Frank often ran into hesitancy about using the approaches that he learned in the Business school to make changes in a hospital. One common criticism was that ideas from Operations Management and Operations Research wouldn't work with processes that deliver health care because medical service settings are fundamentally different from other production or service delivery systems. The delivery of health care is based on a network of knowledge workers, and not machines. Each case is imbued with its own nuances, and while steps are quite similar from one patient to the next, they are not simply repetitive. Many production processes show variability in terms of arrival times for jobs and activity times, but processes in health care involve variability along many additional dimensions all at once. The services involved are delivered in high pressure settings, with grave consequences for mistakes by experts that must make critical decisions in real time.

Over the years of working on these projects, Frank helped to develop a framework for improvement projects (as discussed in Chapter 6). However, that framework leaves a rather large question unanswered. Once we have an accurate depiction of the existing process and a clear proposal for some process modification it is relatively straight forward to collect data, edit a simulation model of a similar setting, and estimate the impact of a proposed change. However, it is not immediately obvious from where ideas for process improvement are going to come.

The critical complication is that managers must have some basis to claim that a change will improve system performance before an exhaustive data set is in place. In other words, we need the ability to make predictions about outcomes before making the change. This is needed to help screen proposals before a lengthy evaluation is done, to get buy-in from the many agents working in the system, and to move forward confident that no harm will be done by a proposed change. Over time Frank learned that improvements in this environment have to be based on a rather deep knowledge about the setting and the processes to be improved. Collecting data for its own sake is not enough. There is a difference between data, and useful information. But there is also a gap between information and deep knowledge. While these three are often confused or assumed to be identical, the differences are key to the task at hand.

In short, <u>data</u> is a concise quantitative or qualitative measure of system state, evolution, or performance. The number "43" standing by itself is useless. However, if this refers to 43 patients who came into the Emergency Department (ED) today, it becomes data. <u>Information</u> can be thought of as data in context. When context is added, such as "43 patients arrived today, compared with 29 yesterday, and the staff levels were not adjusted even though we had long waiting times yesterday," the statement becomes potentially useful information. Data is insufficient as a basis for action. Once data and context are combined to develop information we may find a basis for an action to be taken, such as diverting patients or asking to move workers from one area to another (Kock et al (1996)). By recognizing the context we arrive at what information the data needed to convey.

Taking this a step further, information is not the same as knowledge. <u>Knowledge</u> rests upon an understanding about the domain. A person with knowledge about a situation can understand the implications of incoming information and draw on that understanding to either take an action or ignore that particular stimulus (Zins (2007)). Knowledge has an essential predictive capability. If "piece of information W" is present with "context X," and action "Y" has been appropriate in past similar situations, then it is 80 per cent likely that action "Y" will be appropriate in this situation unless "Z" is present, etc. (Kock et al (1996)).

The need for the predictive power borne of deep knowledge is the key reason that knowledge is essential to process improvement. This also suggests that agents who work in the system on a day to day basis have to be involved throughout the data collection and analysis for improvement projects to have a reasonable chance of success.

Waiting times in an ED may present valuable data. Exposition of the context may transform this data into information. In order for this information to lead to improvement we must combine it with an understanding of how the system works, as well as an appreciation of the repercussions of longer waiting times. This understanding is the knowledge needed to both explain why the current situation is not sustainable and to state why and how much the situation will be improved if we take action "Y."

Fortunately, the practice of medicine includes a culture that routinely deals with large amounts of data and information but also with ways to develop knowledge without having to "reinvent the wheel" at every hospital or clinic. Medical research is carried out at a host of institutions in a very rigorous fashion, and results are made available to the larger community via publications, consulting arrangements, presentations, etc. Other interested parties and organizations use this work as a starting point when they seek ideas on how to improve health related outcomes. This approach lies at the core of the concept of evidence-based medicine. We don't all have to replicate every experiment or build a detailed data set for every case or condition that we see. We can find relevant research and figure out how that maps onto our patient set, caseload, medical service, etc.

Just as this is done to further medical knowledge, a parallel approach can be taken when looking for ideas on how to improve processes that deliver care. For example, hundreds of Discrete Event Simulation (DES) models have been created, validated, and used for research on everything from small private practice clinics, to entire networks of medical facilities. When we look for ideas related to managing waiting times we can leverage this prior work.

12.3 Searching for Improvement Ideas Using Prior Works

If we are interested in mining earlier work from others for suggestions and ideas about how to improve a process, we need to have a good sense of what we are looking for, a strategy to find it, and a way to make use of what we find.

12.3.1 Finding Ideas

As we seek ideas about actions that may improve a process we recognize that virtually any problem that we consider has been seen in some form before and multiple efforts have been made to improve the situation. The internet and specialized online databases provide ready access to more publications than ever before (Vom Brocke et al (2015)). A recent search for "healthcare process improvement" in Google Scholar produced 2,680,000 results. However, when we get more specific about a single issue, in a single setting, we may ultimately be looking for 2 or 3 works that actually tackle the problem of interest in a way that is sufficiently explained and likely to fit our setting. Wachtel and Dexter (2013) discusses the fact that the authors searched for publications that they knew existed about managing an Operating Room suite, only to find that a successful online search depended upon prior familiarity with a vocabulary of terms specific to that discipline. For example, if one is looking for published work with a focus on managing overtime in the Operating Room (OR) suite, one needs to search for articles that include the phrase "overutilized" or "over-utilized" Dexter (2017). This is unfortunate, because most people would not use that exact term in their day to day conversations. As a result, locating the most relevant works can be surprisingly cumbersome.

A large number of databases now exist that may be of use. We have found that Google Scholar and PubMed are excellent starting points and more than sufficient in most cases. However, in many fields more focused databases have also been developed. Here are a few ideas related to conducting a literature search across these databases.

1. Consider starting with literature reviews of similar works that summarize the field.

2. Formulate the question (of interest) and use terms gleaned from the literature reviews to translate it into the vocabulary and syntax that are appropriate to the field and the database.

3. Translate the same question into generic everyday keywords.

4. Search the database using both sets of keywords.

5. If the number of results is too large, add additional terms that narrow the focus toward your specific setting.

6. If the number of results is too small, broaden the vocabulary terms or remove criteria that are more specific to your setting.

7. Save a record of your search strategy so you know what is helpful and what is not and can duplicate or use a different strategy in another database.

8. If these steps are not sufficient, choose a few works that are "close" to what you need and consider the sources listed in them as references (Backward search).

9. Look at a work that might be a precursor to the works that you want, and look at later publications that reference this one (Forward search).

10. Ask for the assistance of a librarian, informationist, or colleague expert in searching.

When searching a vast literature to find an ideal example, it can help to make the question to be addressed as specific as possible. Rather then looking for ways to "reduce waiting time" we may want to ask something like "how do waiting times in an inner-city, outpatient, pain clinic compare under open scheduling versus a fixed appointment schedule?" While this is likely to be a bit too specific, the more similar the setting of a research project is to yours the better.

Recent years have seen an explosion in the number of data bases that catalog scholarly research, and each database will have its own nuances in how search terms are stated and used. Databases that focus on work in Operations Management or Industrial Engineering will have a different interface and reflect a different vocabulary when compared to those in medicine. This is significant because literature searches often boil down to identifying the right set of key words. For example, many doctors are concerned about patients arriving late to appointments. Much of the literature on this topic refers to patient "unpunctuality" because this was the term that early work on the topic employed as it was written in the UK. Most doctors outside of the UK would not use this term and may prefer the term "lateness."

At the same time, a vast literature on production environments addressed by researchers in Operations Management and Operations Research refer to job "tardiness." While these works are most often not focused on patients, the relationship between tardiness and completion times is the main idea that you are trying to understand. Your contribution may be simply in translating insights from works looking at a production setting to your patient service setting.

Consequently, it is often useful to read literature reviews and other work that is close to your topic in order to learn the vocabulary that it used in that research stream. On the other hand, one does need to do this with care as Zamboni et al (2020) has found that critiques of quality improvement efforts suggest that the mixed results can be partly explained by a tendency to reproduce activities without attempting to modify the functioning, interactions or culture in a clinical team, thus overlooking the mechanisms of change.

One strategy to deal with the issue of area-specific word choices is to begin with works that summarize a great deal of the relevant literature for you. These works are often labeled as "Literature Reviews" or "Annotated Bibliographies." Review papers are among the most frequently cited papers in most fields, so finding them is usually not difficult, and most databases allow researchers to search for publications of a specific type, including literature reviews. Reading a few of these works often helps identify the keywords that are more likely to lead to a fruitful search.

After the question is translated into a collection of keywords, multiple databases can be searched to find candidates for consideration. Perusing the titles and abstracts will usually reduce this initial list to a manageable size. In many cases you will find more sources than you need and you can whittle the list down by adding keywords more relevant to your specific setting. On the other hand, if you do not see anything useful, you may have to make the search less specific to broaden the range of outcomes.

One common technique that we have found particularly effective is to use forward and backward searches. Once you find a paper that seems close to what you need, you can easily consider the prior works that the paper cites as references. This is what we mean by a backward search. Similarly, you can find papers written later that reference the work that you have found. This is what we mean by a forward search. Combining these methods is likely to produce a set of works that are closely related to your topic of interest.

Finally, if this approach does not produce fruit with a reasonable amount of effort, it is time to seek professional help. Most large public, and virtually all university libraries employ experts specifically trained to help with these types of searches, and their service can be invaluable.

12.3.2 Screening Ideas

Frank worked on many projects with the Business school students. He recently recanted a story that bears repeating here. A pain medicine physician contacted Frank about working to improve waiting times at a clinic at a hospital affiliated with Virginia Commonwealth University in Richmond, Virginia. Frank set up a virtual meeting with the physician as well as the clinic manager and a nurse to clarify the issue. Frank immediately recalled some of our prior work in pain clinics including Williams et al (2012) and Williams et al (2015). After discussing the problem with the staff, Frank noticed that one concern was the no-show rate for patients in an inner-city, outpatient, pain clinic. Frank searched the literature using PubMed and located several papers that focused specifically on getting patients in a pain clinic to arrive on time in an inner-city hospital. (See Andreae et al (2017b) and Andreae et al (2017a).) He also looked at an effort to use an open access model in a very similar setting. (See Sivanesan et al (2017).)

The doctors in Virginia were looking at almost identical approaches for their setting. The clinic had existing reports on arrival and waiting times. However, this data was not collected with the idea in mind of creating a detailed model. The available data was mostly summary statistics that many Appointment Management Systems (AMS) generate. (See the cases in Chapters 11 and 12 for discussion about related issues.) This is only a fraction of the data that one gets sitting in a clinic for days at a time, recording every entry and exit into various spaces.

However, after Frank carefully considered the results that the prior work reported, he decided that the results did not show strong evidence that the actions taken materially affected clinic performance. As a result, Frank came up with a much simpler idea. The clinic could exercise a bit of extra effort to ensure that the time stamps entered for the next month were accurate and simply try to schedule one extra patient per hour. They could then review the data after 30 days and decide whether it was a good idea to add one more patient to the schedule, and so on. Elaborate studies often do not generate the results that one might wish for. However, the insights gained may be enough to suggest a simpler strategy and can lead in the right direction.

12.4 Closing Comments

As Frank looked back at his experiences working as an internal operations consultant, he realized that it would be easy to get discouraged by seeing so much effort to improve processes with so little documented benefit. Yet Frank believed that his own work had made a difference. So now as a seasoned practitioner of health care operations, he thought about how would he communicate with students who sought his advice.

First, process improvement in health care settings is incredibly important. Demand is growing, the population is aging, and costs are a tremendous burden on the economy. In order to make this system work better, patients and providers have to work together to improve both health outcomes and system performance. As we look to the future, we will have to figure out more ways to get the patients to contribute to efforts to make the system work better. This might be especially important in units that deal with the most complex cases like Academic Medical Centers (AMCs) typically do.

As his experience has shown, it is important to start all improvement projects by working to gain a deeper understanding of the process flows of patients, providers, and information. In addition, we need to understand as much as we can about the inflows and outflows of collections and costs. Only after a clear picture emerges of the business processes can one zero in on one or two essential flow and decision points in the delivery of care that need to be found to answer the question at hand.

When we think about the flows of patients, providers, and other resources, a comprehensive picture or model of the system can be constructed. However, in most instances the required data collection and model validation take much too long. Often the insights gleaned through basic mathematical models and common tools is enough to guide a simple, incremental approach. For example, if productivity is low and we want to schedule one more patient, perhaps it is sufficient to find a good slot for another visit in the appointment schedule by identifying where there is a lull in the action, rather than trying to add capacity.

By focusing on implementing a modest idea in an incremental fashion, we can create a setting where we can demonstrate quantitatively that it leads to a desired outcome. This early win can produce the impetus to improve the timeliness and quality of data collection. By moving toward this evidence-driven paradigm, the commitment to use information derived from data to make informed decisions can be instilled into the ethos of the managers' decision making apparatus.

Ultimately, no matter how good the data collection, the modeling, the analysis, and the recommendations, people make decisions. They have to buy into the improvement project from the start, believe in the output, and be able to communicate the implementation and its outcome to their managers and other stakeholders in the organization. Failing to be people-centric will result in failure of any proposed solution no matter how great the underlying analysis may be.

References

AHA (2017) Aha hospital statistics: fast facts on us hospitals. American Hospital Association, available at: www/aha/org (accessed May 31, 2017)

Alexopoulos C, Goldman D, Fontanesi J, Kopald D, JR W (2008) Modeling patient arrivals in community clinics. Omega 36:33–43

Andreae MH, Nair S, Gabry JS, Goodrich B, Hall C, Shaparin N (2017a) A pragmatic trial to improve adherence with scheduled appointments in an inner-city pain clinic by human phone calls in the patient's preferred language. Journal of clinical anesthesia 42:77–83

Andreae MH, White RS, Chen KY, Nair S, Hall C, Shaparin N (2017b) The effect of initiatives to overcome language barriers and improve attendance: a cross-sectional analysis of adherence in an inner city chronic pain clinic. Pain Medicine 18(2):265–274

Anupindi R, Chopra S, Deshmukh SD, Van Mieghem JA, Zemel E (1999) Managing business process flows, vol 400. Prentice Hall Upper Saddle River, NJ

Bai G, Anderson GF (2016) A more detailed understanding of factors associated with hospital profitability. Health Affairs 35(5):889–897

Bailey N (1952) A study of queues and appointment systems in hospital out-patient departments, with special reference to waiting-times. Journal of the Royal Statistical Society pp 185–199

Bailey N (1954) Queueing for medical care. Applied Statistics 3:137–145

Baker JJ (1998) Activity-based costing and activity-based management for health care. Jones & Bartlett Learning

Bandura A (1969) Principles of behavior modification. Holt, Rinehart, & Winston

Basharin GP, Langville AN, Naumov VA (2004) The life and work of aa markov. Linear algebra and its applications 386:3–26

Begen M, Queyranne M (2012) Appointment scheduling with discrete random durations. Mathematics of Operations Research 36:240–257

Bernard C (1957) An introduction to the study of experimental medicine, vol 400. Courier Corporation

Beronio K, Po R, Skopec L, Glied S (2014) Affordable care act will expand mental health and substance use disorder benefits and parity protections for 62 million americans. Mental Health 2

Bevan G (2006) Margaret l. brandeau, francois sainfort, william p. pierskella (eds.), review of operations research and health care. a handbook of methods and applications, kluwer, 2004.

Blanco White M, Pike M (1964) Appointment systems in out-patients' clinics and the effect of patients' unpunctuality. Medical Care pp 133–145

Boex J, Boll A, Franzini L, Hogan A, Irby D, Meservey P, Rubin R, Seifer S, Veloski J (2000) Measuring the costs of primary care education in the ambulatory setting. Academic Medicine 75(5):419–425

Bohmer RM, Huckman RS, Weber J, Bozic KJ (2007) Managing orthopaedics at rittenhouse medical center. Harvard Business School Case 607-152

Bowers J, Mould G (2005) Ambulatory care and orthopaedic capacity planning. Health Care Management Science 8(1):41–47

Burke E, De Causmaecker P, Berghe G, Van Landeghem H (2004) The state of the art of nurse rostering. Journal of Scheduling 7(6):441–499

Carvalho JV, Rocha Á, Abreu A (2016) Maturity models of healthcare information systems and technologies: a literature review. Journal of medical systems 40(6):1–10

Castiglioni A (2019) A history of medicine. Routledge

Cayirli T, Veral E, Rosen H (2006) Designing appointment scheduling systems for ambulatory care services. Health Care Management Science 9(1):47–58

Chambers C, Dada M (2014) Managing clinical appointments in an academic medical center

Chambers C, Williams K (2017a) Case article—miller pain treatment center—eastern hospital outpatient center. INFORMS Transactions on Education 17(3):116–120

Chambers C, Williams K (2017b) Case—miller pain treatment center. INFORMS Transactions on Education 17(3):121–127

Chambers C, Dada M, Elnahal S, Terezakis S, DeWeese T, Herman J, Williams K (2016) Changes to physician processing times in response to clinic congestion and patient punctuality: a retrospective study. BMJ open 6(10):e011,730

Chambers C, Dada M, González Fernández M, Williams K (2018) Managing clinical appointments in an academic medical center. In: INFORMS International Conference on Service Science, Springer, pp 277–286

Chambers CG, Dada M, et al (2021) Crowdsourcing anaesthesia care. comment on br j anaesth 2016; 117: 276–279. British journal of anaesthesia 127(5):e176–e177

Chao X, Liu L, Zheng S (2003) Resource allocation in multisite service systems with intersite customer flows. Management Science 49(12):1739–1752

Chesney A (1943) The Johns Hopkins Hospital and John Hopkins University School of Medicine: a chronicle. Johns Hopkins University Press

Clark W (1922) The Gantt chart: A working tool of management. Ronald Press Company

CMS (2020) National health expenditures fact sheet. URL https://www.cms.gov/Research-Statistics-Data-and-Systems/Statistics-Trends-and-Reports/NationalHealthExpendData/NHE-Fact-Sheet

Conley W, Chambers C, Elnahal S, Choflet A, Williams K, DeWeese T, Herman J, Dada M (2016) Using real-time location system technology to facilitate process analysis and time-driven activity based costing in a radiation oncology outpatient clinic

Cooper R, Kaplan RS (1992) Activity-based systems: Measuring the costs of resource usage. Accounting horizons 6(3):1–13

Dada M, Mundly V, Chambers CG, Alamdar Yazdi MA, Ha C, Toporcer SE, Zhou Y, Gan Y, Xing Z, Mooney M, et al (2022) Managing prior approval for site-of-service referrals: an algorithmic approach. BMC health services research 22(1):1–7

Dada MM, Chambers C (2019) Healthcare analytics. In: Essentials of Business Analytics, Springer, pp 765–791

Dantas LF, Fleck JL, Oliveira FLC, Hamacher S (2018) No-shows in appointment scheduling–a systematic literature review. Health Policy 122(4):412–421

Dexter F (1999) Design of appointment systems for preanesthesia evaluation clinics to minimize patient waiting times: A reivew of computer simulation and patient survey studies. Anesthesia and Analgesia 89:925–931

Dexter F (2017) Rcl-22 implementing operating room management improvement. Review Course Lectures p 22

for Economic Co-operation O, Development (2020) Health spending (indicator). URL https://doi.10.1787/8643de7e-en

Elnahal S, Conley W, Afonso S, Guss Z, Quon H, Kiess A, DeWeese T, Williams K, Dada M, Herman J (2015a) Defining clinical process value in radiation oncology: A pilot study using a real time location system and discrete events simulation technology. International Journal of Radiation Oncology? Biology? Physics 93(3):E365–E366

Elnahal S, Conley W, Souranis A, Briner V, McNutt T, DeWeese T, Dada M, Chambers C, Herman J, Terezakis S (2015b) Treatment machine workload is associated with near-miss and safety incidents: Analyzing safety with a novel operations management data system. International Journal of Radiation Oncology, Biology, Physics 3(93):E502

Elnahal S, Moningi S, Wild A, Dholakia A, Hodgin M, Fan K, Pawlik T, Herman J (2015c) Improving safe patient throughput in a multidisciplinary oncology clinic. Physician leadership journal 2(2):56

Elnahal S, Blackford A, Smith K, Souranis A, Briner V, McNutt T, DeWeese T, Wright J, Terezakis S (2016) Identifying predictive factors for incident reports in patients receiving radiation therapy. International Journal of Radiation Oncology* Biology* Physics 94(5):993–999

Emerson HP, Naehring DC (1988) Origins of industrial engineering: the early years of a profession. Inst of Industrial Engineers

Erol T, Mendi AF, Doğan D (2020) The digital twin revolution in healthcare. In: 2020 4th International Symposium on Multidisciplinary Studies and Innovative Technologies (ISMSIT), pp 1–7, DOI 10.1109/ISMSIT50672.2020.9255249

Feddock C, Bailey P, Griffith C, Lineberry M, Wilson J (2010) Is time spent with the physician associated with parent dissatisfaction due to long waiting times? Evaluation & the Health Professions 33(2):216–225

Fetter R, Thompson J (1966) Patients' waiting time and doctors' idle time in the outpatient setting. Health Services Research 1(1):66

Fitzsimmons J, Fitzsimmons M (2006) Service management. Tata McGraw Hill Education Private Limited

Flagle C (2002) Some origins of operations research in the health services. Operations Research 50(1):52–60, DOI Some Origins of Operations Research in the Health Services. Operations Research 50(1):52-60. https://doi.org/10.1287/opre.50.1.52.17805

Franzini L, Berry J (1999) A cost-construction model to assess the total cost of an anesthesiology residency program. The Journal of the American Society of Anesthesiologists 90(1):257–268

French J (1946) A History of the University Founded by Johns Hopkins. Johns Hopkins Press

Gantt HL (1919) Organizing for work. Harcourt, Brace and Howe

Gass SI, Assad AA (2005) An annotated timeline of operations research: An informal history, vol 75. Springer Science & Business Media

Glied S, Ma S (2015) How will the Affordable Care Act affect the use of health care services? Commonwealth Fund

Günal MM, Pidd M (2010) Discrete event simulation for performance modelling in health care: a review of the literature. Journal of Simulation 4(1):42–51

Guttmann A, Schull MJ, Vermeulen MJ, Stukel TA (2011) Association between waiting times and short term mortality and hospital admission after departure from emergency department: population based cohort study from ontario, canada. Bmj 342

Hanna MN, Chambers C, Punyala A, Iqbal A, Singh B, Oruc C, Prakash P, Prajapati Y, Wang Y, Shechter R, et al (2019) A model for an institutional response to the opioid crisis. Journal of opioid management 16(1):73–83

Heskett JL (2003) Shouldice hospital limited

Hing E, Hall M, Ashman J, Xu J (2010) National hospital ambulatory medical care survey: 2007 outpatient department summary. Natl Health Stat Report 28:1–32

Hopp WJ, Lovejoy WS (2012) Hospital operations: Principles of high efficiency health care. FT Press

Hosek J, Palmer A (1983) Teaching and hospital costs: the case of radiology. Journal of Health Economics 2(1):29–46

Huang X (1994) Patient attitude towards waiting in an outpatient clinic and its applications. Health Services Management Research 7(1):2–8

Hwang C, Wichterman K, Alfrey E (2010) The cost of resident education. Journal of Surgical Research 163(1):18–23

Jha R, Sahay B, Charan P (2016) Healthcare operations management: a structured literature review. Decision 43(3):259–279

Kaplan R, Anderson S (2003) Time-driven activity-based costing. SSRN 485443

Kaplan R, Porter M (2011) How to solve the cost crisis in health care. Harvard Business Review 89(9):46–52

Kaplan RS (2014) Improving value with tdabc. Healthcare Financial Management 68(6):76–84

Karuppan CM, Dunlap NE, Waldrum MR, et al (2021) Operations management in healthcare: strategy and practice. Springer Publishing Company

Klienrock L (1975) Queueing systems. A wiley-Interscience Publication

Kock NF, McQueen RJ, Baker M (1996) Learning and process improvement in knowledge organizations: a critical analysis of four contemporary myths. The Learning Organization

Kolker A (2010a) Queuing theory and discrete events simulation for health care. Health Information Systems: Concepts, Methodologies, Tools, and Applications 4:1874–1915

Kolker A (2010b) Queuing theory and discrete events simulation for health care: from basic processes to complex systems with interdependencies. In: Health Information Systems: Concepts, Methodologies, Tools, and Applications, IGI Global, pp 1874–1915

Kolker A (2011) Healthcare management engineering: what does this fancy term really mean?: The use of operations management methodology for quantitative decision-making in healthcare settings. Springer Science & Business Media

Kolker A (2013) Interdependency of hospital departments and hospital-wide patient flows. In: Patient flow, Springer, pp 43–63

Kolker A, Story P (2012) Management engineering for effective healthcare delivery: Principles and applications

Laguna M, Marklund J (2005) Business Process Modeling, Simulation and Design. Pearson Prentice Hall, Upper Saddle River, NJ

Lasater KB, Aiken LH, Sloane DM, French R, Martin B, Reneau K, Alexander M, McHugh MD (2020) Chronic hospital nurse understaffing meets covid-19: an observational study. BMJ Quality & Safety

Lee V, Earnest A, Chen M, Krishnan B (2005) Predictors of failed attendances in a multi-specialty outpatient centre using electronic databases. BMC Health Services Research 5(1):1

van Lent WA, VanBerkel P, van Harten W (2012) A review on the relation between simulation and improvement in hospitals. BMC Medical Informatics and Decision Making 12(1):1

Lin C, Albertson G, Schilling L, Cyran E, Anderson S, Ware L, Anderson R (2001) Is patients' perception of time spent with the physician a determinant of ambulatory patient satisfaction? Archives of Internal Medicine 161(11):1437–1442

Little JD (2011) Or forum—little's law as viewed on its 50th anniversary. Operations research 59(3):536–549

Long DM (1991) The johns hopkins hospital. Journal of neurosurgery 75(1):160–161

Lorenzoni L, Belloni A, Sassi F (2014) Health-care expenditure and health policy in the usa versus other high-spending oecd countries. The Lancet 384(9937):83–92

Majeed A (2017) Shortage of general practitioners in the nhs

Mandelbaum A, Momcilovic P, Tseytlin Y (2012) On fair routing from emergency departments to hospital wards: Qed queues with heterogeneous servers. Management Science 58(7):1273–1291

Mawardi B (1979) Satisfactions, dissatisfactions, and causes of stress in medical practice. Journal of the Americal Medical Association 241(14):1483–1486

McCarthy K, McGee H, O'Boyle C (2000) Outpatient clinic waiting times and non-attendance as indicators of quality. Psychology, Health & Medicine 5(3):287–293

Meza J (1998) Patient waiting times in a physician's office. The American Journal of Managed Care 4(5):703–712

Moore JH, Weatherford LR (2001) Decision modeling with microsoft excel. Prentice Hall PTR

Moses H, Thier S, Matheson D (2005) Why have academic medical centers survived? Journal of the Americal Medical Association 293(12):1495–1500

Ortman J, Velkoff V, Hogan H (2014) An aging nation: the older population in the united states. Washington, DC: US Census Bureau pp 25–1140

Ozcan YA (2009) Quantitative Methods in Health Care Management: Techniques and Applications, vol 36. John Wiley & Sons

Ozcan YA (2017) Analytics and Decision Support in Health Care Operations Management. John Wiley & Sons

Perros P, Frier B (1996) An audit of waiting times in the diabetic outpatient clinic: Role of patients' punctuality and level of medical staffing. Diabetic Medicine 13:669–673

Peterson SM, Harbertson CA, Scheulen JJ, Kelen GD (2019) Trends and characterization of academic emergency department patient visits: A five-year review. Academic Emergency Medicine 26(4):410–419

Prentice JC, Pizer SD (2007) Delayed access to health care and mortality. Health services research 42(2):644–662

Sainfort F, Blake J, Gupta D, Rardin R (2005) Operations research for health care delivery systems. WTEC Panel Report

Schmidt E, Dada M, Ward J, Adams D (2001) Using cyclic planning to manage capacity at alcoa. Interfaces 31(3):16–27

Seals B, Feddock C, Griffith C, Wilson J, Jessup M, Kesavalu S (2005) Does more time spent with the physician lessen parent clinic dissatisfaction due to long waiting times? Journal of Investigative Medicine 53(1):S324–S324

Shortle JF, Thompson JM, Gross D, Harris CM (2018) Fundamentals of queueing theory, vol 399. John Wiley & Sons

Singer AJ, Thode Jr HC, Viccellio P, Pines JM (2011) The association between length of emergency department boarding and mortality. Academic Emergency Medicine 18(12):1324–1329

Singh S, Rydland KJ, Chambers C, Mundlye V, Kumian E, Williams KA, Dada M (2022) Implications for cost and access of site-of-service referrals for ancillary medical services in a us medicaid population: analysis of claims data from maryland, usa. BMJ open 12(6):e058,104

Sivanesan E, Lubarsky DA, Ranasinghe CT, Sarantopoulos CD, Epstein RH (2017) Modified open-access scheduling for new patient evaluations at an academic chronic pain clinic increased patient access to care, but did not materially reduce their mean cancellation rate: A retrospective, observational study. Journal of clinical anesthesia 41:92–96

Sloan F, Feldman R, Steinwald A (1983) Effects of teaching on hospital costs. Journal of Health Economics 2(1):1–28

Sprague LG (2007) Evolution of the field of operations management. Journal of Operations Management 25(2):219–238

Stiefel M, Shaner A, SD S (1996) The edwin smith papyrus: the birth of analytical thinking in medicine and otolaryngology. Laryngoscope 116(2):182–188, DOI 10.1097/01.MLG.0000191461.08542.A3

Strickland J (2010) Discrete Event Simulation using ExtendSim 8. Simulation Educators, Colorado Springs, CO

Tai G, Williams P (2012) Optimization of scheduling patient appointments in clinics using a novel modelling technique of patient arrival. Computer Methods and Programs in Biomedicine 108(2):467–476

Taylor D, Whellan D, Sloan F (1999) Effects of admission to a teaching hospital on the cost and quality of care for medicare beneficiaries. New England Journal of Medicine 340(4):293–299

Thomas S, Glynne-Jones R, Chait I (1997) Is it worth the wait? a survey of patients' satisfaction with an oncology outpatient clinic. European Journal of Cancer Care 6(1):50–58

Vieth TL, Rhodes KV (2006) The effect of crowding on access and quality in an academic ed. The American journal of emergency medicine 24(7):787–794

Vom Brocke J, Simons A, Riemer K, Niehaves B, Plattfaut R, Cleven A (2015) Standing on the shoulders of giants: Challenges and recommendations of literature search in information systems research. Communications of the association for information systems 37(1):9

Wachtel RE, Dexter F (2013) Difficulties and challenges associated with literature searches in operating room management, complete with recommendations. Anesthesia & Analgesia 117(6):1460–1479

Welch J, Bailey N (1952) Appointment systems in hospital outpatient departments. The Lancet pp 1105–1108

Williams J, Matthews M, Hassan M (2007) Cost differences between academic and nonacademic hospitals: a case study of surgical procedures. Hospital topics 85(1):3–10

Williams K, Chambers C, Dada M, Hough D, Aron R, Ulatowski J (2012) Using process analysis to assess the impact of medical education on the delivery of pain services a natural experiment. The Journal of the American Society of Anesthesiologists 116(4):931–939

Williams K, Chambers C, Dada M, McLeod J, Ulatowski J (2014) Patient punctuality and clinic performance: observations from an academic-based private practice pain centre: a prospective quality improvement study. BMJ open 4(5):e004,679

Williams K, Chambers C, Dada M, Christo P, Hough D, Aron R, Ulatowski J (2015) Applying jit principles to resident education to reduce patient delays: A pilot study in an academic medical center pain clinic. Pain Medicine 16(2):312–318

Wilson JT (1981) Implementation of computer simulation projects in health care. Journal of the Operational Research Society 32(9):825–832

Zamboni K, Baker U, Tyagi M, Schellenberg J, Hill Z, Hanson C (2020) How and under what circumstances do quality improvement collaboratives lead to better outcomes? a systematic review. Implementation Science 15(1):1–20

Zandbelt LC, Smets EM, Oort FJ, Godfried MH, De Haes HC (2004) Satisfaction with the outpatient encounter. Journal of general internal medicine 19(11):1088–1095

Zhang X (2018) Application of discrete event simulation in health care: a systematic review. BMC health services research 18(1):1–11

Zins C (2007) Conceptual approaches for defining data, information, and knowledge. Journal of the American society for information science and technology 58(4):479–493

Index

Academic Medical Center, 180
Academic Medical Center
  AMC, 39, 64, 128, 145, 147, 149, 161, 185
  appointment schedule, 187
  capacity, 145
  AMC, 31
Activity, 2, 55, 129
Activity Time, 44
Activity Time
  distribution, 83, 162
Activity Time, 6, 23, 28, 29, 59, 61, 80
Activity Time
  attending, 145, 161
  CDF, 68
  distribution, 64, 68, 69, 88, 134, 157, 166,
    183, 187
Affordable Care Act, 127
Appointment Management System
  AMS, 199
Appointment Schedule
  open, 17
Arrival Process, 142, 162
Arrival Rate, 5, 13, 15, 17
Attending, 6, 31, 37, 38, 55, 64, 128, 140, 147,
    181
Attending
  processing time, 143, 165

Batch Size, 6
Blocking, 171, 173
Bottleneck, 5, 10, 86, 136
Bottleneck
  example, 20

Capacity, 5, 10, 12, 130
Capacity
  example, 20

Census, 7, 15
Centers for Medicare and Medicaid Services
  CMS, 169
Check-In, 15, 29, 31, 46, 56, 82, 117, 156, 181,
    186
Check-Out, 15, 29, 46, 82, 117, 156, 181, 187
Clinic
  AMC, 129, 137
  check-in, 129
  check-out, 129
  hernia, 25
  outpatient, 129
  vital, 129
  waiting time, 130
  walk-in, 12, 15, 129
  walk-in example, 17
Clinical Assistant
  CA, 56, 57
Cost, 10, 54, 57
Cost
  ABC Example, 111
  attending, 112
  example, 22
  labor, 20
  medicare cost report, 109
  overtime, 66, 67
  rooms, 60, 111
  waiting, 66–68
Cost to Charge Ratio, 109, 112, 114, 116
Critical Path Method
  backward pass, 46, 48
  CPM, 27, 43, 50
  critical activities, 44
  critical path, 43
  dependencies, 44
  EFT, 44, 48, 50
  end, 50

EST, 44, 48, 50
  example, 46
  forward pass, 44, 48
  LFT, 44, 48, 50
  LST, 44, 48, 50
  predecessor, 44
  slack time, 44, 45, 48
  start, 50
  sucessor, 44
Critical Time, 5, 12, 22
Critical Time
  example, 20
Cycle
  composite job, 66, 69
Cycle Time, 4, 12, 28, 80, 121, 137, 139, 154,
    158, 160
Cycle Time
  length of stay, 13
  queue, 98
  stable, 13
  theoretical, 21

Data, 233
Data Collection, 28
Decomposition, 65, 67, 74, 75, 115
Diagnosis Related Group
  DRG, 110, 116
Discrete Event Simulation, 149
Discrete Event Simulation
  DES, 132, 133, 136, 137, 141, 145, 149, 154
  schematic, 157, 159, 163, 169, 172
Double-Booking, 33, 39, 63

Electronic Medical Record
  EMR, 29
Emergency Department, 12
Emergency Department
  blocking, 172
  simulation, 169
Entry Time, 28
Exam, 32, 35, 36, 117, 124, 129, 156
Exit Time, 28

Face Time, 11, 29, 138, 147, 201
Face Time
  state dependent, 166
Flow Time, 3
Flow Unit, 2, 4, 5, 7, 12, 15, 129

Gantt Chart, 27, 31, 33, 41, 50, 55, 73, 154
Gantt Chart
  academic medical center, 38, 40, 41
  private practice, 31, 35, 36, 117

Henry L. Gantt, 31
Heuristic, 61, 67, 71, 73, 75, 85, 115
Heuristic
  length-gap, 71
  length-gap +, 72
  length-gap ++, 72
  length-ratio, 71
  length-ratio +, 72

Information, 233
Intensive Care Unit
  ICU, 12, 153, 172
International Classification of Diseases
  ICD, 110, 116

Johns Hopkins Outpatient Center
  JHOC, 50

Knowledge, 234

Lead Time, 7, 10
Length of Stay, 4, 13, 172
Little's Law, 13
Little's Law
  insurance example, 16
  lab example, 16
  queues, 93
  walk-in clinic example, 17
  x-ray lab example, 14

Makespan, 8, 41, 43, 44, 48, 55, 121, 130, 148,
    154, 156, 158, 160
Medicare, 127
Metric, 3, 9, 12, 24, 160, 180

Network, 44, 46, 47
No-Show, 33, 63, 187
Nurse, 31

Operating Room
  OR, 12
Operations Management, 1, 53, 114, 128, 132,
    146, 233
Operations Research, 1, 62, 131, 149, 233
Optimization, 61
Organisation for Economic Cooperation and
    Development
  OECD, 107
Overtime, 159

Parallel Processing, 33, 54–56, 58, 64, 145,
    167
Patient Type
  new, 181

Patient Type, 165
Patient Type
  consult, 201
  follow up, 201
  new, 17, 18, 47, 62, 64, 112, 113, 129, 147,
    155
  nursing, 201
  on treatment visit, 201
  return, 17, 18, 47, 62, 64, 112, 113, 129,
    147, 181
Physician's Assistant, 181
Physician's Assistant, 181
Pre-Processing, 140, 146, 156
Private Practice, 31, 145, 179, 181, 185
Private Practice
  activcity times, 181
  capacity, 145
  Process Flow, 181
Process, 3, 80, 129
Process
  cost, 10
  improvement, 10
  stable, 12, 13, 86
Process Analysis, 2
Process Analysis
  emergency department, 25
  instrument preparation example, 18
Process Management, 8
Process Management
  assessment, 9
  goals, 11
Process Map, 3, 17, 44, 50, 55, 64, 80, 83, 133,
    148, 154
Process Map
  academic medical center, 31, 64, 186
  clinic, 129, 130
  private practice, 34, 64

Queue, 80
Queue
  arrival process, 87
  arrival rate, 85, 86
  birth-death process, 91
  configuration, 87
  discipline, 88
  inter-arrival-time, 81
  memoryless, 81
  MM1, 94
  MMs, 96
  service rate, 85
  source, 87
  theory, 136

utilization, 85

Real Time Location System
  RTLS, 29, 30, 135, 200
Resident, 31, 54, 64, 128, 130, 137, 140, 147,
    186
Resource, 3, 10, 80, 129
Resource
  pooling, 162, 164
Resourse
  sharing, 58, 60, 114, 155
Route, 3, 80, 129
Rush Order Flow Time, 21

Schedule, 132
Schedule
  cyclic, 147
Setup Time, 6
Shouldice Clinic, 26
Simulation, 61
Start Time Distribution, 160

Takt Time, 4, 12
Teaching, 31
Throughput, 4, 11, 12, 28, 55, 80, 121, 154
Time Driven Activity Based Costing
  TDABC, 115, 123
Turnover, 7, 12

Unpunctuality, 142, 143, 157, 160, 183, 184,
    232
Unpunctuality
  distribution, 159
Utilization, 8, 28, 37, 41, 55, 121, 137, 158
Utilization
  atttending, 122
  CA, 122
  labor, 8, 39
  nurse, 122
  room, 122

Vitals, 31, 36, 46, 117, 156, 181, 186

Waiting Time, 11, 84, 134, 137, 138, 145, 148,
    154, 156, 199, 200
Waiting Time
  distribution, 84
  queue, 99
Work In Process
  census, 13
  WIP, 7, 14, 80